MW00857000

Liturgical Theology in Thomas Aquinas

Liturgical Theology in Thomas Aquinas

Sacrifice and Salvation History

FR. FRANCK QUOËX († 2007)

TRANSLATED AND EDITED BY
ZACHARY J. THOMAS

Foreword by Dominic M. Langevin, OP

The Catholic University of America Press
Washington, D.C.

The paper used in this publication meets the requirements
of American National Standards for Information Science—
Permanence of Paper for Printed Library materials,
ANSI Z39.48-1992.
∞

Cataloging-in-Publication Data is available
from the Library of Congress
ISBN: 978-0-8132-3755-8
eISBN: 978-0-8132-3756-5

Contents

Foreword

Human beings search for the source of life and happiness. Sometimes, they stumble about in lives of routine, and sometimes, they spring forward in feats of the fantastic. Philosophers anguish, and psychologists advise. But for the human person, as well as for the smallest ant and the largest galaxy, the start and finish are very simple: God.[1] The proper human response can only be similarly simple: the worship of God.

The life and work of Fr. Franck Quoëx (1967–2007) testify to this fundamental truth, the truth of the Christian religion, the truth of worship. Fr. Quoëx was born in the Savoy region of France and spent time as a student, seminarian, priest, professor, and pastor in many areas of the old heartland of Catholic Christendom: Tuscany, Rome, Bavaria, Paris, Liechtenstein, Switzerland. He first entered seminary studies at the age of nineteen. He immersed himself in the Christian culture that is the cult—the worship—of God. He studied its history and practiced its ways, attaining a renown for both activities at a young age.

Quoëx was attached to the forms and texts of the *Usus antiquior*, the Extraordinary Form of the Roman Rite. Though for Quoëx, as a historian and practitioner of the liturgy, he is perhaps best described as a man of the *Usus antiquiores*, for he had learned well the many variances that have characterized Christian worship over the centuries.

---

1. See Thomas Aquinas, *Summa contra Gentiles*, III, ch. 17–18 and 24.

His historical acumen was appreciated across the spectrum of academic liturgists, whether of a more traditional bent or a more progressive bent, such as the important French Dominican, Pierre-Marie Gy.[2] Historical sensitivity is essential to Christian liturgical science and expression, even if persons sometimes come to differing prudential conclusions about the historical data's contemporary consequences. Quoëx, as a classical man of the Roman Rite, was a proponent of doctrine, tradition, sobriety, solemnity, and *humanitas*.

A properly ecclesiastical historian—and particularly a student of the various historical expressions of the liturgy—must study the eternal God and his providential ways. And so, besides his historical research, Fr. Quoëx was a theologian of the liturgy. For a doctorate in sacred theology, he wrote a dissertation entitled "Le Rite et le Royaume: Culte et histoire du salut selon Thomas d'Aquin" (Rite and Kingdom: The Exterior Acts of Cult [or Worship] and Salvation History according to Saint Thomas Aquinas")," composed under the direction of Fr. Ambrosius Eszer, OP, and successfully defended in 2001 at the Dominican Order's Pontifical University of St. Thomas Aquinas (the Angelicum) in Rome. This work served as the basis for the publication in several journals of the articles translated and assembled here. The chapters demonstrate Quoëx's Thomistic spirit, which could understand the Angelic Doctor's broad theological vision and sympathetically tease out the meaning of the thirteenth-century Dominican's more obscure medieval references. For the latter, Quoëx's knowledge of the liturgical sources and history is invaluable, bringing together the best of modern historical-critical research and Scholastic theological judgment. Furthermore, readers will benefit from Quoëx's ability to integrate insights scattered throughout the various texts of Aquinas.

Learning the liturgy with St. Thomas Aquinas offers numerous advantages. Thomas spent his entire conscious life in environments marked by solemn Catholic liturgy: first as a boy who lived

2. E.g., Pierre-Marie Gy, "Bulletin de liturgie," *Revue des Sciences philosophiques et théologiques* 81, no. 3 (1997): 491–92.

and studied at the famous Benedictine abbey of Monte Cassino, and then as a man who joined the Order of Friars Preachers. As a top mind, under obedience to be the best professor and scholar that he could be for the salvation of souls, the Dominican Thomas was not habitually supposed to attend the monastic-style conventual liturgies of his Order. And yet, as a young man, even against great opposition, he chose this clerical community as his home. Its solemn, contemplative worship imbued and reinforced his own personality. In the Dominican Thomas, prayer and study, faith and reason, contemplation and action went together. The liturgy thus helped him throughout his life to affirm his unique focus: God. It helped him to affirm as a middle-aged man—but a man already, it turns out, at the end of his life—that he wanted only one thing from God: God himself. "*Non nisi te.*"

As a worshipper, therefore, Thomas had that experiential wisdom that comes only from personal communication with the living God. And as a scholar, Thomas communicated the truth that we need to be saints, we who are students of worship.

Fr. Quoëx, over the course of the studies presented here, illuminates several features of Aquinas's wisdom on worship. For instance, the liturgy is transcendent, centered on the Blessed Trinity and on the God-man, Jesus Christ, who suffered death but now reigns gloriously. This vertical focus should be obvious to the student and practitioner of worship, but often it is not, at least in many contemporary Catholic celebrations in the developed Western nations. St. Thomas and Fr. Quoëx helpfully put God and the sacred at the center of worship.

This liturgical transcendence does not mean in the least that men and women are disadvantaged or deprived. Rather, the worship of God elevates the human person. Chapter 1 of this book describes this dynamic by explaining the human virtue of religion, which interiorly and exteriorly renders to God his due. While God is the object of worship, he is not the beneficiary, for he cannot change or be changed. Rather, the worshippers benefit. Collectively, this is precisely why our liturgy should be solemn and demanding: God's dignity deserves as much, and so does our Christian dignity. Good liturgy dignifies the dignified.

In this respect, Fr. Quoëx's work in chapter 1 to demonstrate the natural basis of religion and worship is especially important. In our secular and secularizing age—one that has forgotten so much about God and a godly way of life—it is essential to learn why man should aim for more than earthly happiness, why man is better than brute beasts, why man is capable of so much more than even the best computers, namely, why man should worship God. Chapters 2 and 3 further explore this human endeavor by showing how God has aided it over the course of salvation history, from the earliest days recorded in the Old Testament, through the earthly perfection achieved in the New Law of Jesus Christ, and moving forward toward the heavenly perfection of the eternal liturgy. The vision of Quoëx the theologian is herein able to integrate the data of Quoëx the historian.

Certain parallels may be observed—as Quoëx explicitly did in these pages—with another great recent theorist of Christian life and liturgy, Joseph Ratzinger. The latter, a sensitive student of the human condition, was raised in the supportive Catholicism of Bavaria but then exposed to the harsh atheism and nihilism of, first, Nazi Germany and, then, postmodern Europe. In works such as *The Spirit of the Liturgy*, Ratzinger attempted to incite a new vision for man, a revolution against the secular revolution. Ratzinger and other representatives of the twentieth-century's *ressourcement* movement drew strength from the Church Fathers, theological doctors who certainly offer much of value to the Christian worshipper. Ratzinger's efforts must be commended for their importance and wide appeal. At the same time, for the Christian who wishes to develop or deepen this theology of the liturgy beyond Ratzinger, to where does one turn? One would be admirably aided by recourse to that medieval *Doctor Communis*, St. Thomas Aquinas, who could be called the last of the Fathers, for he so well captured and synthesized the great minds of the preceding Christian centuries.

Chapter 3 develops the idea that Jesus, in his humanity, instanti-ated the virtue of religion. Christ is "God's religious man," the exem-plar for Christ's adopted brethren. Through right worship, the Chris-tian becomes more like Christ. In this, Quoëx weaves Aquinas's theology with the (priestly) spirituality of the seventeenth-century French School (which includes such luminaries as Cardinal Pierre de Bérulle, Charles de Condren, Jean-Jacques Olier, and St. John Eu-des). The permanent sacramental characters conferred by Baptism, Confirmation, and Holy Orders play key roles in the worship of the Christian, as chapter 4, drawing on the work of St. Thomas, explains. Sacramental character is the Christian's configuration to Christ in his priesthood. It is through the power of that priesthood that Chris-tian worship is true and salvific.

In Christ's priesthood, the Christian worshipper mounts with Christ to the Upper Room and then to the height of Calvary. He does so in the Holy Sacrifice of the Mass, to which the final three chapters of Quoëx's study are devoted. As Christ is offered substantially in the Eucharist for the benefit of the Christian, so the Christian is en-abled to fulfill his human capacity for worshipping the one God. Be-cause the Eucharist is a "representative image" of Christ's Passion and communicates the salvific "effect of the Passion," the Mass is a true, sacramental sacrifice (chapter 5).[3] As such, the Christian—whether participating in Christ's priesthood through the sacrament of Holy Orders or through the sacrament of Baptism—benefits from active attention accorded to the liturgical rites of the Mass, as described in detail by St. Thomas and Fr. Quoëx (Appendices I & II).

The Christian life is both theological and liturgical. This excel-lent volume of Thomistic liturgical theology helps us toward the one thing necessary: God.

Dominic M. Langevin, OP
Dean of the Pontifical Faculty of the Immaculate Conception
Washington, D.C.

---

3. Thomas Aquinas, *ST*, III, q. 83, a. 1.

Translator's Preface

Fr. Franck Quoëx received a doctorate in theology at the Angelicum, defending a thesis entitled *Les Actes extérieurs du culte dans l'histoire du salut, selon saint Thomas d'Aquin* in 2001. He was subsequently professor of liturgy at the International Seminary of the Priestly Fraternity of St. Peter in Wigratzbad, Germany. As a historian of the liturgy of the Middle Ages, he obtained a further degree at the *École pratique des Hautes Études* (*Paris-Sorbonne, Section des Sciences historiques et philologiques*), editing a memoir of the liturgical manuscripts of the *Bibliothèque capitulaire de Verceil*. He died of cancer in 2007, at the age of thirty-nine.

In his early career, Fr. Quoëx published a series of essays based on his dissertation in the French journal *Sedes sapientiae*, and later a two-part study of Aquinas's *expositio missae* in the *Revue thomiste*. His untimely death prevented him from assembling these writings into a book, but they represent a sufficiently complete synthesis to justify their inclusion, as chapters, in the present volume, in order to make more widely available his insights into St. Thomas's sacramental theology. We have supplied the introduction and conclusion from his doctoral dissertation as a crucial frame for the first five chapters, leaving the *Revue thomiste* articles as an appendix.

Though the chapters do cohere, the book is of course not a deliberately crafted monograph, but rather is a set of essays. In general, Quoëx exposits St. Thomas reverentially, not seeking to disagree with him. At the same time, he notes the absence of the theme of thanksgiving in St. Thomas's Mass commentary, and he sounds a critical note about St. Thomas's arguments in favor of the multiple signs of the cross in the Eucharistic prayer. Quoëx's style is straightforward and lucid, and he generally does not enter into more impassioned theological engagement with the questions being raised, though of course his perspective shines through. He often does not take the further step of clarifying the ramifications for the Church today of what he is presenting. Undoubtedly, there are numerous instances in which much more could be said, as for instance in his discussion of St. Thomas on image and representation, or in his reflections on the active and passive sacramental character received by the faithful in Baptism.

While readers will gain tremendously from Quoëx's insights, a few more prefatory remarks about avenues that Quoëx did not explore will be helpful. For instance, the volume could have been enhanced by a discussion of Church according to St. Thomas, not least in order to relate St. Thomas's discussion of Christ as priest to his understanding of Christ as Head of the Church and as mediator between God and man. There could also have been a more detailed discussion of the Eucharist as sacrament, as distinct from a sacrifice. This would have allowed for deeper reflection upon the Eucharist as the "sacrament of charity," as well as an examination of how St. Thomas employs Augustine's account of sacrifice. There are other loose ends, such as how the non-ordained are also "actors" in the Eucharistic sacrifice (given Quoëx's emphasis on the sacramental character received by the ordained priest alone), in light of what Aquinas has to teach about spiritual priesthood in question 82 of the Tertia pars. Similarly, in discussing the virtue of religion, Quoëx's presentation could be enriched by linking justice more concretely to charity. While Quoëx is no longer with us to expand upon his views, we can hope that readers of this text will find it an indispensable baseline for going further into these topics and into the whole of St. Thomas's rich and perennially relevant teaching on the cultic dimensions of Eucharistic worship.

This collection of essays has much to offer us about the exterior act, the exterior cultic act, and especially sacrifice, throughout the history of salvation in light of St. Thomas's theological synthesis. Without being the final word by any means, Quoëx's insights will be of significant value for all students of St. Thomas's sacramental and Eucharistic theology, as Fr. Langevin's foreword has made clear.

All translations of Fr. Quoëx's quotations from French authors are mine unless otherwise noted, and the English Dominican version of the *Summa* has been used throughout.

I thank the journals *Sedes sapientiae* and *Revue thomiste* for the permission to translate and republish the following articles:

Chapter 1: "Les fondements anthropologiques du culte, selon saint Thomas d'Aquin," *Sedes sapientiae* 81 (Autumn 2002): 49–82.

Chapter 2: "Le culte dans l'ancienne alliance, selon saint Thomas d'Aquin," *Sedes sapientiae* 82 (Winter 2002): 53–80.

Chapter 3: "Le Christ, religieux de Dieu, selon saint Thomas d'Aquin," *Sedes sapientiae* 83 (Spring 2003): 11–34.

Chapter 4: "Les sacrements, signes du culte divin," *Sedes sapientiae* 86 (Winter 2003): 16–44.

Chapter 5: "Le sacrifice eucharistique, sacrement de la passion du Christ selon saint Thomas," *Sedes sapientiae* 89 (Autumn 2004): 13–42.

Appendix I: "Thomas d'Aquin, mystagogue (I): L'*Expositio missæ* de la *Somme de théologie* (IIIa, q. 83, a. 4–5)," *Revue thomiste* 105, no. 2 (2005): 179–225.

Appendix II: "Thomas d'Aquin, mystagogue (II): L'*Expositio missæ* de la *Somme de théologie* (IIIa, q. 83, a. 4–5)," in *Revue thomiste* 105, no. 3 (2005): 435–72.

The author dedicated the final two articles in memory of Fr. Pierre-Marie Gy, OP.

Liturgical Theology in
Thomas Aquinas

Introduction

The present study was born of the author's dual interest in the history of liturgy and sacramental theology.[1] For more than half a century now, medieval historians have been growing more aware of the fact that liturgy was an integral part of medieval life. As a result, interest in the history of Christian worship has grown steadily. No history of cult can be complete, however, without a serious knowledge of the history of doctrine and especially of developments in sacramental theology. Without it, the historian of worship cannot account for the evolution of a given rite at a certain moment in time. He would not, for example, be able to explain the appearance of gestures of Eucharistic veneration if he did not have in mind the aftermath of Berengar of Tours's (†1088) denials and, later, the Albigensians' Manichean hostility toward the sacrament of the Lord's Body, and the resulting urgency for Scholastic theologians to affirm the presence of the *Christus totus* under the Eucharistic veils.

The work of the liturgist, therefore, and in a particular way that of the medieval liturgist, should always be situated at the frontier of

---

1. Translator's note: Throughout this book, the French word *culte*, (from Latin *cultus*) and its adjectival form *cultique* are translated as "cult, cultic" rather than the more common English word "worship." As a term borrowed from anthropology, cult refers to a system of religious devotion and its rites. It has nothing to do with "the occult." The reader will find, however, that all quotations from the *Summa*, which are taken from the English Dominican version, prefer the term "worship." Translations from non-English sources are mine unless otherwise noted.

1

history and theology. The liturgist must observe, as Fr. Pierre-Marie Gy has written, "the give-and-take between celebrated liturgy and theology, ever keeping the one in mind while studying the other."[2]

From this perspective, a study of the liturgical theology of the most important master of the school, whose doctrine achieved such an authoritative status that it entered into the formulations of the Magisterium—in particular in the constitution *Sacrosanctum Concilium* of the Second Vatican Council—will prove to be of no small use to the liturgist. It will provide him with the doctrinal foundations that will enable him not only to give an account of the cultic conceptions of the thirteenth century, but also to distinguish the influence these conceptions have had on the history of a range of liturgical developments that took place in the second half of the thirteenth century and lasted far beyond it.

The thirteenth century marked a turning point for Western liturgy, as it did for philosophical reflection and dogmatic systematization, political theory, and sacred art. Located at the heart of what C. Vogel has called the "epoch of progressive unification"[3] of the Western liturgy, extending from the reforms of Gregory VII (1085) to the immediate pre-Tridentine period (1485),[4] the thirteenth century saw the definition and standardization of a number of liturgical books and practices, processes that affected the general structure of the rite as well as a great majority of its details, and that were to remain unchanged for several centuries.

In the case of the rite of Mass, for example, Innocent III ordered the compilation of a missal for the use of the Roman Curia at the dawn of the thirteenth century.[5] Subsequently, this missal was widely

2. Pierre-Marie Gy, *La liturgie dans l'histoire* (Paris: Cerf, 1991), 12. On the interdisciplinary study of liturgy, see the current state of the question in Eric Palazzo, *Le Moyen Âge: Des origines au XIIIᵉ siècle* (Paris: Beauchesne, 1993), 21–25.

3. Cyrille Vogel, *Medieval Liturgy: An Introduction to the Sources*, trans. William George Storey and Niels K. Rasmussen (Washington, DC: Pastoral Press, 1986).

4. In 1485, the papal master of ceremonies, A. Patrizi Piccolomini, published the *editio princeps* of his pontifical. The work's strictly "Roman" orientation and the working method of its editor foreshadowed the character of the post-Tridentine liturgical books.

5. See Stephen J. P. van Dijk, *The Ordinal of the Papal Court from Innocent III to*

diffused by the Franciscans during the course of the century, and then transplanted in Avignon at the dawn of the fourteenth century. This vast spread, in combination with other influences created the conditions for its use by the whole Church, and it would go on to serve as the basis of the 1570 edition of the missal. In the same way, the Dominican liturgy established by Master General Humbert of Romans in 1256,[6] when Thomas Aquinas was just beginning to teach in Paris, would remain in use almost unchanged for several centuries.

During his childhood spent with the Benedictine monks of the abbey of Monte Cassino and then throughout the course of his life in the Dominican Order, Aquinas lived in daily contact with liturgical prayers and ceremonies. Dominican legislation, as Fr. A. González Fuente has shown, provided for the communal and solemn celebration of both the Eucharistic sacrifice and the Divine Office.[7] In his teaching, St. Thomas often revealed his dependence on the liturgical customs he practiced: he quoted them as *auctoritates* and theological *loci* in his demonstrations;[8] he used them to explain and justify doctrine; and here and there, especially in the (unfinished) treatise

---

Boniface VIII and Related Documents, Spicilegium Friburgense 22 (Fribourg: Éditions universitaires, 1975).

6. See Louis Rousseau, *De ecclesiastico officio Fratrum Praedicatorum secundum ordinationem Humberti de Romanis* (Rome: A. Manuzio, 1927).

7. Antolín González Fuente, *La vida litúrgica en la Orden de Predicadores: Estudio en su legislación; 1216–1280*, Dissertationes historicae 20 (Rome: Institutum Historicum FF. Praedicatorum, 1981). The author emphasizes that "the central and exclusive character the Order's legislation gives to establishing and maintaining liturgical life is focused above all in the community's solemn celebration thereof. It is important to emphasize this from the start, because the entire efficacy of liturgical prayer is conceived and carried out—and always will be carried out—only in its solemn celebration. Legislation continually bases the importance of liturgical prayer with respect to contemplation and action on the community's solemn celebration of the liturgy, despite some texts that might seem to distract from this point. Care for communal liturgical celebration has reached even the most minor of the Dominicans Order's legislative acts on the subject.... The Order of Preachers clearly insisted on this central role of the liturgy, embracing in several general chapters Saint Benedict's dictum that the Divine Office must be placed before all other things" (371).

8. See Hyacinthe-Marie Hering, "De loco theologico liturgiae apud S. Thomam," *Pastor Bonus* 5 (1941): 456–64. See also Cipriano Vagaggini, *Il senso teologico della liturgia* (Rome: San Paolo, 1965), 538–55.

on the sacraments in particular, he commented on them, therefore arguably meriting the title of *mystagogue*.[9]

In the case of the Mass rite, for example, the Angelic Doctor commented on the *ordo* of Innocent III, the same one used in the papal chapel, for which Thomas had composed the Office and Mass of Corpus Christi. He held Innocent III in high regard and quoted from his treatise *De sacro altaris mysterio*,[10] composed when the latter was still Cardinal Lothar of Segni, in works ranging from the *Commentary on the Sentences* to the *Summa theologiae*'s treatise on the Eucharist[11]—though less frequently in the latter. In his treatise, Lothar, trained in the theological school at Paris, seems to embark upon a classical explanation of the papal Mass, but actually presents a genuine study of the theological doctrine of the Eucharistic sacrifice, grafting a scholastic-theological work onto the liturgical-ceremonial commentary. Cardinal Lothar's work proved to be highly influential. Hugh of Saint-Cher,[12] and especially Durandus of Mende at the end of the century,[13] drew on the treatise's liturgical material, while Thomas Aquinas chose to integrate certain liturgical-theological data from Innocent III's treatise into his own doctrinal synthesis.[14]

9. On this subject, see Pierre-Marie Gy, "La documentation sacramentaire de Thomas d'Aquin," *Revue des sciences philosophiques et théologiques* 80 (1996): 425–31.

10. Innocent III, *De sacro altaris mysterio*, also known under the title *De missarum mysteriis*, PL 217, col. 775–914. See the critical edition and French translation *Les mystères des messes: Présentation, édition critique et traduction française*, ed. and trans. Olivier Hanne, 2 vols. (Huningue: Presses universitaires Rhin & Danube, 2022); see also David Wright, "A Medieval Commentary on the Mass: *Particulae* 2–3 and 5–6 of the *De missarum mysteriis* (ca. 1195) of Cardinal Lothar of Segni" (PhD diss., University of Notre Dame, 1977). A partial English translation is forthcoming in *The Mysteries of the Mass; The Four Images of Marriage*, trans. David M. Foley (Kansas City, MO: Angelus Press, 2023).

11. See Thomas Aquinas, *Summa theologiae* [*ST*] III, q. 78, a. 1, 1um; q. 81, a. 3, sed contra; q. 82, a. 2; q. 79, a. 4, sed contra.

12. Hugh of Saint-Cher (✝ 1263), *Tractatus super missam seu Speculum Ecclesiae* (or *Expositio missae*), in *Opuscula et textus historiam ecclesiae eiusque vitam atque doctrinam illustrantia*, ed. Gisbertus Sölch, Series liturgica 9 (Münster: Aschendorff, 1940).

13. William Durandus, bishop of Mende (✝ 1296), *Rationale divinorum officiorum*, vol. 3, bk. 4, ed. A. Davril and Timothy M. Thibodeau, Corpus Christianorum Continuatio Mediaevalis [CCCM] 140 (Turnhout: Brepols, 1995).

14. For the influence of Innocent III's treatise *De sacro altaris mysterio* on Aquinas's

Aquinas gave an account of the liturgical usages he received from previous centuries, but it is also beyond question that the authority of his teaching, from the end of the thirteenth century up to the close of what J. A. Jungmann called the "Gothic period," influenced the creation and development of liturgical usages for the celebration of the sacraments.

One would be hard pressed, for example, to maintain that our Doctor's making the Eucharist the veritable keystone for his organization of the seven sacraments did not contribute to fixing the rites of ordination in a perspective more strictly linked to confecting the Eucharist, a change that obscured, though did not deny, the ancient conception inherited from the *Apostolic Tradition* (c. 215) and the Roman sacramentaries of the seventh and eighth centuries, which saw in the *secunda dignitas* essentially the task of cooperating with the episcopal order. St. Thomas always maintained that priesthood was conferred by the *traditio instrumentorum*,[15] the handing over to the candidate of the material of the Eucharistic sacrifice while the bishop pronounces: "*Accipe potestatem offerre sacrificium Deo missasque celebrare.*"[16] This theological opinion was elevated to the status of a principle in the Pontifical of William Durandus (1293–1295), whose importance in the history of the Roman liturgy is well known. It then passed along with the substance of Durandus's Pontifical into the *Liber pontificalis* of Patrizi Piccolomini (1485), and thence into the *Roman Pontifical* of 1595, to be overturned only in 1948 by Pius XII.[17] In the same way, the orientation of the priesthood to the Eucharistic

---

Eucharistic doctrine, see Michele Maccarrone, *Studi su Innocenzo III* (Padova: Editrice Antenore, 1972), 404–10.

15. See Thomas Aquinas, *Commentary on the Sentences* IV, d. 24, q. 1, a. 2, 2um; and *Summa contra Gentiles* [*SCG*] IV, ch. 74. On the history and development of this doctrine, see Angelo Lameri, *La Traditio Instrumentorum e delle insegne nei riti di ordinazione*, Bibliotheca ephemerides liturgicae subsidia 96 (Rome: Edizioni Liturgiche, 1998).

16. William Durandus, *Pontificale*, in *Le pontifical de Guillaume Durand*, vol. 3 of *Le pontifical romain au Moyen Âge*, ed. Michel Andrieu, Studi e Testi 88 (Rome: Vatican Library, 1940), 370, no. 17.

17. Pius XII, Apostolic Constitution *Sacramentum Ordinis* (November 30, 1947), in *Acta Apostolica Sedis* 40 (1948): 5–7.

celebration, on the one hand and, on the other, the positions that St. Thomas adopted concerning the value of the words of consecration taken in isolation, surely influenced the manner of modern Eucharistic concelebration, with its more marked insistence on the *sacramental* function that the concelebrant has received in his priestly ordination.

All of these reasons have convinced us of the obvious historical interest of the study of St. Thomas Aquinas's theology of cult. We use the expression "theology of cult" advisedly, because our purpose is not to survey everything in the Angelic Doctor's works that in any way concerns the various manifestations of Christian worship, and thus arbitrarily to try to cast our Doctor as a sort of liturgist.

For, as Fr. P.-M. Gy has emphasized in relation to St. Thomas's frequent reliance on the sacramental theology of St. Bonaventure's *Commentary on the Sentences,* Aquinas develops his reflection

with a very different balance than that of the Franciscan master between the spiritual element and the intellectual element. The latter element gives power and rigor to his theological thought, even though it occasionally renders the historical complexities of the sacramental tradition more difficult for him to perceive.[18]

That is why we would like to analyze St. Thomas Aquinas's theological reflections on the external acts of worship through the eyes of a liturgist, namely in order to bring out the doctrinal substance of the "rite," and especially of the sacramental sign. An understanding of the doctrinal status of the cultic sign informed by the fruits of historical research could serve as a foundation for, or at least contribute to, a deeper study of the liturgical rites that grew up and developed over the late Middle Ages, and were in the sixteenth century fixed for an enduring span of history.

The *Summa theologiae* will constitute the first and principal focus of our research, not so much in the interest of circumscribing

18. Pierre-Marie Gy, "Divergences de théologie sacramentaire autour de saint Thomas," in *Ordo sapientiae et amoris,* ed. Carlos-Josaphat Pinto de Oliveira (Fribourg: Éditions universitaires, 1993), 433.

our investigation to a single work, but rather because the theological work of the Angelic Doctor's maturity presents us, in the matter of the theology of cult, developments for which there are no equivalents in terms of abundance or systematic quality in the other theological works, indeed not even in his scriptural commentaries.

Our investigation of the Thomistic theology of the external acts of worship will focus on three treatises from the Summa, which we enumerate according to the order of exposition—*secundum ordinem disciplinae*, says the Prologue of the *Summa*—that is to say, according to the order of the grand divisions of our Doctor's work. These three treatises are in the *Prima secundae*, the treatise on the Old Law (questions 98–105), especially questions 101 to 103, which relate to the ceremonial precepts; in the *Secunda secundae*, the treatise on the moral virtue of religion (questions 81–100), especially questions 84 to 86; in the *Tertia pars*, the treatise on the sacraments, "*De sacramentis in communi*" (questions 60–65). The treatise on the Old Law, in essence an exposition of biblical theology, and the treatise on the sacraments, which is a direct extension of the mystery of the Incarnation, should both be considered according to the order of the mysteries, that is, according to the sequence of salvation history—not following the order of doctrinal and sapiential systematization, but rather the order of the progressive revelation of God's plan in its three historical stages: before the Mosaic Law, under the Law, and under the regime of grace.[19] Consequently, our study is structured around the historical order of Revelation, endeavoring to analyze the cultic regimes proper to the various stages of the Mystery's manifestation. This decision represents our view in the larger discussion over the *Summa*'s structure.

The modern debate over the *Summa*'s structure was born out of a recognition that, beyond the basic threefold division of the material, there is another pattern, which Fr. M.-D. Chenu has identified with the neo-Platonic scheme of *exitus* and *reditus*: the emanation

---

19. See *ST* II-II, q. 1, a. 7; q. 174, a. 6; *ST* III, q. 61, a. 3, 2um.

of all things from God and their return to him as the first princi-ple.[20] Taking stock of the discussions, corrections, and clarifications that have since multiplied around this theory,[21] we choose to fol-low the indications of Fr. Marie-Vincent Leroy. He distinguishes a *theological* part, which considers the Being of God in himself (*ST* I, q. 1–43), and an *economic* part, which looks at God's external work; Fr. Leroy applies the *exitus-reditus* scheme to this latter part, which covers all the rest of the *Summa*. The *exitus* is manifested in the cre-ation of angels and men (*ST* I, q. 44–119), while the *reditus* embrac-es the whole movement of man's return to God, of man insofar as he is the image of God, but also insofar as, wounded by sin, he can at-tain full communion with God only through Christ, who is the cen-ter of history.[22]

We hold with Fr. Yves Congar that

the plan of the *Summa* follows the stages by which God has realized, in a progressive and more and more perfect and intimate way, the mystery of his Presence and Indwelling in his creation.[23]

A place is given within the *Summa theologiae*'s sapiential organiza-tion, therefore, to the historical stages of the restoration of human nature and the principal elements of salvation history. Among the many pages of biblical theology it presents, we shall focus for the

20. Marie-Dominique Chenu, *Introduction à l'étude de saint Thomas d'Aquin* (Mon-treal: Institut d'études médiévales, 1954), 255–76. For a more general account of the re-lation between the *exitus-reditus* schema and salvation history, and the place of cult in this economy, see Cardinal Joseph Ratzinger, *The Spirit of the Liturgy*, trans. John Saward (San Francisco: Ignatius Press, 2000), 29–34.

21. For a synthesis of the discussion that has taken place bearing on the *Summa*'s plan in the wake of Fr. Chenu's work, see Jean-Pierre Torrell, *Saint Thomas Aquinas*, vol. 1, *The Person and His Work*, trans. Robert Royal (Washington, DC: The Catholic University of America, 2005), 153–56. See also Albert Patfoort, *Saint Thomas d'Aquin: Les cléfs d'une théologie* (Paris: FAC, 1983); and *La Somme de saint Thomas et la logique du dessein de Dieu* (Saint-Maur: Parole et Silence, 1998).

22. Marie-Vincent Leroy, review of Fr. A. Patfoort's book *Saint Thomas d'Aquin: Les cléfs d'une théologie*, in *Revue thomiste* 84 (1984): 298–303.

23. Yves-Marie Congar, "Le sens de l'économie salutaire dans la théologie de saint Thomas d'Aquin," in *Festgabe J. Lortz*, vol. 2, ed. E. Iserloh and P. Manns (Baden-Baden: B. Grimm, 1958), 81.

purposes of this study on the treatise on the Old Law, on the life of Jesus,[24] and, as an extension of the mystery of the redeeming Incarnation, on the treatise on the sacraments.

Our task, therefore, is to consider the function and role of worship in its external and sensible dimension and in the whole vast historical movement of man's return to God. However, since salvation history is nothing other than the progressive restoration of man's nature, it seems necessary, before unveiling the various stages of this restoration, to consider man as he is, that is, as God created him, with his natural capacity to express his orientation toward the Creator through acts of the moral virtue of religion. Thus, we will first lay out the anthropological foundations for the acts of worship, sketching the outlines of this perennial "natural religion," which the cultic economy of Revelation raises to the order of grace. We will do this by pointing out within the treatise on religion the questions that relate to the value of the external acts of religion. Then we will proceed to describe several of these acts (adoration, sacrifices, oblations, etc.), highlighting those points at which St. Thomas's "religious anthropology" converges with contemporary research in this field.

Once the anthropological foundations have been established, we shall then proceed, in a second and more developed part, to an analysis of the cultic economy of salvation history. First, we shall expound the ritual theology of the Old Testament, the first stage of revelation, as it is presented in the treatise on the Old Law. We shall discuss the status of the ceremonial precepts, their literal and figurative *raison d'être*, their number, their various forms (sacrifices, holy

---

24. See Henri de Lubac, *Exégèse médiévale: Les quatre sens de l'Écriture*, vol. 4 (Paris: Aubier, 1964), 286: "By the same token, St. Thomas shows that he does not underrate the value of history in the divine economy as much as some have believed, even though his most systematic thought is hardly open to the category of history. His Christology does not have that purely formal and abstract character which it will sometimes assume later on: in him (as in Suarez) the properly theological (and not only pious) interest in the mysteries of Christ's life is still alive; he studies these mysteries in their concrete unfolding, at the same time as he situates them in their dominant place in the unfolding of salvation history." See also Jean-Pierre Torrell, *Le Christ en ses mystères: La vie et l'œuvre de Jésus selon saint Thomas d'Aquin* (Paris: Desclee, 1999).

things, sacraments, etc.), but also their transitory character in reference to the One whom they only announced: Christ, the *fructus legis*.[25]

The coming of Christ is the center of the divine plan of salvation. The incarnate Word inaugurates the new economy: the redemptive cult. Question 22 of the *Tertia pars*, dedicated to the priesthood of Christ, will be the subject of the third chapter devoted to Christ's cult. Further, the central theme of the offering of the redemptive sacrifice and its eternal consummation will often require us to study several questions on Christ's Passion.

Finally, we will analyze the cult of the Mystical Body, a worship that is based in the sacraments of the Church. In a first section, Thomistic sacramental theology, defined by the concept of sign, will show us how, because of the very constitution of the sacramental reality, God operates in the work of man's sanctification in a way so proportionate to him that one can speak, with Fr. Chenu, of a true "sacramental anthropology."[26] In a second section, we will show that the sacraments accomplish man's sanctification only insofar as they are acts of the cult of Christ and of the Church. Relying on the theology of the sacramental character developed in the *Summa*, we will highlight the cultic dimension of sacramentality and the orientation of the various sacraments, along with their complex of "sacramentals," to the celebration of the most perfect of all, the Eucharist, sacrament of the Lord's Passion. From these studies will come the possibility of offering in conclusion some Thomasian landmarks on the profound nature of the Christian liturgy—a simple contribution to the intelligibility of ritual conceptions and practices of which the Angelic Doctor was the witness and which he illustrated in his own way.

While St. Thomas's theology of worship is inscribed within a specific historical period, we do not believe that it should be limited to it. Since the field of worship concerns, as we shall see, both moral

25. *ST* I-II, q. 102, a. 6, 5um.
26. Marie-Dominique Chenu, "Pour une anthropologie sacramentelle," *La Maison-Dieu* 119 (1974): 85–100.

action and the history of salvation, Aquinas offers a doctrine of cult that may be considered relevant because it answers questions many Christians have about the meaning and value of liturgical acts. In addition to the historical interest of this study, its originality consists in seeking a complete vision of what one may call "rituality" in Thomas's thought. This project admittedly advances a position in stark contrast to several contemporary liturgical-theological tendencies, which would see in most rites only a superfluous array of symbols charged with a paganizing (not to say pharisaical) "religiosity"; or else, while allowing them a relative necessity, would not grant them any objective theological or spiritual meaning.

The method adopted in this study consists in simply following St. Thomas's order of exposition in each of the treatises and questions we analyze, noting, underlining, even comparing them with parallel passages in the *Summa* or in other works of our Doctor. This approach will allow us to lay out and grasp Thomas's thought on the external dimension—namely, the liturgical—of a cult that, although performed by man, is also the cult of Christ and of his Church, the only one acceptable to the Father.

The choice, guided by contemporary methodology, of quoting the text of St. Thomas in a vernacular translation allows us to make room more easily for this same text in the body of the study, while in the notes we quote the original text in the Leonine edition.[27] Let us add finally that if the text of the *Summa theologiae* is our basic text, we will sometimes refer to the *Commentary on the Sentences* and the *Summa contra Gentiles*, if only to underline the evolution discernible in these works that precede the *Summa theologiae*. In the same way, other parallel places, in particular the *Super Boetium de Trinitate*, the *Commentary on the Letter to the Hebrews*, the *Compendium theologiae*, etc., will

27. On the text of the *Tertia pars*, see the remarks of Fr. Pierre-Marie Gy, "Le texte original de la *Tertia pars* de la *Somme théologique* de saint Thomas d'Aquin dans l'apparat critique de l'édition léonine: Le cas de l'eucharistie," *Revue des sciences philosophiques et théologiques* 65 (1981): 608–16. See also Mauro Turrini, "Raynald de Piperno et le texte original de la *Tertia pars* de la *Somme de théologie* de saint Thomas d'Aquin," *Revue des sciences philosophiques et théologiques* 73 (1989): 233–47.

serve us to specify, compare, and support this or that point of our analysis of the text of the *Summa*.

Our study of St. Thomas's religious anthropology draws on the work of historians of religion such as G. van der Leeuw, M. Eliade, and others. The following chapters on salvation historical realities, such as the cultic theology of the Old Law, the components and definition of Christian sacraments, the cultic dimension of the sacramental character, the nature of the Eucharistic sacrifice, etc., include abibliography that captures both the contemporary renewal of Thomistic studies and the body of theological reflection on the liturgy carried out by the "Liturgical Movement."

1

------:------

The Anthropological Foundations of Cult
according to Thomas Aquinas

At the dawn of the twentieth century, after the work of H. Hubert
and M. Mauss on the nature of sacrifice,[1] and especially after the
publication of E. Durkheim's study on the primitive forms of religious life among the tribes of Australia,[2] a new science was born
that was quite distinct from the simple history of religions: religious
anthropology. Rather than studying the life of a particular tribe or
society from a religious perspective, the new science set out to discover the general laws of *religious man* and to define the notion of
the *sacred*, while taking into account all the variety of cultures and
multiplicity of religious data.

In Durkheim, and after him in R. Caillois,[3] the sacred was treated
essentially as a kind of prohibition (the *taboo*). R. Otto defined it as
the *wholly other*, at once terrifying and fascinating.[4] G. van der Leeuw
and especially M. Eliade greatly furthered studies of the sacred by

1. Henri Hubert and Marcel Mauss, "Essais sur la nature et la fonction du sacrifice,"
Année sociologique, no. 2 (1889): 29–138.

2. Emile Durkheim, *The Elementary Forms of Religious Life* (London: George, Allen,
& Unwin, 1915).

3. Roger Caillois, *Man and the Sacred* (Champaign: University of Illinois Press,
2001).

4. Rudolf Otto, *The Idea of the Holy* (Oxford: Oxford University Press, 1958).

presenting the phenomenon in all its complexity, going beyond a view of the sacred as the merely irrational to take into account all of the forms of its manifestation throughout history.[5] Thus arose the scientific recognition of the existence, apart from technical or profane activity, of another sort of activity specific to the human condition: symbolic activity, which men experience in religious acts. Thus religion came to be viewed as man's handling of the sacred, as a manifestation of the relationship that man conducts with the divine omnipotence revealed to him by the forces of the cosmos, and whose superiority he, as a naturally religious being, spontaneously perceives.

Moving out from the internal sense of the transcendence of the divine and man's total dependence on *mystery*, religion translates outwardly into ritual, an act that involves the handling of sacred things, language, action, and word. The aim of contemporary religious anthropology is to understand the religious fact in what Roger Bastide calls "its living unity, as a total cultural activity,"[6] with various modes of expression at the service of a given form of cult.[7]

The methods of religious anthropology have proven useful for the study of Christian liturgy. They are used by historians of liturgy in the Middle Ages such as P.-M. Gy, J.-Y. Hameline, E. Palazzo, J.-C. Schmitt, and others.[8] Furthermore, philosophers such as

5. Gerardus van der Leeuw, *L'homme primitif et la religion* (Paris: PUF, 1940); *Religion in Essence and Manifestation: A Study in Phenomenology*, trans. J. E. Turner (Princeton, NJ: Princeton University Press, 2014); Mircea Eliade, *The Sacred and the Profane: The Nature of Religion* (New York: Harcourt, 1987); see also *Images and Symbols* (Princeton, NJ: Princeton University Press, 1991); *History of Religious Ideas*, 3 vols. (Chicago: University of Chicago Press, 1981).

6. Roger Bastide, "Anthropologie religieuse," *Encyclopedia universalis*, vol. 2 (Paris: Encyclopedia Universalis, 1990), 551.

7. See Julien Ries, *Trattato di antropologia del sacro*, vol. 1, *Le origini e il problema dell'Homo religiosus* (Milan: Jaca Book, 1989).

8. Pierre-Marie Gy, *La liturgie dans l'histoire* (Paris: Cerf, 1991); Jean-Yves Hameline, "Eléments d'anthropologie, de sociologie historique et de musicologie du culte chrétien in Enjeux du rite dans la modernité," *Recherches de sciences religieuses* 78, no. 3 (1990): 397–424; Eric Palazzo, *Liturgie et société au Moyen Âge* (Paris: Beauchesne, 2000); Jean-Claude Schmitt, *Le corps, les rites, les rêves, le temps: Essais d'anthropologie médiévale* (Paris: Gallimard, 2001), 31–126.

S. Rouvillois and Catherine Pickstock,[9] and theologians like Marie Dominique Chenu and Aidan Nichols,[10] have contributed to a profound reflection on the nature of the liturgy in relation to the challenges and problems of modernity. From various points of view, all these studies highlight the fundamental importance of *ritual* in the Christian life. Although Christianity is a *spiritual* religion, it has not therefore dispensed the believer from the practice of external acts of cult or from the handling of *sacred* things. This is an extremely important observation, for it invites the liturgical theologian to base his definition of the liturgy on the notion of cult, which falls in the domain of the virtue of religion.

But is Christianity, in which man is opened to the presence and goodness of a self-revealing God, really a *religion*, in the classic sense? In other words, a sacred administration of ritual relations that man sustains with the transcendent Mystery whose existence he intuits and fears? What contribution can Christian reflection, arising as a result of the analysis of purely external behaviors, make to a definition of religion so rooted in the sensible world? Will it offer accommodation or rejection—more or less disguised—of rituality?

At first blush, with regard to the conclusions of religious anthropology, it seems that the religious ideas of Christianity are worlds apart from others that so often slip into idolatry, superstition, and magic. Nevertheless, on the other hand, can Christianity, named after One who, though God, became man and established his cult among men, initiate a religious life that does not take into account

9. Samuel Rouvillois, *Corps et sagesse: Philosophie de la liturgie* (Paris: Fayard, 1995); Catherine Pickstock, *After Writing: On the Liturgical Consummation of Philosophy* (Oxford: Blackwell, 1998).

10. Marie-Dominique Chenu, "Pour une anthropologie sacramentelle," *La Maison-Dieu* 119 (1974), 85–100; Aidan Nichols, *Looking at the Liturgy: A Critical View of Its Contemporary Form* (San Francisco: Ignatius, 1996). [Translator's note: Several recent works merit a place in these lists, such as Uwe Michael Lang, *Signs of the Holy One: Liturgy, Ritual, and Expression of the Sacred* (San Francisco: Ignatius, 2015) and *The Roman Mass: From Early Christian Origins to Tridentine Reform* (Cambridge: Cambridge University Press, 2022); Michael Fiedrowicz, *The Traditional Mass: History, Form, and Theology of the Classical Roman Rite* (New York: Angelico, 2020); and Claude Barthe, *A Forest of Symbols: The Traditional Mass and its Meaning* (New York: Angelico, 2023).]

the structure of reality? Has it not been natural to men of all times to conceive of the conduct of their relationship to God in ways that involve acts of cult?

To respond to these questions, of such deep interest to the liturgical life of the Church, we propose to mine the resources offered by the teaching of Thomas Aquinas on the virtue of religion, found in its most complete form in the *Summa theologiae* (II-II, q. 80–100). Here, in the wake of the treatise on the virtue of justice, Aquinas constructs—and is perhaps the first to do so—a genuine treatise on the virtue of religion, bringing together and ordering in an organic synthesis the various acts of religion that he has studied separately until this point.[11] With the realism and careful analysis that are his hallmarks, he traces the thread that unites into one virtue the internal and external acts man uses to render to God the homage of his cult.

St. Thomas thus exposes the deep roots of cult in human nature, in abstraction from the various forms it has taken in the several theological states of humanity. As Fr. Bonino has observed, this approach "shows St. Thomas's vivid sense of the consistency of natural order and the methodological necessity for the theologian to treat first what belongs to the common requirements of human nature in the religious order before tackling their concrete historical forms."[12]

Nevertheless, the obligation to first locate the anthropological

---

11. Thus, in the *Commentary on the Sentences* (III, d. 9, q. 1, a. 3, q^a 3), Thomas distinguished the acts of homage according to how they secure the various goods we owe to God: the spirit, the body, and external goods. In the *Commentary on Boethius's De Trinitate* (q. 3, a. 2), he classed the acts of cult according as they were acts of the spirit, acts of the body, or acts "by which we are ordered to our neighbor because of God." In the *Summa contra Gentiles* (III, chs. 119 and 120) he treated the ceremonial precepts as so many determinations through divine law of acts that are owed to God by natural law. But while affirming the primacy of internal acts, Thomas was concerned above all to prove the fittingness of the external acts contained in the law. Here the major distinction between internal and external acts of a single virtue remained implicit, but was not treated in a systematic manner. This distinction would later serve to structure the treatise on the moral virtue of religion" in the *Summa theologiae*.

12. Serge-Thomas Bonino, "Le sacerdoce comme institution naturelle selon saint Thomas d'Aquin," *Revue thomiste* 99, no. 1 (1999): 37.

foundations of the acts of cult is based on logical anteriority alone. There is no question here of laboriously building out of the observations of religious anthropology a conceptual system of the external acts of religion, onto which the cultic realities of salvation history must then be grafted. When Thomas treats acts of the virtue of religion, he clearly does not mean to postulate a hypothetical "pure nature." Rather, he hews closely to the principle that grace does not take the place of nature or render its fulfillment useless, but rather elevates and perfects it.

In this chapter, we will follow the *Summa theologiae*'s treatise on religion—without neglecting relevant texts elsewhere—in an attempt to discover the role of the external acts of cult. First we will consider the nature of the virtue of religion as presented in the first articles of question 81, so that we can situate the external acts as acts of this virtue properly speaking (a. 7). Second, we will proceed to analyze several of these acts: adoration, sacrifices, and oblations, then sacred persons, places, and things. Finally, we will be in a good position to underscore the social dimension of the external acts of the virtue of religion and thus the existence of a genuine cultic society.

ACTS OF CULT IN THE VIRTUE OF RELIGION

The Virtue of Religion

The treatise on religion of the *Summa theologiae* (II-II, q. 80–100) stands within the broad study of the moral virtues, more precisely in the first place among the virtues auxiliary to justice.

Every virtue that involves relations with other people belongs to justice. Justice, in St. Thomas's words, is the "habit whereby a man renders to each one his due by a constant and perpetual will,"[13] demanding that what is due to another be rendered to him exactly in order to establish an equality between the one who owes and the one to whom something is owed. Thus the virtue of justice is the

13. *ST* II-II, q. 58, a. 1.

constant will to satisfy, by a proportionate external act, other people's *right* and legitimate needs,[14] irrespective of the inner dispositions of the subject. Aquinas makes the virtue of religion a poten-
tial part of justice, respect for what is due to others. But if religion
involves a relation to others, and when the other is God himself, the
conditions that define justice, strictly speaking, namely the relation
of equality, cannot be met completely. Man does not have the capacity to establish a relation of equality proportionate to the divine
rights; he cannot give God anything that he does not already owe
him.[15]

Consequently, the definition of the virtue of religion will have to
take into account a Nature that is superior, untouchable, *divine*, to
which the will of man is ordered in a constant and perpetual disposition through rendering "service and ceremonial rites or worship."[16]
Departing from the usual expression of the anthropologists, the essence of religion for St. Thomas does not consist in a creature's feeling of terror in the face of divine and inaccessible realities—which
the English language expresses by the word *awe*—but rather essentially regards the relation of man to God, of the creature to the Creator. In fact, the feeling that one must perform a debt of homage toward the supreme Being is only a sentiment, not a virtue; though it
is a feeling that religion will order and make its own.[17]

In his search for a definition of religion, the Angelic Doctor resorts to etymology. He points out the Greek term *eusebeia*: "*Eusebeia* means 'good worship' and consequently is the same as religion."[18]
Eusebeia has to do with internal piety, respect or love for the gods;
it is also the science of the service of God and of sanctity. In Latin, among the various etymologies he lists, Aquinas seems to prefer
that of Isidore (who owes it to Cicero): "A man is said to be religious

---

14. *ST* II-II, q. 58, a. 11.
15. *ST* II-II, q. 80, a. 1.
16. *ST* II-II, q. 80, a. 1.
17. *ST* II-II, q. 81, a. 2, ad 2.
18. *ST* II-II, q. 80, a. 1, ad 4.

from *religio*, because he often ponders over and, as it were, reads again [*relegit*], the things which pertain to the worship of God."[19]

The object of religion, therefore, is the divine cult. But what are we to understand precisely by the word *cult*? Returning to etymology, our Doctor links the Latin verbal form *colo* to the act of cultivating, taking care of, or honoring parents, country, and the divinity. Applied to religion, the term indicates a special honor given to God. Because religion considers God insofar as he is "the first principle of the creation and government of things,"[20] therefore "only those acts belong to it which pertain to the reverence of God by reason of their specific character."[21] The act of the intellect by which the creature acknowledges God's superiority and his own dependence is motivated by the desire to give to God the exclusive homage which is his in the order of justice.[22] Cult, the proper object of religion, consists entirely in this will to offer homage. Out of reverence for God, religion proposes certain acts, both internal and external, by which man orients himself to his final end.

Reverence for God is therefore the formal reason for divine worship, and all the acts of cult have no other purpose than to signify this reverence: "The end of religion is to pay God reverence."[23] As St. Thomas points out, *reverentia* calls for service (*obsequium, servitus*): "By the one same act man both serves and worships God, for worship regards the excellence of God, to Whom reverence is due, while service regards the subjection of man who, by his condition, is under an obligation of showing reverence to God."[24] God's lordship over man can be signified only by an act of man, clearly expressive of his dependence. This act is cult, the very object of religion, a type of service the Greek language calls *latria*.[25]

---

19. *ST* II-II, q. 81, a. 1. The citation from Isidore is taken from *Etymologies*, 10.
20. *ST* II-II, q. 81, a. 3. See also a. 1, ad 4.
21. *ST* II-II, q. 81, a. 4, ad 2.
22. *ST* II-II, q. 81, a. 4.
23. *ST* II-II, q. 81, a. 2.
24. *ST* II-II, q. 81, a. 3, ad 2.
25. *ST* II-II, q. 81, a. 1, ad 3.

The twin notions *reverentia-obsequium* constitute the object of religion, namely cult. Under the word *cult*, therefore, is contained the ensemble of actions, both internal and external, proper to the virtue of religion. Externally, the moral virtue of religion will be signified by "rites of offering or participation in divine things."[26] These rites will do nothing less than translate the essential and primary religion of the soul, at first simply in accord with the laws of religious psychology, before they are taken up in a superior way in the order of salvation history.

Does Religion Require External Acts?

As he begins to consider separately the various acts of the virtue he has just defined (*ST* II-II, q. 81, a. 7), the Angelic Doctor asks why external acts of *latria* are justified. Even to field this question puts emphasis on the relation between these two types of acts proper to the same virtue of religion.

All three of the objections advanced are based on an exclusively "spiritualist" conception of religion that would dismiss external acts of cult as unnecessary. As the first objection would have it, because God is a spirit, those who adore him should adore him "in spirit and truth" (Jn 4:24), which they would not be doing if they performed acts involving the body. Furthermore, how can one render homage to something so great by means of external acts, which seem more suited to relations of respect between equal or inferior human beings? Finally, because it is not fitting to treat immortal beings the same as mortal beings, should not bodily acts be excluded from divine cult and not counted among the works of religion?

Having heard these objections, we will follow the text of article 7 to prove the necessity of external acts of cult before moving to discuss their role as signs.

26. *ST* II-II, q. 81, a. 3, ad 2.

The Necessity of External Acts of Cult

St. Thomas emphasizes at the outset that if we give honor to God, it is "not for His sake, because He is of Himself full of glory to which no creature can add anything, but for our own sake." It is not that the purpose of the act of homage is not to honor God, the final end of the religious man. But God does not gain any increase of his essential glory through acts of homage, whether internal or external. The only profit accrues to the one who performs the acts of religion. As Cajetan observed, "by our worship God is glorified in us and in all that is external to him, but not in himself."[27] Since the practice of the moral virtue of religion orders man to God by orienting him immediately to his end,[28] it is man who benefits from the acts of this virtue. When he gives witness to his honor and reverence for God, when he puts himself in a state of essential dependence in relation to his first Principle and supreme Good, he is completely fulfilled. For man's perfection consists precisely in subordinating himself to God through religion, the most eminent of the moral virtues.

To illustrate the state of perfection of the religious man, which is to say the man who is justly ordered to God in glorifying him and giving him public praise, Thomas uses two comparisons: the man ordered to God is like the body when vivified by the soul and like the air when it is illuminated by the sun; in other words, when between a creature and his Creator harmony is established. But we should not understand these two images to imply a sanctifying influence. We are still considering the cult of natural religion, whose workings we must understand before considering its elevation to the supernatural order.

To be ordered to God, continues the Angelic Doctor, "the human mind needs to be guided by the sensible world, since 'invisible

27. See Cajetan's commentary on ST II-II, q. 81, a. 7 in Tommaso de Vio Cajetan, *Summa totius theologiae S. Thomae de Aquino*, ed. Serafino Capponi (Hildesheim: Georg Olms Verlag, 2000–2003), 191.

28. "Religion approaches nearer to God than the other moral virtues" (*ST* II-II, q. 81, a. 6).

things ... are clearly seen, being understood by the things that are made,' as the Apostle says (Romans 1:20). Wherefore in the Divine worship it is necessary to make use of corporeal things."

God is invisible, and yet our reason can grasp him. The basis for this argument is the conception of knowledge found throughout the work of St. Thomas, here cast in the formula: "The human mind, in order to be united to God, needs to be guided by the sensible world." Made up of a soul and a body, man can know nothing without the use of his senses. The spectacle of creation that fills his senses guides him toward knowledge of the first Principle. The gaze of his intellect reveals the *invisibilia*, the invisible mysteries of God. In the same way, through acts in conformity with his constitution as a rational animal, the virtue of religion orders man to God. The manner of honoring God must necessarily correspond to the mode of being of him who performs these acts of homage, but also to the spiritual nature of Him who is honored, so that he may receive and accept the homage.

Though God is a spirit, he is also the creator of man's body. Thus in the act by which man manifests his service to the Divine Majesty, there must be a corporal dimension, one subordinated to the spirit.[29] From a certain natural instinct, man renders his cult to God according to his own proper mode of being, and to fail to recognize the dual dimensions (spiritual and corporeal, internal and external) of man's cult would be to repudiate human nature and deny the goodness of God's handiwork.[30] The acts of worship that man renders according to the modalities of his own being are connatural to him.

29. Among others, see *ST* I-II, q. 101, a. 2 (in the treatise on the Old Law): "The Divine worship is twofold: internal, and external. For since man is composed of soul and body, each of these should be applied to the worship of God; the soul by an interior worship; the body by an outward worship: hence it is written (Psalm 83:3): 'My heart and my flesh have rejoiced in the living God.' And as the body is ordained to God through the soul, so the outward worship is ordained to the internal worship, [which] consists in the soul being united to God by the intellect and affections."

30. See the remark in *SCG* III, ch. 119, no. 5: "It is not astonishing if heretics who deny that God is the author of our body condemn such manifestations. This condemnation shows that they have not remembered that they are men when they judge that the

The divine law does nothing more than specify these connatural obligations, correcting a number of errors due to sin and ordering the acts of cult within the plan of salvation history, making them figures of the acts of Christ.

The External Acts of Cult as Signs

But do the external acts of religion have value in themselves, by the mere fact of their materiality? Can the practice of religion be reduced to rituality? Here we must avoid a danger that is at the root of the errors of idolatry, a superstitious ritualism verging on magic, which would have religion consist in the practice of bodily acts alone.[31] From this point of view, God could profit from all our bodily obligations, deeming them acceptable in themselves. But we have seen that such acts add nothing to God. Rather, they benefit man, who finds his perfection by relating to God with his body and soul. Because the flesh is subordinate to the spirit, the creature's religious homage must be principally interior. External homage, the homage of everything that man is and of everything that he possesses, can only signify the principal and primary cult, the cult in spirit and truth.

In the *Summa theologiae*, when the time comes for Thomas to give an account of the economy of external acts, he brings the notion of sign deliberately to the fore. This choice, decisive for the definition of sacrament, is for St. Thomas the culminating point of his teaching regarding the acts of cult.

Since visible realities are ordered to manifesting one principal

---

representation of sensible objects to themselves is not necessary for inner knowledge and for love."

31. "Superstition is a vice contrary to religion by excess, not that it offers more to the divine worship than true religion, but because it offers divine worship either to whom it ought not, or in a manner it ought not" (*ST* II-II, q. 92, a. 1). "On the other hand if that which is done be, in itself, not conducive to God's glory, nor raise man's mind to God, nor curb inordinate concupiscence, ... all this must be reckoned excessive and superstitious, because consisting, as it does, of mere externals, it has no connection with the internal worship of God" (*ST* II-II, q. 93, a. 2).

invisible reality, the notion of symbol or sign is best able to give an account of the relative character of bodily realities in the practice of divine cult. Since man is so constituted that he cannot rise to God except by means of sensible things, it follows that the essential reason for the use of these things in cult is to express the religion of the soul. But to establish the interdependence of interior religion and its bodily manifestations even more strongly, the Angelic Doctor emphasizes the law of signification: cultic signs are necessary not only in order to translate interior religion, but they also serve to "arouse man's mind ... to the spiritual acts by means of which he is united to God."[32]

These signs are *owed*, though in a secondary fashion. They, too, belong to the virtue of religion. They help man give to God the debt of cult in an integrally human mode, "that man may serve God with all that he has from God, that is to say, not only with his mind, but also with his body."[33] Subordinated to the interior acts, the cultic signs are proportionate, to the extent required by the virtue, to that Other who is God, Creator of the body and soul. They render him the debt of homage insofar as they manifest the absolute lordship of the Creator over the creatures who honor him.

Because they express and stimulate interior religion, the signs are clearly secondary, entirely ordered to fostering acts that belong to the virtue of religion in themselves, not in a relative but in a principal way.[34] Interior and external acts are both proper and immediate acts of the virtue of religion: *proper and immediate* because they are uniquely characterized by the special psychology of the virtue of religion and produced without the mediation of subordinate virtues.

---

32. *ST* II-II, q. 81, a. 7. See also q. 84, a. 2, apropos of the external marks of adoration. The function of the external act to stimulate acts of the spirit is a constant theme of Thomistic doctrine. Thus Thomas had already claimed in the *Commentary on the De Trinitate* (q. 3, a. 2) that "certain corporeal actions ordered to cult" are necessary, on the one hand, so that man may serve God with his whole being, but also so that he may be stirred up and incite others to "spiritual acts ordered to God."

33. *ST* II-II, q. 83, a. 12.

34. *ST* II-II, q. 81, a. 7.

But all cultic signs are subordinated to the two interior acts that Aquinas now studies: devotion (q. 82) and prayer (q. 83).

Devotion, the principal act of the virtue of religion, is "the will to give oneself readily to things concerning the service of God."[35] An act of the will by which the subject offers himself to God in service, devotion imposes a certain modality on human acts; it chooses the acts that are favorable to the prompt execution of what leads to God's honor. Consequently, it is at the heart of all acts of religion, of the interior act of prayer itself as well as all the exterior acts, where it exists virtually "as the motion of the mover is found virtually in the movements of the things moved."[36]

While devotion is an act of the will, prayer for its part regards the intellect, which it subordinates by raising it toward God. Prayer is a formulation of reason, by which the reason asks God for something that does not depend on itself but on his good will. In prayer, Thomas observes, man subjects much more than his body and the external goods used in God's service: he submits his intellect.[37] And when he does so, man proves once more the need to include external acts in the process, for example, in verbal expression.[38]

Sacred Signs

Although they are ultimately relative, the external signs of religion, in virtue of the immaterial and principal realities that they signify in the sensible order, are nonetheless *sacred*, removed from the profane, set apart. In fact, the sign is not only the mode in which interior religion is expressed outwardly, but also the means by which man enters into relation with God. As a consequence of the relation of the signifier to the reality signified, the sign possesses genuine religious value.

This notion is worked out indirectly in article 8, where the whole

---

35. *ST* II-II, q. 82, a. 1.
36. *ST* II-II, q. 82, a. 1, ad 2.
37. *ST* II-II, q. 83, a. 3, ad 3.
38. See *ST* II-II, q. 83, a. 12.

question of the essence of religion culminates. Having given all his attention to the external act in the previous article, Thomas here examines the nature of the relation between *religion* and *holiness*. The logical proof becomes the occasion for an analysis of the requirements of religion, under the aspect of the two dispositions required by *holiness*: purity and firmness. The religious soul is *pure* because it withdraws itself from inferior goods whose contact and alliance dishonor it. The religious soul is *firm* because it applies itself with constancy to those very things of God for the sake of which it detached itself from transitory goods. The truly holy and religious soul guards a purity in its contact with God that readies it for cult and a steadfastness that keeps it firm in its intention.

Although the notion of holiness here is taken in a primarily spiritual sense, as a virtuous activity of the religious soul, it naturally extends into the domain of the external acts of the virtue of religion. These too are holy actions. They are meant to express the soul's state of purity and firmness in its adherence to God. In external cult, the performance of sacred ceremonies and actions involves more than ritual exactness; it should proceed from the soul's religion. As it moves the body in carrying out ritual practices, the soul is grounded in holiness, wishing principally to render to God a spiritual cult that is signified and stimulated by the rite. Rites can be called holy insofar as they participate in religious holiness in the cultic mode proper to them.

The text offers another valuable remark: because holiness is attributed to everything that is involved in the divine cult, interior and external, in the external realm it extends to every reality placed in the service of God. Thus, "not only men, but also the temple, vessels and such like things are said to be sanctified through being applied to the worship of God."[39] We can already say that what modern religious anthropology means by the general term *sacred* cannot sufficiently account for the essence of religion. The *sacred* is really

---

39. *ST* II-II, q. 81, a. 8.

nothing more than a symbol and external sign. In order for us to appreciate it for what it truly is, we must measure it by the standard of interior religion.

THE VARIOUS FORMS OF
EXTERNAL CULT

After studying the two interior acts of devotion and prayer, St. Thomas proceeds to analyze the external acts. He lists three major categories: *actions, gifts,* and *sacred things.*[40] We will consider first the acts of adoration by which religious man subjects his body to God, then the acts by which he submits his possessions to the Divine Majesty, namely sacrifices and oblations. Finally, we will examine sacred things, the places and objects that relate to the sacrificial act, as they are discussed in the treatise on religion. As Aquinas remarks, a consideration of sacred things will require an analysis of the sacraments. However, although sacrament remains an act of religion (rising from man to God), it is also an *act of Christ* for the sanctification of souls.[41] Thus St. Thomas refers his reader to the treatise on the sacraments in the *Tertia pars.*[42]

Adoration

The *principal* intention of the bodily act of adoration is to offer interior homage,[43] which manifests itself *in a secondary way* through exterior signs of humility: "when we genuflect we signify our weakness

40. Within each of these three distinctions, he gathers the various forms of worship that relate to each one. First he will look at bodily gestures, such as adoration (q. 84). Then he will move on to study the categories of gifts given to God: sacrifices (q. 85), oblations (q. 86), tithes (q. 87), and vows (q. 89). Finally, he considers the use of sacred things, such as the use of the Divine Name in oaths (q. 89), adjuration (q. 90), and invocation (q. 91).

41. See *ST* III, q. 60, a. 5: "In the use of the sacraments two things may be considered, namely, the worship of God, and the sanctification of man."

42. See *ST* II-II, q. 89, prologue.

43. Aquinas treats adoration in *ST* II-II, q. 84. See also *Commentary on the Sentences* III, d. 9, q. 1, a. 3, q^a 3; and *Summa contra Gentiles*, III, ch. 119, no. 4, and ch. 120, no. 10.

in comparison with God, and when we prostrate ourselves we pro-
fess that we are nothing of ourselves."[44] The humility of the devout
soul is manifested through the humiliation of the body. The interior
posture of the heart honoring its God has a corresponding external
posture that is related to it, flowing from it and manifesting it. Further, the external posture incites the soul to submit itself to God.[45]
The act of adoration does not possess the quality of homage from
the sole fact of being performed in its materiality, but rather insofar
as it is spiritualized and signifying, carried out as a function of interior adoration. The spiritual order and the sensible order unite; the
former is the end of the latter. The external act is due insofar as its
purpose is above all to signify the soul's respect.

Does God alone deserve adoration? Does not man offer signs of
respect toward certain creatures because of their perfection or authority? Thomas distinguishes religion or *latria* from the cult called
doulia. *Latria* consists in adoring the supreme and uncreated excellence, whereas *doulia* moves us to render certain signs of reverence
to eminent creatures. These signs can amount to what our Doctor
calls "adoration," but then we must understand this term according
to its proper use in the medieval liturgical vocabulary: adoration was
an act of homage consisting in prostrating oneself before a power invested with a sacred character, whether pontifical or royal. Such a
sign of humility, therefore, did not signify an act of divine homage—
though in our times it would seem particularly reserved for divine
honor. "It was with the reverence due to an excellent creature that
Nathan adored David."[46] From this we understand that the meaning
of bodily adoration depends rather on the intention of the one who
offers it than on the mere external quality of the action.

But according to St. Thomas there is a type of homage reserved
for God that cannot be offered to any other, even if that other be
the most perfect image of God on earth. He has in mind the act of

44. *ST* II-II, q. 84, a. 2, ad 2.
45. *ST* II-II, q. 84, a. 2.
46. *ST* II-II, q. 84, a. 1, ad 1.

sacrifice, an action that possesses in itself an exclusively latreutic significance.[47]

Sacrifices

St. Thomas had already developed a doctrine on the essence of sacrifice in his treatment of the value of rituals in the Old Law.[48] He established that the act of sacrifice, which signifies an exclusively divine homage, is a ritual offering of a particular type that manifests the most fitting posture of the soul before God. In question 85 of the treatise on religion, our Doctor expounds the excellence of sacrifice.

The Universal Practice of Sacrifice

Before any definition, St. Thomas makes the observation that offering sacrifice is a universal phenomenon. We encounter it in every historical period and in every place, always and everywhere. Now, he argues, "that which is observed by all is seemingly natural. Therefore the offering of sacrifices is of the natural law."[49] It was, of course, outside the intention of the Angelic Doctor and probably beyond the competence of the science of his time to delve into the relevant historical and geographical facts. What concerned him was rather to point out what in the performance of the sacrificial act is in conformity with human nature and religious psychology. In this regard, his insistence is noteworthy; seven times in the body of the article he uses expressions referring to the idea of nature, such as *naturalis ratio, in rebus naturalibus, naturaliter, ex naturali ratione*, among others.

The fact of sacrifice is grounded in the consciousness man has

47. *ST* II-II, q. 84, a. 1, ad 1. And St. Thomas cites St. Augustine: "Many tokens of Divine worship are employed in doing honor to men, either through excessive humility, or through pernicious flattery; yet so that those to whom these honors are given are recognized as being men to whom we owe esteem and reverence and even adoration if they be far above us. But who ever thought it his duty to sacrifice to any other than one whom he either knew or deemed or pretended to be a God?" (*De civitate Dei*, bk. 10, ch. 4).

48. See *SCG* III, ch. 119, no. 2; ch. 120, no. 10; then in the treatise on the Old Law: *ST* I-II, q. 102, a. 3.

49. *ST* II-II, q. 85, a. 1, s.c.

of his state of need and dependence on One who is superior, from whom he has received all things and to whom in justice he owes submission and respect. Sacrifice is the manifestation of this state of humble dependence. This expression of homage must be carried out in a manner proportionate to the nature of man, namely, through the use of sensible signs: "Hence it is a dictate of natural reason that man should use certain sensibles, by offering them to God in sign of the subjection and honor due to Him."[50] The sacrificial act thus consists in a sensible reality signifying the interior homage of total dependence that is given by the spiritual creature to its Creator.

Beyond the order of religious psychology there is that of moral obligation. As a religious act of natural law, sacrifice is owed to God. All men are bound to offer the interior sacrifice by which the rational creature offers to God the goods of his soul. With regard to the external signification of sacrifice—the oblation of external goods "offered to God in protestation of our subjection to God"—man's obligation varies with the different theological states of humanity: "For those who are under the Law are bound to offer certain definite sacrifices according to the precepts of the Law, whereas those who were not under the Law were bound to perform certain outward actions in God's honor, as became those among whom they dwelt, but not definitely to this or that action."[51] If a man who is ignorant of the divine law does not know the full power of sacrifice, or even if, as a result of the blinding effects of sin, his sacrificial practice is tainted with errors or grave faults, he still grasps the power of sacrifice "implicitly."[52]

The Exclusively Latreutic Nature of Sacrifice

The natural fact and the duty of the sacrificial act rest on the act's intrinsic religious value. Sacrifice is the most perfect act of religious homage. External sacrifice is actually, according to St. Augustine's

50. *ST* II-II, q. 85, a. 1.
51. *ST* II-II, q. 85, a. 4.
52. *ST* II-II, q. 85, a. 4, ad 2.

word, the "sacred sign of the invisible sacrifice."[53] It is the sign of man's gift of all that he possesses and of all that he is. Now the gift of himself, spiritual sacrifice, is owed only to God. Therefore, the sign of this gift, the external act of sacrifice, can be offered only to God.[54]

Invested with all the latreutic exclusivity of the invisible sacrifice, the external sign must consist in a particular mark that of itself signifies, by virtue of either human or divine institution, the interior homage of the one who offers it. This mark can never be shown in the honor of anyone else, even of the most excellent spiritual creatures, without giving offense, just as, in the temporal order, to usurp a mark of honor that signifies the honor owed to the sovereign would be "a crime of high treason (lèse-majesté)."[55]

Unlike the case of adoration, no intention can qualify the homage of sacrifice. The significance inherent in the act itself, by virtue of its positive determination, reveals the moral quality of the external act. We have seen that external acts, which are owed in themselves, possess a proper religious value because of their role in signifying the interior acts of devotion and of prayer. In the same way, sacrifice is not the simple exteriorization of the interior act, but has in itself a proper value as homage, absolute and exclusively latreutic homage. All the moral value of sacrifice thus comes from the fact that it is directly and uniquely oriented to God,[56] signifying—unlike the other acts of religion—an exclusively divine homage. Therefore it is the most perfect of all the acts of cult.

Sacrifices: Offering and Consecration

The set-apart character of sacrificial homage is expressed by appropriate sensible signs. It is more than the presentation of a simple of-

53. See *ST* II-II, q. 81, a. 7, ad 2: "These external things are offered to God, not as though He stood in need of them, ... but as signs of the internal and spiritual works, which are of themselves acceptable to God. Hence Augustine says (*De civitate Dei*, bk. 10, ch. 5): 'The visible sacrifice is the sacrament or sacred sign of the invisible sacrifice.'" See also *ST* II-II, q. 94, a. 2.

54. *ST* II-II, q. 85, a. 2.

55. *ST* II-II, q. 85, a. 2.

56. *ST* II-II, q. 85, a. 3.

fering. Actually, the term "oblation" alone—in St. Thomas a synonym for offering—does not suffice to designate the act of sacrifice in its totality: "Oblation is properly the offering of something to God even if nothing be done thereto, thus we speak of offering money or bread at the altar, and yet nothing is done to them. Hence every sacrifice is an oblation, but not conversely."[57]

The part of the sacrificial act that corresponds to a simple oblation is the fact of freely offering something to God, bringing to him some reality that one has received from him. However, the sacrificial offering is distinguished from a simple offering precisely in that the religious will that animates the act does not intend to present an indeterminate homage, but to satisfy the whole of the debt. Over and above partial offerings, its intention is to make the offering *par excellence*, a total offering; in this way the sovereign dominion of God will be recognized not over one good in particular, but over all the goods of creation, and especially over man himself. When offering a sacrifice, man humbles himself before God and makes a profession of his total dependence. This homage is so unique that it cannot be offered to any creature and thus could not be designated merely by the term oblation, which is too generic. Citing the book of Leviticus (Lv 2:1), St. Thomas speaks precisely about the *oblation of sacrifice*.

What is it about the ritual action, beyond the simple act of offering, that is significatory in an exclusive sense, permitting us to distinguish sacrifice from oblation? As the word indicates, the *sacrificium* is a *sacrum facere*. It means *to make* something *sacred*, to perform a ritual action "*circa res Deo oblatas,*" "on" the things offered and "around" them; in a word, to *consecrate* them. The act that distinguishes sacrifice from simple oblation consists in a kind of setting apart, a rite of *consecration* of the goods offered. A sacrifice properly speaking "requires that something be done to the thing which is offered to God, for instance animals were slain and burnt, the bread is broken, eaten, blessed."[58]

57. *ST* II-II, q. 85, a. 3.
58. *ST* II-II, q. 85, a. 3, ad 3.

Therefore, sacrifice includes a genuine offering and, further, an action performed over the thing offered. Sacrifice certainly includes oblation, but an oblation of a particular type, one in which, over and above the offering of matter, there is added something distinct. The significatory value of the rite is what distinguishes sacrifice from simple oblation—hence the determination of this rite is important. Sacrifice takes place when, in the very act of offering, the thing offered is treated as the material not of a simple rite of presentation, but of a special rite, *a sacred action* that in its very symbolism constitutes a mode of homage that is exclusively latreutic.

After an attentive reading of the text, it does not seem necessary to conclude that the *sacrum facere* must involve immolation *per se*. It is enough that something be done—*aliquid fit*. But there is a strong sense that the action should be transformative in some way and therefore that the putting to death of offered animals will be the most exclusive and fitting act because it is the most highly signifying. Both the sacrificial economy of salvation history and the history of sacrifices confirm this intuition. As we shall see, in Thomas's mind, the putting to death of animals is oriented with surprising directness toward the sacramental immolation of Christ.

Toward Christ's Sacrifice

In sacrifice the rational creature acknowledges the sovereign dominion of God by an act clearly expressive of his own mode of existence. Man offers something to God not because the thing offered has material value for God, but rather as an expression of the interior intention that inspires his act of offering. It is this intention, this interior sacrifice, that is signified in a formally latreutic manner by the sacrificial ritual.

The Old Law did nothing more than determine this act of natural religion and enable it to be a figure for Christ. The redemptive sacrifice of Christ took up, through its divine-human operation, both the figurative sacrifices of the Law and the inefficacious sacrifices of natural religion. For sin had not canceled out the act of sacrificial

oblation that is connatural to man. It had only modified its conditions, its capacity to be accepted. In the state of original justice,
God had accepted mankind's homage of subjection when it was still
graced and whole. Once man became separated from him by sin,
God no longer accepted man's sacrifice in itself, but only insofar as it
was taken up by Christ. It was in this way that he deigned to accept
Abel's gifts, the sacrifice of Abraham, and the offering of the High
Priest Melchisedech. By virtue of the redemptive Incarnation, Christ
restored the relation between God and mankind, by both his interi-
or offering and the external offering of Calvary. For he performed an
act on Calvary: the redemptive sacrifice, the bloody immolation of
the Word of God, an act of submission to the will of the Father in his
suffering, agony, and death.

We are well aware that the cultic realities of the moral virtue of
religion alone cannot account for the supernatural realities and the
transcendence of the Christian cult. Nevertheless, because of the
connatural necessity for man to offer sacrifice, it is possible to understand how the sacrifice of the God-man must take up the sacrifice
of man so that the sacrifice of man, by becoming that of Christ, can
be made acceptable.[59] The figurative determinations of the Old Law
have ceased, but the obligation of the sacred act of sacrifice remains
because it is due by natural law. This act was accomplished once and
for all on Calvary but is sacramentally represented on the altar until
the end of time: "Our Lord wished to leave to his beloved spouse the
Church a visible sacrifice (as the nature of man demands) by which
the bloody sacrifice which he was to accomplish once for all on the
cross would be re-presented...."[60]

When translating the excellence of sacrifice into the supernatural
order, one can already glimpse that the offering of Christ himself in
a "sweet-smelling" sacrifice forms, in its sacramental representation,

---

59. This is the basis for the necessity, in the liturgy of the Mass, of a rite of offertory
that refers our sacrifice to that of Christ.

60. Council of Trent, Session 22 (DS 1740), cited in *Catechism of the Catholic Church*,
2nd ed. (Vatican: Libreria Editrice Vaticana, 2012), no. 1366.

the center of the religious life of the cultic society of the Church. Consequently, we also understand that Eucharistic theology cannot neglect the profoundly human and thus ritual nature of the sacramental celebration of the sacrifice of Christ.

Oblations

St. Thomas dedicates a whole question of the treatise on religion to the oblations and first-fruits (*ST* II–II, q. 86), two distinct types of offerings united by the fact that they are presented to God, while the tithes go for the subsistence of the ministers of the cult.

We have already pointed out that oblation (or offering) consists in presenting some good to God with the intention of honoring him. Various things may be offered, all with some relation to the sacrificial action or to the practice of cult; for example, an offering for the use of the clergy. Due to the partial nature of the honor, an offering, unlike sacrificial oblation, has a certain undetermined character. It is given freely and spontaneously, in strong contrast with the rigorous determination of the matter and rite of sacrifice. St. Thomas emphasizes that it is precisely because the offering is essentially voluntary and spontaneous that it cannot be determined by law.[61] Though there exist obligatory offerings, the nature of their obligation could not stem from the character of the act of offering itself, but from fittingness and convention.

In this question of the treatise on religion, Aquinas refers more than once to the cultic and canonical uses of the Church. Earlier, in the treatise on the Old Law, he mentioned the role of non-sacrificial offerings in the organization of the Mosaic cult. In the two treatises, oblations are always seen as dedicated to cult. Even though they may be related to the practical needs of the cult and its ministers, the offerings are presented to God himself. Though God's ministers receive them, it is not because they are immediately intended for them, but because they are the intermediaries between God and the

---

61. *ST* II-II, q. 86, a. 4, ad 3.

people, assigned to perform the functions of the divine cult to which the offerings belong as homage.

In fact, the offerings are not more or less deputed to the divine cult but are wholly acts of homage. As acts of cult that the religious man renders to God by the use of external goods, the offerings also have value as signs of interior religion. They manifest, in the partial and undetermined mode proper to them, the generosity of the soul in the service of its Lord, for the cult of whom man reserves a part of his possessions.[62]

Sacred Persons, Places, and Things

In response to an objection raised about the abusive practice of selling offerings to laymen, St. Thomas affirms that "once they are consecrated, oblations such as sacred vessels and vestments cannot be granted to the use of the laity."[63] The act of offering makes the thing pass from the realm of the profane to the mysterious and symbolic domain of the sacred. The object offered is henceforth removed from common use, consecrated. It belongs to the divine world and becomes a means of entering into contact with God.

Therefore, the act of sacrifice permits us to account for the existence of *sacred realities*. It is because sacrifice is a sacred action exclusively set apart for God that, in order to increase the quality of this devotion and separateness of which sacrifice is the highest sign, ministers, temples, and objects are themselves separated from the profane realm to become holy and sacred.

The Priest, Sacred Minister

The treatise on religion allows us to perceive how the priestly function, independently of the forms it has taken in the history of salvation, corresponds to the basic needs of every religious society. Priesthood arises from an essential human need for a hierarchical

---

62. See *ST* I-II, q. 102, a. 3, ad 13.
63. *ST* II-II, q. 86, a. 2, ad 3.

and sacral organization of a category of men who are deputed to the cult of God. As such it is a natural institution that the order of grace assumes and elevates.

To explain the nature of the priesthood, several texts from his *Commentary on the Sentences*, various scriptural commentaries, and the *Summa theologiae* put forward the notion of *mediation*.[64] The priest is the intermediary between God and the people through a twin movement of ascent and descent. On the one hand, he brings to God the prayers, oblations, and sacrifices of the people; on the other hand, he is the interpreter, among men, of the divine will.[65]

Sacrifice is the act of cult *par excellence*. Consequently it is the heart of the priestly function. St. Thomas emphasizes this repeatedly: the connection is so intimate between the priestly function and the act of sacrifice that the priest is essentially ordered to offer sacrifice.[66]

Sacred Places and Objects

When treating the acts of adoration, St. Thomas asks whether they should be done in a particular place. He begins by recalling that the most relevant thing is the soul's devotion. However, although "the mind internally apprehends God as not comprised in a place," acts of adoration, because they are acts of the body, should be done in a determined and sacred place. The determination of this place is not the principal element but a question of fittingness.[67]

To prove this fittingness, the Angelic Doctor puts forward several reasons of a psychological nature. Just as it is connatural to man to

64. See *Commentary on the Sentences* IV, d. 5, q. 2, a. 2, q^a 2, ad 2; d. 13, q. 1, a. 1, q^a 1; d. 25, q. 2, a. 1, q^a 1; *Commentary on the Letter to the Hebrews* at 3.1, 5.2, 8.2, and 9.4; and *ST* III, q. 102, a. 4, ad 6; q. 22, a. 1, ad 1; q. 22, a. 4; q. 26, a. 1, ad 1.

65. *ST* II-II, q. 86, a. 2.

66. On the connection between priestly function and sacrifice, see Thomas, *Commentary on the Sentences* IV, d. 13, q. 1, a. 1, q^a 1, ad 1; and d. 24, q. 3, a. 2, q^a 1, ad 1; *Commentary on the Letter to the Hebrews* on 5:6 and 7:12; *ST* III, q. 22, a. 4, corp. and ad 2. "For every priest is ordained to offer sacrifice" (*Commentary on the Letter to the Hebrews*, ch. 3, lect. 1).

67. *ST* II-II, q. 84, a. 3.

manifest and encourage the soul's religion by means of sensible realities, so it is fitting—and a fact observable in all societies and civilizations[68]—to set apart a dwelling in honor of the divinity and to use there the objects that are also reserved for cult. The treatise on the Old Law develops this point: "The divine worship regards two things: namely, God, Who is worshipped, and men, who worship Him. Accordingly God, Who is worshipped, is confined to no bodily place; wherefore there was no need, on His part, for a tabernacle or temple to be set up. But men, who worship Him, are corporeal beings: and for their sake there was need for a special tabernacle or temple to be set up for the worship of God. . . . , that through coming together with the thought that the place was set aside for the worship of God, they might approach thither with greater reverence."[69]

Furthermore, it is fitting to pray in a place set apart for divine cult precisely because of its sacrality. To make a place for cult is to separate it from the profane realm by an act of consecration, making it a house of sacred actions. It is thus highly recommended to pray in the temple in preference to any other place, "on account of the sacred mysteries and other signs of holiness contained therein."[70] Mysteries and signs of holiness will actually stimulate devotion in those who pray in the temple. Also, the presence of other adorers will arouse fervor through imitation.

The Cultic Society

The beneficent confluence of (a) other adorers in the temple, (b) the universal obligation of sacrifice, (c) the public character of the priesthood, and (d) the possibility of transmitting offerings through the

---

68. See *ST* I-II, q. 102, a. 4: "Hence too it is customary among men for kings and princes, who ought to be reverenced by their subjects, to be clothed in more precious garments, and to possess vaster and more beautiful abodes. And for this reason it behooved special times, a special abode, special vessels, and special ministers to be appointed for the divine worship, so that thereby the soul of man might be brought to greater reverence for God."

69. *ST* I-II, q. 102, a. 4, ad 1.

70. *ST* II-II, q. 84, a. 3, ad 2.

ministers of cult, bring out another essential dimension of the external cult: the social character of religious homage. St. Thomas does not envisage religion as taking place primarily in the realm of the private conscience. The text of the treatise on religion and parallel texts in previous works suggest rather than systematically expound the public dimension of cult. When considering the subject of the virtue of religion, Thomas always takes man in the fullness of his human nature: a rational, social, political, and naturally religious animal. Moreover, the family, city, and even the state, because they belong to God by nature, have religious duties.

This is the traditional understanding, that of St. Thomas, and it is also the conclusion to which historians of societies and religions have been led by their empirical observations. Without addressing here the problem of the relation between divine and human law, we must observe with Fr. Labourdette that, according to this perspective, "every socially organized group, just as any more or less perfect familial or political society, is a *liturgical, cultic community*. A human people is always at the same time, in some way, a 'people of God.' Whether they claim a divine origin or historic election, or claim that the place they inhabit belongs specially to God or to some other god of their own, every people has a god; even further, it belongs to God and is *sanctified* by this belonging as compared with all other peoples. This is an absolutely constant fact."[71]

The Angelic Doctor's doctrine on sacrifices and oblations makes it evident that nature itself is the founder of a genuinely cultic human society and of the principle—stemming from the doctrine of sacrifice—of the special consecrated (set-apart) status of sacred persons, places, and objects. This cultic or sacral society is eminently hierarchical, and the deepest reason for this hierarchy is the transcendence of the mysteries the priest dispenses. Set up as "mediator ... 'between' the people and God" the priest-hierarch is appointed "to set forth the Divine teachings and sacraments before the people; and

71. Michel Labourdette, *Cours de théologie morale: Vertus rattachées à la justice* (Toulouse: Parole et Silence, 1961), 326.

besides to offer to the Lord things appertaining to the people, their prayers, for instance, their sacrifices and oblations."[72]

The Sacred: Cultic Holiness

Aquinas has taken a realist stance toward the sacred that is found in all historical religious phenomena, as shown by many studies in modern anthropology. But because his account of the sacred supposes its ordination to the interior act as the principle of the external act that is owed, he avoids the pitfall of a superstitious materialization of the sacred. Thus persons, places, and things are called holy and sacred because they signify the holiness—purity and firmness—of the religious soul who offers the sacrifice while using determined places and instruments.

This conception of the sacred also avoids the danger of an intellectualist devaluation of the ontological subsistence of sacred realities, which, like all the actions attributed to the virtue of religion, are "holy" not only because they come into cult in the mode of presentation, but also because they receive *something divine*.[73] The debt of homage rendered in cult is accompanied by a certain sanctification that proceeds from the cult and is ordered to it. For this reason, the holiness of cultic objects and realities may be rightly described by the term *sacramentum*—even before the arrival of the supernatural perfection of the Christian sacrament. Now these cultic objects require a definite rite that signifies their role in the divine cult and the sanctification that they receive from on high. Thus certain particular rites consecrate persons and things to the service of the cult, conferring upon them a significant mark, a sacred *character*, a *fittingness for cult*, in a word, a cultic holiness that is, nonetheless, entirely external.

We can already glimpse how much the idea of cultic deputation through "consecration," once transposed into the order of the divine

---

72. *ST* II-II, q. 86, a. 2.

73. "To [worship and service] belong all acts ascribed to religion, because, by them all, man bears witness to the Divine excellence and to his own subjection to God, either by offering something to God, or by assuming something Divine" (*ST* II-II, q. 81, a. 3, ad 2).

Incarnation, will be able to account for the cultic identity of the Church. For the sacraments of Baptism, Confirmation, and Holy Orders have as their immediate object the production of a mark of supernatural consecration in the soul: the character. This latter, in a manner proper to each sacrament received, deputes the subject to the divine cult.[74] Consequently, the Church is the cultic society *par excellence*: all her members, by virtue of the sacramental characters, participate in various degrees in the priesthood of Christ. All render to God the cult due to him, and the only one acceptable to him, in the name of Christ, who lives and acts in them.

THE SACRED: SIGN OF THE RELIGION OF THE HEART

In our review of the *Summa theologiae*'s treatise on religion, we have tried to present the thought of St. Thomas Aquinas on the external acts of religion. They belong to the acts required by the debt of religion, connatural to religious man and formally due in their corporeal dimension. But since in man bodily realities are ordered to the moral and spiritual dimension, the external acts of cult are due only in a secondary way insofar as they are *signs* that encourage and manifest the principal interior religion, which is composed of acts of devotion and prayer.

We have pointed out a hierarchy of external cultic realities: acts of adoration, vocal prayer, sacrifices, oblations, and so forth. Aquinas stresses the preeminence of sacrifice, underlining its connaturality, defining its exclusively latreutic nature, and analyzing its internal constitution. Further, there are ministers, places, and objects separated from profane use and put into a state of "cultic holiness," the *sacred*, by rites of consecration; these are ordered to the sacrificial offering and to the other public acts of religious homage rendered in the name of the society of men.

74. See *ST* III, q. 63, a. 1.

Therefore, the sacred, to which religious anthropology too often reduces the essence of religion, stands in the order of sign. The sacred is not the whole of religion, which is principally interior, but it is a good word to designate the vast ensemble of external realities that have been separated from the profane order, marked out by the symbolic seal as belonging specially to God and deputed in an exclusive manner to his cult. As signs, sacred realities are, therefore, means of entering into communication with God and this in a two-fold sense: by serving to render to God the religious debt of homage and by taking up some of the holiness of the One for whom they have been set apart.

These preliminary discussions have touched upon religion only as a moral duty, considering manifestations of cult insofar as they are connatural to religious man, abstracting from the cultic regimes of salvation history. But as several allusions made in the treatise to contemporary Church practices suggest, St. Thomas certainly does not want to remove the acts of the virtue of religion from the cultic economy of Revelation. Rather, he has chosen first to put forward the work of creative Wisdom in human reason.

Without recourse to Revelation, the practice of cult went through serious alterations. However, apart from the superstitious practices and the various deformations he has denounced,[75] and which we witness in the history of religions, we believe with St. Thomas that it is still possible to find value in the natural and persistent manifestations of the moral virtue of religion that sin and superstition have not been able to erase. In this sense, the observations of St. Thomas founded on an Aristotelian metaphysics are not contradicted by the research of religious anthropology.

The conclusion is obvious: the manifestation in history of God's plan for salvation does not change or overturn the anthropological foundations of the acts of the virtue of religion, but rather affirms and elevates them. Salvation history is rooted in man's natural

75. See *ST* II-II, q. 92 (superstition in general), q. 93 (undue worship), q. 94 (idolatry), q. 95 (divination), and q. 96 (magic).

condition as creative Wisdom established it. The order of grace, despite its radical novelty, makes use of the religion that is in the heart of man. The life of theological virtue has no more destroyed natural religion than faith has abolished the requirements of reason. Grace has assumed religion and along with it all the external acts that manifest and encourage it, according to the peculiar economy of the various moments in salvation history.

Of course, the notion of "natural religion" discussed here is insufficient to account for the superiority of the spiritual cult inaugurated by Christ. For one who is concerned about the profound nature and spirit of the liturgy, making the cult of the true God depend on the categories of religious anthropology alone would be a grave error. But would it be any less an error to conceive of the Christian liturgy without the rituality that the Creator himself has placed in the mind and heart of man?

2

Cult in the Old Dispensation according to St. Thomas

According to St. Thomas Aquinas, the destiny of mankind—its return to God (*reditus*)—is intimately related to the act of creation (*exitus*). As many studies of the *Summa theologiae*'s organization have shown, behind the systematic organization of sacred doctrine lies a grand schema of *exitus-reditus*.[1] The presence of this schema in the *Summa* clarifies "the meaning of the salvific economy,"[2] according to Fr. Congar, or to use the phrase of Fr. Albert Patfoort, "the logic of God's design."[3] After having contemplated, in the first part (*Prima pars*), the Being of God in himself and the work of creation, the Angelic Doctor dedicates the remainder of the *Summa* to the vast movement of man's return to God. In this he takes man as he is; certainly the image of God, but also having a nature wounded by sin, a being subject to the law of time, incapable of entering into

1. The debate over the plan of the *Summa Theologiae* has essentially consisted in nuancing the affirmation of Fr. Marie-Dominique Chenu (*Introduction à l'étude de saint Thomas d'Aquin*), who first identified the presence of a neo-Platonic schema of *exitus* and *reditus* in the *Summa*. For a summary of the discussion, see Jean-Pierre Torrell, *Saint Thomas Aquinas*, vol. 1, *The Person and His Work*, trans. Robert Royal (Washington, DC: The Catholic University of America, 2005), 153–56.

2. Congar, "Le sens de l'économie salutaire dans la théologie de saint Thomas d'Aquin," 73–122.

3. Patfoort, *La Somme de saint Thomas et la logique du dessein de Dieu*.

full communion with God except through the mediation of Christ. Man's return to God is thus inscribed within history, the history of salvation.

In the progressive economy of revelation, what is the function of the exterior acts of religion whose moral importance we have highlighted in our previous chapter? St. Thomas teaches us that "external worship should be in proportion to the internal worship, which consists in faith, hope, and charity"[4]; thus it would seem that rites become more perfect to the degree that the cult they signify becomes more spiritual. What, then, is the proper substance of the rites? Do they become less necessary or even superfluous? Isn't the very notion of ritual something "Pharisaical," something that ought to be overcome in favor of a purified religion, of exterior forms that are simple and spontaneous? Such questions touch very closely upon the nature of the Christian liturgy. They are no less important in the present moment when, following the publication of Cardinal Ratzinger's *The Spirit of the Liturgy*, the time is ripe for a reflection on the present state of the divine cult in the Church.[5]

As a contribution to this reflection, we will study the teaching of the Universal Doctor on the cultic economy of salvation history. Tracing the progress of man from one theological state to another, this teaching distinguishes two great cultic moments in salvation history: the cult of the Old Law, a "corporeal" and imperfect cult in which the mediation of Christ and the Church is only prefigured, and the cult of the New Law, a spiritual cult, the cult of Christ himself, whose saving actions are commemorated and *represented* in an efficacious manner by the sacraments of the Church.

We will begin by examining the cultic theology of the Old Law as presented in the treatise on the Old Law at the beginning of the

---

4. *ST* I-II, q. 103, a. 3.

5. Cardinal Ratzinger, *The Spirit of the Liturgy*. For an overview of the debate occasioned by the work's publication, see the review of Fr. Pierre-Marie Gy, "L'esprit de la liturgie du Cardinal Ratzinger est-il fidèle au Concile, ou en réaction contre?," *La Maison-Dieu*, no. 229 (2002): 171–78, then the Cardinal's reply: "L'esprit de la liturgie ou la fidélité au Concile, Réponse au Père Gy," in *La Maison-Dieu*, no. 230 (2002): 114–20.

second part (*Prima secundae*) of the *Summa*. In this treatise, although the Angelic Doctor here and there points out the connaturality of certain exterior acts as subordinated to the interior acts of religion—a fact that has its origins in natural law[6]—he is primarily concerned with the ritual economy of the first stage of salvation history and, more precisely, with the cultic precepts of the Mosaic Law. These questions, among the longest in the *Summa*, take up the nature of the ceremonial precepts (q. 101), their literal and figurative causes (q. 102), and finally their transitory duration insofar as they are entirely relative to the perfect cult of Christ (q. 103).

THE NATURE OF THE CEREMONIAL PRECEPTS

As a result of original sin, the precepts of the natural law, whose influence was ruined by the "law of concupiscence," no longer suffice to direct men in virtue. Their religious life having fallen prey to superstition and idolatry, the benefits of revelation were necessary.[7] But before decreeing a law for an entire people, God manifested himself to Abel, Melchizedek, Abraham, and other prophets. Between the original sin and the gift of the Law, there was thus an intermediate period, which was nothing more or less than the age of the Law inscribed universally into human nature.[8] Without fixing anything in writing, God ordained certain definite ways to honor him. But the prescribed cult already took on the figurative meaning that would characterize the cult of the Law to come. Thus, when Abel, Noah, Melchizedek, and Abraham offered a sacrifice, the same divine will that had revealed to them the particular manner in which they were to offer it conferred a certain supernatural quality on this sacrifice, so that it already constituted a profession of faith in Christ, who was to come.

---

6. See *ST* I-II, q. 99, a. 3.

7. Thomas Aquinas, *On the Ten Commandments*, prologue.

8. St. Thomas designated this period simply as coming "*ante legem*, before the law," in *ST* II-II, q. 174, a. 6 (the article in which he treats the degrees of prophecy in salvation history).

Nevertheless, as time passed and the hour of the redeeming Incarnation approached, it became more urgent to enter into a more perfect understanding of the Divine Mystery and thus to give specific determination to the cultic precepts that would serve to signify the faith. God no longer taught only a few men but an entire people, to whom he gave a number of ceremonial precepts. To the initial stage of the economy of salvation, a stage of spiritual infancy,[9] there thus corresponds a whole cultic regime. Though already illuminated by some supernatural knowledge of God, this cult is, nevertheless, as all the Old Law, in a state of imperfection,[10] for it is entirely relative to the perfect cult that only Christ is able to fulfill.

Precepts ordered to the divine cult

In his discussion of the principle that justifies the ceremonial precepts, St. Thomas first points out the fact that they established a relationship with God. The ceremonial precepts, however, are distinguished from the moral precepts of religion in that they do not receive their authority from reason. Human morality is defined by reason, but the ceremonial precepts oblige by virtue of a divine decision to fill in what was lacking in the natural law. Thus, for example, God adds to the natural law the obligation to offer certain specific victims.[11]

Since they are determinations of the moral precept of religion, ceremonial precepts do not possess religious value in themselves, that is, in the material fact of their performance. They acquire value by reason of the divine authority that has promulgated them and the religious intention of the men who perform them. In the divine plan of salvation, "it ... is a matter of ceremonial precept that man should show some fitness for the divine worship."[12]

9. See *ST* I-II, q. 91, a. 5; q. 99, a. 5.
10. *ST* I-II, q. 98, a. 1.
11. *ST* I-II, q. 99, a. 4, ad 2; q. 104, a. 1.
12. *ST* I-II, q. 104, a. 1, ad 3.

A Figurative Cult

If the ceremonial precepts are mysterious and obscure, the reason is that God has willed them to be figurative in this way. Contrary to Maimonides's opinion, however, their mystical sense does not exclude their practical, cultic, and literal dimensions, but adds to and completes them.[13]

In order to demonstrate the figurative dimension of these precepts, our Doctor considers them in light of the reality of which they are shadows. Setting out to paint the great canvas of salvation history, he begins by reminding us that exterior cult is subordinate to interior cult. The former has gone through various regimes following mankind's progress in knowledge (*cognitio*) and love (*affectio*) of God. Each of these various regimes of union with God entails "so many ways [for mankind] to apply [its] external actions to the Divine worship."[14] In order to better define the nature of these cultic regimes, St. Thomas first points out the nature of exterior cult in the state of beatitude, in a brief but very dense sketch. In heaven, when the soul is reunited to the glorified body, "the human intellect will gaze on the Divine Truth in Itself." This face-to-face encounter will take place without the mediation of any figure, for everything will be present. Thus the exterior cult "will not consist in anything figurative, but solely in the praise of God, proceeding from inward knowledge and affection."[15] In this life, since we have not entered into the full light of eternity, "we need the ray of Divine light to shine upon us under the form of certain sensible figures." Thus, in our present condition it is unavoidable that the cult that men render to God in history be determined by the notion of "figure."

The two covenants have two corresponding regimes of sensible mediation. The cult of the Old Law is the figure of the cult of Christ and of the future beatitude. The cult of Christ and the Church is the

13. *ST* I-II, q. 101, a. 1, ad 4.
14. *ST* I-II, q. 101, a. 2.
15. *ST* I-II, q. 101, a. 2.

fulfillment of the figures of the Old Law, but is itself the earthly figure of the heavenly Jerusalem.

Under the Old Law, faith and hope pertained not only to the state of glory, but also to the ways and means necessary to approach it. Thus the corresponding cultic regime "needed to be figurative not only of the future truth to be manifested in our heavenly country, but also of Christ, Who is the way leading to that heavenly manifestation."[16] Relying upon a great number of figures adapted to men unable to comprehend his plan of salvation, God made use of a genuine pedagogy to prepare humanity in its childhood for the coming of Christ and his gift of grace. It was Christ who from the beginning gave the figures their consistency and proper value, though they could not confer any sort of justification by themselves since Christ was not yet immolated and glorified. According to the Letter to the Hebrews (7:19): "the law made nothing perfect." The whole value of the imperfect cult could derive only from the perfect cult of which it was the type and anticipation.

Under the New Law, the purpose will no longer be to prefigure the way of salvation, that is, Christ, as something in the future, but to commemorate it "as something past or present" (*per modum praeteriti vel praesentis*). This cult is more than a shadow, it is "the very *image* of the things," to use the term of the Letter to the Hebrews (10:1). The image (*imago*) has the fundamental property of similitude (*similitudo*), which is to say something between difference and absolute equality, or in this case between the Old-Testament shadow and the light of glory.[17] But there is another essential property of the image: imitation (*imitatio*). The image reflects the model (*exemplar*) to which is it subordinated, as in a mirror. In this sense the image, which differs from the reality, is still a figure. Thus the cult of the New Law is the image of certain supernatural realities past and present, but also a figure of the future glory.

---

16. *ST* I-II, q. 101, a. 2.
17. See *ST* I, q. 35, a. 1, ad 1; Thomas, *Commentary on the Sentences* I, d. 28, q. 2, a. 1.

A Diversity of Precepts

Once he has outlined the figurative value of the cultic precepts, St. Thomas asks about their great number.[18]

To the objection that a great number of rules constitutes a burden that is difficult to bear and takes away from the spiritual character of the divine cult, the Angelic Doctor begins by opposing the general state of the people to whom these precepts were given. Every people is composed of those "inclined to evil" and others "inclined to good, either from nature or from custom, or rather from grace." The first sort must be constrained by precepts, while the second "have to be taught and improved by means of the precepts of the law."[19] Under the Old Testament, these two categories of persons had need of numerous ritual laws.

Certain elements of the people had a tendency to idolatry. The history of Israel shows how much this evil was to be feared. To prohibit the myriad ways of partaking in this sin, it was necessary to promulgate a great number of precepts. This ceremonial economy manifests a sort of divine pedagogy, one that was extremely realistic, making use of the most corporeal and tangible aspects of cult—which are also the most subject to deviating into superstition. The Old Law thus permitted men who were inclined to evil, weighed down by the flesh and little capable of raising themselves up to the spiritual cult, to offer the homage of a true cult to the only true God, even while grasping no more than its sensible dimension.[20]

These acts were beneficial also for the just, who acquitted themselves of the debt of religion by acts that manifested and stimulated their interior devotion. The practice of all these rites "thus turned

---

18. (*ST* I-II, q. 101, a. 3.)

19. *ST* I-II, q. 101, a. 3. See also Thomas, *Commentary on the Sentences* IV, d. 1, q. 1, a. 5, q^a. 2, ad 2; and *Commentary on the Letter to the Romans*, ch. 5, lect. 6, where three sorts of man are distinguished among the Hebrew people: the sinners (*duri*), those making progress (*proficientes, mediocres*), and the perfect (*perfecti*).

20. See the distinction in Thomas's *Commentary on the Letter to the Romans*, ch. 5, lect. 6: while the law is given "as a scourge" to men inclined to evil, it is granted to those making progress "a pedagogue" (trans. Larcher, 184–85).

their mind to God in many ways, and more continually." Finally, the diversity of these rites had the quality of announcing "the mystery of Christ, which was foreshadowed by these ceremonial precepts; brought many boons to the world; and afforded men many considerations, which needed to be signified by various ceremonies."[21] Under the veil of precepts and signs, where average men and those inclined to evil saw nothing but constraints, God already revealed to the perfect the mystery to come and the gift of his grace.[22]

Nevertheless, the ceremonies "were weak and imperfect, both for representing the mystery of Christ, on account of its surpassing excellence, and for subjugating men's minds to God."[23] This incapacity was another reason in favor of their multiplication. Since their power to dispose men to attain the end was imperfect, no precept could suffice on its own to perform the debt of cult, much less to manifest the excellence of the mystery to come. Just as a doctor administers more remedies to make up for the absence of one effective remedy, yet without the desired goal being achieved, so has God established dispositive precepts that are complex and imperfect.

The classification of the precepts established by Aquinas became more precise as he moved from the *Summa contra Gentiles* to the *Summa theologiae*. In the former case, our Doctor included the exterior act of the moral virtue of religion and its preceptive determination in the Old Law in one treatment.[24] In the *Summa theologiae*'s treatise on the Old Law (q. 101, a. 4) he considers principally the

21. *ST* I-II, q. 101, a. 3.
22. See Thomas, *Commentary on the Letter to the Romans*, ch. 5, lect. 6: "For the perfect the Law regarding ceremonies was a sign" (ibid., 185). See also the passage of the *Gloss* Thomas cites in *Commentary on the Sentences* IV, d. 1, q. 1, a. 5, q^a 2, ad 2: "for the manifestation and witness of grace, and the signification of future things" (trans. Mortensen, 7:42).
23. *ST* I-II, q. 101, a. 3, ad 1.
24. *SCG* III, ch. 119. St. Thomas first distinguishes *sensible sacrifices*, sacred signs instituted "so that man may be reminded that he ought to refer both his own being and all his possessions to God as end, and thus to the Creator, Governor, and Lord of all" (no. 2). Then, certain sensible things serve man as means of sanctification, consecrations or *sacraments*, which "are applied to man through sensible things whereby he is washed, or anointed, or fed, or given drink, along with the expression of sensible words" (no. 3).

determination of the precepts in salvation history, the moral value of the act being reassigned to the study on the virtue of religion.

St. Thomas begins his enumeration of the precepts with the category of *sacrifices*. Insofar as they are the most perfect acts of homage rendered to God, they are a special feature of the exterior cult.[25] Here he also mentions the other kinds of offerings, namely oblations and gifts.[26] Sacrifice is distinguished as a special offering, one over which a sacred and signifying rite of latreic homage is performed.

The sacrificial act requires the presence of persons deputed to its performance, consecrated or sanctified persons. Thus offering sacrifice causes the "sanctification" not only of certain categories of persons, but also, in a certain manner, of an entire people. Those forms of sanctification that are ultimately cultic are here defined as the "sacraments" (*sacramenta*) of the Old Law. Here we can discern the outlines of the sacramental character proper to the New Law, which is a genuine deputation to a spiritual cult. In addition, as a result of the ritual mark they receive, the subjects of the *sacraments* must manifest their state of consecration by their exterior comportment, "and to this pertain the 'observances,' for instance, in matters of food, clothing, and so forth."[27]

Finally, the practice of cult requires objects and places for the offering of sacrifices. These instruments, such as the tabernacle and its utensils, belong to the category of what Aquinas calls sacred things (*sacra*), which means things that have been consecrated and reserved entirely for the divine cult, *sacred signs* of the religion of Israel.

Finally, he distinguishes the various sensible practices by which our attention is directed toward God, "such as prostrations, genuflections, vocal ejaculations, and hymns" (no. 4).

25. *ST* I-II, q. 101, a. 4: "The worship consists specially in sacrifices, which are offered up in honor of God."

26. *ST* I-II, q. 101, a. 4, ad 5.

27. *ST* I-II, q. 101, a. 4; see also the response to the fourth objection: "Those things which pertained to the mode of life of the people who worshipped God, retained the common designation of observances, in so far as they fell short of the above. For they were not called sacred things, because they had no immediate connection with the worship of God, such as the tabernacle and its vessels had. But by a sort of consequence they were matters of ceremony, in so far as they affected the fitness of the people who worshipped God."

THE PURPOSE OF THE CEREMONIES

After defining and enumerating the ceremonial precepts, St. Thomas clarifies their significance in the divine plan of salvation. To do this, he resorts to the Divine Wisdom, the supreme reason of all things. Since everything that proceeds from the Divine Wisdom is necessarily ordered to it as to its end, the precepts given by God were in some way proportionate to the end that he proposed for himself.[28] Our analysis of the nature of the precepts has taught us that this end is twofold. On the one hand, the precepts must order the cult of the people God has chosen for himself; on the other, they must prefigure the mystery of Christ. This dual purpose suggests that one must distinguish a plurality of senses in the explanation of the precepts, which can be reduced to two: the *literal* sense and the *figurative* or *spiritual* sense.[29]

The Literal Sense and the Spiritual Sense

There is a temptation to accord no more than a figurative value to the old rites, one entirely relative to the coming of the Redeemer. But just like the historical facts of the Old Testament, the rites too contain a literal meaning:[30] the words they use express certain precise things, valid and intelligible in themselves,[31] in keeping with the time in which they took place.

St. Thomas explains the literal historical reasons for the precepts

28. *ST* I-II, q. 102, a. 1.

29. The plurality of the senses of Scripture is a matter of such importance in the exposition and comprehension of sacred doctrine that our Doctor addresses it in the first question of the *Summa theologiae*: "The author of Holy Writ is God, in whose power it is to signify His meaning, not by words only (as man also can do), but also by things themselves. So, whereas in every other science things are signified by words, this science has the property, that the things signified by the words have themselves also a signification" (*ST* I, q. 1, a. 10). See also *Commentary on the Letter to the Galatians*, ch. 5, lect. 7.

30. *ST* I-II, q. 102, a. 1.

31. See Marie-Dominique Chenu, "La théologie de la loi ancienne selon saint Thomas," *Revue thomiste* 61 (1961): 493: "When reading the *Summa*, one cannot help but be struck by the almost tenacious persistence of St. Thomas to discover "reasons" and rational "causes" for the precepts.... We are certainly dealing with *Biblical* theology here, but

as part of the religious education of Israel. By this organization of cult, men inclined to evil would be kept from idolatry, and the ordinary man would be suitably ordered to God. All, even the most perfect, would find in the practice of the precepts many means to celebrate God's benefits, to engrave them on their memory, to inculcate in themselves an understanding of the divine excellence, and also "to point out the disposition of mind which was then required in those who worshipped God,"[32] all features necessary for a more perfect practice of the moral virtue of religion.

But even though Aquinas brings a certain focus to his literal interpretation of Scripture that many of his contemporaries, with their penchant for allegory, did not have, he did not neglect the figurative exegesis of the patristic tradition. Certain particular prescriptions, he observes, "have no literal cause, but only a figurative cause; whereas in the abstract [*in communi*] they have a literal cause."[33] Such ritual precepts acquire a rational cause only when understood in a general sense, as part of the larger system of cult.

The interpretations offered by St. Thomas in this domain give great importance to the figurative sense of Scripture: one must know how to "keep the spiritual senses, i.e., the offspring, and set aside the observance of the letter, i.e., the mother."[34] Aquinas shares this spiritual understanding of Scripture, as Fr. de Lubac noted, with the whole patristic and medieval tradition.[35] This tradition followed a typological exegesis that considered Scripture to be the narrative of God's economy in history, founded on the indispensable literal

---

theology nonetheless, which is to say a passionate search of all possible intelligibility in the word and words of God: *intellectus fidei.*"

32. *ST* I-II, q. 102, a. 2.

33. *ST* I-II, q. 102, a. 2, ad 3.

34. *ST* I-II, q. 102, a. 6, ad 8.

35. For Henri de Lubac, St. Thomas belonged to "the family of those who followed Origen and Augustine, and all of whose work hearkened in its own way to the wishes of someone like Rabanus and Garnier." He proves to be "the simple and faithful echo, right down to the smallest detail, of a long tradition. His means can often be different and also more potent than those that many before him had at their disposal. From them to him, though, the spirit of the thing has not changed." De Lubac, *Medieval Exegesis*, trans. Mark Sebanc (Grand Rapids, MI: Eerdmans, 1998), 1:221.

reading of the facts, whose purpose was the spiritual understanding of God's mysteries.

The Law being "only a shadow of the good things to come and not the true form of these realities" (Heb 10:1), it is above all the spiritual and transcendent significance of the cultic precepts that requires attention, more than their transitory particularity. The whole cultic economy of the Old Law is oriented, clarified, and perfected through the cult of the new and eternal Covenant sealed in the blood of the Savior Jesus Christ.[36] Seen in this light, the spiritual sense of the precepts includes all the riches of the realm conquered by Christ. St. Thomas accepts the following distinctions among the spiritual senses: certain precepts prefigure the mysteries of Christ, in which case they require *allegorical* or *mystical* interpretations. Others relate more to the moral life of the faithful and depend on a moral or so-called *tropological* sense of Scripture. Finally, others, called *anagogical*, point forward to the state of future glory.[37]

In writing the Law, the sacred author obviously proposed certain prescriptions that would serve the religious practice of his Israelite contemporaries. However, all the religious value of his concrete designs were only a reflection of the profound designs for which they prepared the way. In other words, since the spiritual sense was the sacred author's intention, then, as J. Gribomont has written, we must look "for an authentic extension of the literal sense, for those realities that truly correspond to the inchoative religious meanings of the letter."[38] Thus the Angelic Doctor admitted that every faithful Israelite,

36. For a treatment of the fulfillment of the Old Covenant according to Thomistic Christology, see Matthew Levering, *Christ's Fulfillment of Torah and Temple: Salvation according to Thomas Aquinas* (Notre Dame, IN: University of Notre Dame Press, 2002).

37. *ST* I-II, q. 102, a. 2. See also *ST* I, q. 1, a. 10; *Quodlibetal Questions*, VII, q. 6, a. 2; *Commentary on the Letter to the Galatians*, ch. 5, lect. 7.

38. Jean Gribomont, "Le lien des deux testaments selon la théologie de saint Thomas," *Ephemerides theologicae lovanienses* 22 (1946): 78–79: "In reality, in order to determine the aspect of the 'thing' that deserves to be considered, one must appeal not to a more or less Platonic gnosticism, but to the most rigorous critical exegesis, aiming to bring out precisely what constituted the permanent religious value of the so-called 'thing' in the eyes of the author."

however imperfect, who dedicated himself to the cultic prescriptions according to the letter, had access to an "implicit knowledge" of the profound spiritual meaning that was hiding under the veil of the figures.[39] By practicing in a literal manner all that had been prescribed in the cultic order—that is, by offering the sacrifices, receiving the ritual consecrations, respecting the observances, and religiously making use of the sacred things—the faithful Israelite was permitted some sort of perception of the supernatural realities of which the precepts were the signs.[40]

St. Thomas was careful to avoid a certain strand of medieval allegorism that, remaining at the most material surface of the text, amounts to nothing more than "a perpetual extrapolation of the literal contents of the Bible."[41] However, he was not always innocent of certain accommodative exegetical extrapolations, a result of his epoch's relatively weak scientific exegesis of the "letter."[42] This method of treating cultic figures will be transposed and taken up again in

---

39. *ST* I-II, q. 101, a. 2, ad 1.

40. "We see that there is a middle way between, on the one hand, a conscious awareness of an image as being an image—for example, the awareness that we have today of Israel as a type or figure—and on the other hand, the simple awareness of the *res*. This middle way is a perception of that aspect of a thing which makes that thing a sign, sharing in some deeper reality; yet this perception does not involve an abstraction from one's immediate knowledge of the thing" (Gribomont, "Le lien des deux testaments," 76).

41. "What in fact is the allegorical domain of Bede, the *fundamentum aedificii*, as Hugh of Saint Victor calls it? It is the most material surface of the text or, more exactly, of its words, taken without consideration of the narrative that, by enclosing [the text] within certain propositions, gives the words their significance, the *prima significatio narrationis*. There is no grammatical, logical, or literary analysis. The veils of the tabernacle? Their length is a figure for the long-suffering patience of the Church, their width is her charity, and lo! just as its width was four cubits, so there are four Gospels that teach us this charity, while its height of twenty-eight cubits represents four times the seven days of the week that ends in the Sabbath, and also Psalm 28, which is about the completion of the tabernacle. And so forth. There is no historical foundation in this pulverization of the text; no consideration of the *proprietas verborum*." Marie-Dominique Chenu, "Les deux âges de l'allégorisme scripturaire au Moyen Âge," *Recherches de théologie ancienne et médiévale* 18 (1951): 25–26.

42. On Aquinas's method of exegesis, see, among others, Marie-Dominique Mailhiot, "La pensée de saint Thomas sur le sens spirituel," *Revue thomiste* 59 (1959), 617ff.; de Lubac, *Exégèse médiévale*, 4:272ff.

the *Tertia pars*, in reference to the rites of the Christian liturgy, and especially the rite of the Eucharist.[43] In fact, we find there the same desire to explain the rites of the Church in a literal manner matched with a "trans-historic" theological and spiritual reading of the sacramental celebration. Nevertheless, despite the weak historical documentation and the imaginative character of certain allegories, the method remains remarkable for its even-handedness, and may even point the way forward toward a more complete understanding of the liturgy today.

ANALYSIS OF SEVERAL CULTIC PRACTICES

Now we will consider several examples. From our liturgical, or, more precisely, Eucharistic perspective, we will first follow Aquinas's exposition of the *sacrifices* (*ST* I-II, q. 102, a. 3), then, among the *sacraments* of the Mosaic Law, his commentary on the Paschal Lamb (a. 5); finally, we will briefly mention the ordinance of the *holy things* and *observances* (a. 4).

The Sacrifices

The literal explanation of the ceremonies relating to the sacrifices hinges on how they contribute to the practice of the virtue of religion. Article 3 sorts the ceremonies into two categories: some relate to the proper organization of divine cult and others to the preservation of the people from the sin of idolatry.

First, the divine cult must be ordained and signified. The act of sacrifice has two components: the offering of goods in order to properly dispose the offerer, then the act of consecration of these goods which thus become holy things.[44] Because the sacrificial act is the sign by which the soul attests that God is the first principle and last end, the cultic realities attached to it should signify the submission and spiritual purity of the religious man. Now, how could the various

---

43. See *ST* III, (q. 83, a. 2–5.)
44. *ST* II-II, q. 85, a. 3.

sacrificial rites of the Old Testament, which all consisted in the offering and slaying of an animal, signify the proper ordering of the soul to God and the purity of his dispositions? Would it not have been fitting to signify the submission of the soul of the offerer by the oblation of living animals? St. Thomas's reply is brief and simple. The religious man offers to God, as a sign of his absolute dependence, from the animals he possesses. If these animals are put to death and burned, it is because "God gave them to man for food [and] it is by being cooked that they are made fit for human consumption."[45]

As for the spiritual purity of the offerer, St. Thomas is quite insistent on the point that the realities intended to signify this purity are themselves characterized by a certain purity and perfection in the order of creation. Relying on the zoological science of his day and often citing extensively from Maimonides, he distinguishes the animals proper to each sacrifice, especially those destined for the sacrifices for sin, in a very literal way. The "licit" animals belong to species most fit for human nourishment and are distinguished by their cleanness and propriety as food. By reason of their particular perfection, they thus signify the spiritual health of the religious man who offers them in sacrifice. As for the unacceptable animals, they are savage and refractory to human service and wallow in uncleanness. From the quality of the animal, the Angelic Doctor passes to several ritual details of the sacrifices. Thus, in the *holocaust*, the victim was entirely burned as a sign of absolute reverence, "so that as the whole animal by being dissolved into vapor soared aloft, so it might denote that the whole man, and whatever belongs to him, are subject to the authority of God, and should be offered to Him."[46]

In addition to their role in signifying the divine cult, the precepts also have a pedagogical value, educating the chosen people in the cult of the true God, in order that "the human mind ... recognize no first author of things other than God, nor place its end in any

---

45. *ST* I-II, q. 102, a. 3, ad 5.
46. *ST* I-II, q. 102, a. 3, ad. 8.

other."[47] To turn mankind from the worship of false gods, the sacrificial practices were made distinct from those of the idolaters: The animals offered to other divinities were discarded in favor of those that the Egyptians believed it baneful to sacrifice. Moreover, these had to be immolated in a particular manner, their blood and fat were given neither to the offerers nor to the priests for their benefit, the consumption of certain parts of the sacrificed animal was reserved to these latter, the offerings of honey and leavened bread were prohibited, etc.

Nevertheless, at this precise moment of salvation history, the multiple sacrifices possessed, of themselves, in their materiality and literal nature, no acceptable value in the eyes of God. Only the mystery that they announced, the reality of which they were nothing but shadows—the Redemptive Sacrifice—conferred upon them a certain spiritual value. In order to fully comprehend the *raison d'être* of the figurative sacrifices, it is thus necessary to situate them in light of the true and unique sacrifice by which Christ the Sovereign Priest has reconciled wounded humanity to God, offering himself to the Father as a victim of propitiation.

Thus, for example, the slaying of animals prefigured the immolation of the Redeemer, while pouring the blood of victims over the base of the altar announced the effusion of his blood. The bread offered by those who could not perform the offering of animals represented his flesh. The other products of the earth that were permissible for offering all had a mystical signification tied to the person of the holy Victim: the vine represented his blood, the grace of Christ was figured by the oil, his knowledge by the salt, and the perfection of his prayer by the incense.

Sometimes, like St. Augustine and so many ancient and medieval masters, St. Thomas goes beyond a spiritual reading based rigorously on the sacred text. He puts forward an exegesis that today we would consider very imaginative, but which his contemporaries loved. For

---

47. *ST* I-II, q. 102, a. 3, corp.

example, citing the Gloss on Leviticus, he lingers for a while to point out how the offered animals fittingly prefigure some particular trait of the virtues and mysteries of Christ: the calf evokes "the strength of the cross" and the lamb the Savior's innocence; the ram foreshadows his headship, and so on. Other times, a fundamental allegorical sense gives rise to very subtle secondary constructions. Thus, observing that those who could not offer animals had to offer bread, or flour, or an ear of grain, he is not satisfied to relate the offering of bread to the offering of Christ, the true bread of life, but goes on to find reasons to explain the flour and grain: "He was indeed an ear of grain, as it were, during the state of the law of nature, in the faith of the patriarchs; He was like flour in the doctrine of the Law of the prophets; and He was like perfect bread after He had taken human nature."[48]

The spiritual sense consists not only in the prefiguration of the person and life of Christ, but also in the prefiguration of Christian moral doctrine. For example, as sin has been the cause of man's chastisement and also of the expiatory death of the Son of God on the cross, in the same way the slaying of the victim "signified the destruction of sins: and also that man deserved death on account of his sins; as though those animals were slain in man's stead, in order to betoken the expiation of sins."[49] In the order of sacrifices, Thomas adds, the sacrifice for sin came in second place after the holocaust, for "man is bound to God, chiefly on account of His majesty; secondly, on account of the sins he has committed."[50]

The Sacraments of the Old Law

With respect to their efficacy, the "sacraments" in question were nothing more than exterior signs, symbolic rites of participation in or reception of a sanctity in the cultic order.[51] Each of these sacred signs prefigured the grace of Christ in its own way. Since the reality was yet

48. *ST* I-II, q. 102, a. 3, ad 12.
49. *ST* I-II, q. 102, a. 3, ad 5.
50. *ST* I-II, q. 102, a. 3, ad 10.
51. *ST* II-II, q. 81, a. 3, ad 2.

to come, they could not contain it. They did not imprint on the souls of those who received them any sacred character, nor did they elevate them to the supernatural order. They only conferred upon them, in the mode of ritual consecration, a sort of exterior sanctity that deputed them to render the true cult to God and disposed them specifically for the offering of sacrifices.

St. Thomas distinguishes two categories of subjects in the sacraments, divided according to their role in the performance of divine cult: the people and the sacred ministers. Though all are deputed to divine cult, still, the ministers of cult require a consecration and certain very special dispositions. After positing this hierarchical principle, Aquinas lists three cultic functions that the sacred ministers and the people must perform according to their state; the various sacraments correspond to each one.[52] First, everyone must be put in a state to render cult to God: in a general manner through *circumcision*, and in a reserved manner through *sacerdotal consecration*. Next, it is necessary to perform acts of cult in an effective manner; for the priest, this meant essentially the offering of *sacrifices*, an offering that, along with the consumption of the gifts, highlights the nature and sanctity of the sacrament; on the part of the people, sacramental participation is realized principally in consumption of the *Paschal lamb*. Finally, it was necessary to be pure from every uncleanness that might forbid one from exercising the divine cult; to this end, several *rites of purification* were practiced by the sacred ministers as well as the people.

St. Thomas thus distinguishes four sacraments in the Old Law—circumcision, the paschal lamb, sacerdotal consecration, and rites of purification—in prefiguration of Baptism, the Eucharist, Holy Orders, and Penance. For "all these things had reasonable causes, both literal, in so far as they were ordained to the worship of God for the time being, and figurative, in so far as they were ordained to foreshadow Christ."[53]

---

52. *ST* I-II, q. 102, a. 5.
53. *ST* I-II, q. 102, a. 5.

The Paschal Lamb

According to the literal sense, after the sacrificial offerings proper
to the sacred ministers, the consumption of the Paschal lamb was
the most expressive of the sacred signs, the most characteristic of
the cult. The Paschal meal was meant to recall the time when God
delivered his people from Egypt: "By celebrating this banquet they
declared that they belonged to that people which God had taken
to Himself out of Egypt."[54] This meal is therefore a genuine sacred
drama, a ritual and dramatic renewal of that former meal of the last
hour in Egypt. Both the nature of the meal (unleavened bread, roast
meat) and the bearing of the diners (girded loins, sandals on the
feet, etc.) represent the haste of those soon to depart. In the same
way, eating bitter herbs recalled the bitterness drunk by the Hebrews in the land of Egypt. The Paschal meal was also an occasion
to display horror for idolatry, for during the flight from Egypt, the
Hebrews were commanded to sprinkle their lintels and door posts
with the blood of a lamb, "as though declaring that they were averse
to the rites of the Egyptians, who worshipped the ram. Wherefore
they were delivered by the sprinkling or rubbing of the blood of the
lamb on the door-posts, from the danger of extermination which
threatened the Egyptians."[55]

Moreover, according to the spiritual sense, none of the Old
Law's sacramental figures is more clearly oriented toward the principal sacrament of the New Covenant, the Eucharist, than the Paschal
lamb. The Angelic Doctor explains each of the phases of the Jewish
Passover from this illuminating perspective. It is worth citing the entire text, dividing it into its elements:

The sacrifice of the paschal lamb signified the sacrifice of Christ according
to 1 Corinthians 5:7: "Christ our Pasch is sacrificed."

The blood of the lamb, which ensured deliverance from the destroyer, by
being sprinkled on the transoms, signified faith in Christ's Passion, in the

54. *ST* I-II, q. 102, a. 5, ad 2.
55. *ST* I-II, q. 102, a. 5, ad 2.

hearts and on the lips of the faithful, by which same Passion we are delivered from sin and death, according to 1 Peter 1:18: "You were ... redeemed ... with the precious blood ... of a lamb unspotted."

The partaking of its flesh signified the eating of Christ's body in the Sacrament;

The flesh was roasted at the fire to signify Christ's Passion or charity. And it was eaten with unleavened bread to signify the blameless life of the faithful who partake of Christ's body, according to 1 Corinthians 5:8: "Let us feast ... with the unleavened bread of sincerity and truth."

The wild lettuces were added to denote repentance for sins, which is required of those who receive the body of Christ.

Their loins were girt in sign of chastity.

The shoes of their feet are the examples of our dead ancestors.

The staves they were to hold in their hands denoted pastoral authority.

Finally it was commanded that the paschal lamb should be eaten in one house, i.e., in a catholic church, and not in the conventicles of heretics.[56]

The immolation of Christ, which is the center of the New Covenant, was prefigured not only in the paschal lamb but also in the sacrifice for sins, a propitiatory sacrifice signifying the particular manner of the redemptive Passion. In this case also, our Doctor analyzes the nature of the victims, the various moments of their sacrifice, and the ritual gestures. Even the consumption of the sacrificial material in the Old Law signified the Eucharistic communion that was to come.

Sacred Things and Observances

By *sacred things* is meant "special times, a special abode, special vessels, and special ministers" appointed for divine cult.[57] In the religious life of God's people, the sacred things served to express and inculcate the reverence due to God, but also to wipe out idolatry and to signify religious purity. Moreover, they had a hidden spiritual sense pointing to future realities. Thus the Holy of Holies in the

56. *ST* I-II, q. 102, a. 5, ad 2.
57. *ST* I-II, q. 102, a. 4.

temple signifies "either the glory of heaven or the spiritual state of the New Law to come. To the latter state Christ brought us; and this was signified by the high-priest entering alone, once a year, into the Holy of Holies."[58]

Now, not only the various objects destined for cult must be set apart, but also the entire people of God and especially the priests. To this end the *observances* were established. For "in that people's, and especially the priests', mode of life, there needed to be certain special things befitting the divine worship, whether spiritual or corporeal."[59] The literal explanation of these numerous observances will thus consist in establishing their proper relation to cult. They may require, for example, abstinence from certain animal meats thought to be impure or blemished in some way and thus unfitting for the sacrificial oblation. Also, the children of Israel had to use certain vestments that were strictly different from those of the pagans, so as to protect them against the lusts of the idolaters. As for the spiritual explanation, it will involve discovering in the *observances* the shadow of some trait relating to Christ or the Christian moral life.[60]

THE DURATION OF THE PRECEPTS

We will now consider the duration of the ceremonies of the Old Law (*ST* I-II, q. 103) under the three aspects of their moral quality, their power of sanctification, and their manifestation of the mystery of salvation.

Our presentation of the spiritual sense of the precepts has shown

---

58. *ST* I-II, q. 102, a. 4, ad 4.

59. *ST* I-II, q. 102, a. 6.

60. Here too we see how the medieval mode of figurative exegesis shows great subtlety of imagination. Consider how it justifies why ruminants without cloven hooves were forbidden for eating, but not other kinds: "The animal that chews the cud and has a divided hoof, is clean in signification. Because division of the hoof is a figure of the two Testaments: or of the Father and Son: or of the two natures in Christ: of the distinction of good and evil. While chewing the cud signifies meditation on the Scriptures and a sound understanding thereof; and whoever lacks either of these is spiritually unclean" (*ST* I-II, q. 102, a. 6, ad 1).

us the transitory character of Israel's cult, insofar as it was oriented toward a future justification through Christ. Nevertheless, it seems important to point out—in the wake of what we have said previously about the anthropological foundations of cult—what literal analysis of the precepts has never ceased to confirm, which is the moral value of the exterior acts of cult insofar as they are due signs of the soul's virtue of religion. For the divine law, just as the first revelations made to Abel, Melchizedek, and Abraham, has done nothing less than determine and orient the religious attitude inherent in human nature.

Thus, without prejudice to the spiritual and transitory quality that was proper to them, the ceremonial precepts corresponded to man's connatural need to express the interior acts of his spirit through exterior activities, here designated under the name of ceremonies.

Consequently, when the ceremonial precepts of the Old Law disappeared, replaced by the Christian cult, the obligation to perform exterior acts of religion did not thereby cease. Rather, it became the object of a more perfect determination, enriched by the efficacy of Christ's sacrifice.

Shadows and figures of a perfect cult, the ceremonial precepts would become obsolete with Christ's coming. Article 2 of this question gives the deepest reason for their disappearance: their incapacity to accomplish anything other than a material and exterior sanctification. In fact, the "sacraments" of the Law did nothing more than purify men from corporeal uncleanness that prevented them from approaching the cult, remedying certain exterior irregularities. According to the words of the Letter to the Galatians (4:9), they were only "weak and beggarly elements," "justices of the flesh imposed until the time comes to set things right." (Heb 9:10). These corporeal purifications were not able to cleanse the soul from sin because "at no time could there be expiation from sin, except through Christ."[61] Ineffective by themselves, they did nothing more than prefigure

---

61. *ST* I-II, q. 103, a. 2.

the justification that was to come in Christ: "Since the mystery of Christ's Incarnation and Passion had not yet really taken place, those ceremonies of the Old Law could not really contain in themselves a power flowing from Christ already incarnate and crucified, such as the sacraments of the New Law contain."[62]

Nevertheless, in the time of the Law and even in the time of the revelations that preceded it, "it was possible for the minds of the faithful, to be united by faith to Christ incarnate and crucified."[63] In essence, God communicated to them the theological gift of faith in the mystery of the coming redemption, a true cleaving to Christ. In this sense, the rites of the Old Law allowed one to make a certain contact with Christ: "Hence in the Old Law certain sacrifices were offered up for sins, not as though the sacrifices themselves washed sins away, but because they were professions of faith which cleansed from sin ... , as though the sin were forgiven, not in virtue of the sacrifices, but through the faith and devotion of those who offered them." As opposed to Christian sacraments, which *apply* the fruits of the redemption (to those who are disposed), the ceremonies could no nothing more at that time than signify the expiation of sins that would come through the unique sacrifice of Christ. And yet the ancients, by making an implicit act of faith in the Redeemer under the figures of the sacrifices, could even then participate in that divine expiation.

The mystery of Christ is the cause of the whole history of salvation. Péguy expressed it well: "All the Old Testament goes towards John the Baptist and towards Jesus. But all the New Testament comes from Jesus. It is like a great arch which rises from two sides towards the keystone, and Jesus is the keystone."[64] This mystery has been gradually communicated. After the imperfect regime of the

---

62. *ST* I-II, q. 103, a. 2.
63. *ST* I-II, q. 103, a. 2.
64. Charles Péguy. *The Mystery of the Holy Innocents.* Translated by Pansy Pakenham, in *The Mystery of the Holy Innocents and Other Poems* (Eugene, OR: Wipf and Stock, 2018), 133. Original language edition: *Charles Péguy: Œuvres poétiques complètes* (Paris: Éditions Gallimard, 1975), 784.

figures, God manifested himself through his perfect image, the Word who was made flesh and suffered, meriting grace and glory for mankind. The whole cultic economy of world history is oriented toward the celebration of this supernatural mystery, whose final consummation is beyond history in the state of glory. And as is the case for all exterior cult, we must measure the spiritual value of the ceremonial precepts by the standard of interior cult, which "consists in faith, hope and charity. Consequently, exterior worship had to be subject to variations according to the variations in the internal worship."[65]

Thus in the Mosaic cult, a ritual regime proportioned to humanity's second theological state, "faith and hope regarded heavenly goods and the means of obtaining them—in both of these considered as things to come. Such was the state of faith and hope in the Old Law."[66] Once the mystery of redemption became manifest in the fullness of time, the cultic regime of the Old Covenant had to cease, since faith and charity, though continuing to pertain to heavenly goods considered as things to come, also henceforth pertain to "the means of obtaining heavenly goods as things present or past."[67] Jesus Christ, the way of salvation, the *type* of the Old Testament figures, has fulfilled all figures by his death on the cross, and his blood has rendered them void: "The prescriptions of the Law must have ceased then altogether through their reality being fulfilled. As a sign of this, we read that at the Passion of Christ 'the veil of the temple was rent' (Matthew 27:51)."[68]

Henceforth, the "bodily cult" cedes its place to the cult celebrated "in spirit and truth"—to the *verum sacrificium*[69]—without, however, obliging the connatural exterior act of sacrifice in this life to

---

65. *ST* I-II, q. 103, a. 3. See also *ST* I-II, q. 101, a. 1 and 2; *Commentary on the Sentences* IV, d. 1, q. 1, a. 2, q^a 5, and q. 2, a. 5, q^a 1 and 2.

66. *ST* I-II, q. 103, a. 3.

67. *ST* I-II, q. 103, a. 3.

68. *ST* I-II, q. 103, a. 3, ad 2.

69. "The sacrifices of the Old Testament were not accepted by God, for it is written that 'for the law made nothing perfect' (Heb 7:19). And 'it is impossible for the blood of bulls and goats to take away sins' (Heb 10:4). That is why it was necessary for the *true sacrifice* to appear and be made manifest" (*Commentary on the Psalms*, 39.8).

disappear. Rather, henceforth the latter has been assumed by Christ and elevated to the supernatural order of the sacraments of faith, so that it represents in an efficacious manner the perfect and sanctify-ing cult of the sovereign High Priest.

Though it represents the saving works accomplished by Christ in a temporal manner for the spiritual good of the faithful, the Chris-tian cult remains a figure; in its prayers and actions, in the great poem of images and sacred symbols, it manifests a cult that is beyond the veil of history: the liturgy of the heavenly Jerusalem. The consum-mation of the mystery is, in the final analysis, a trans-historical re-ality. Because the mystery is revealed slowly in history, history has become a theophany that leads in the footsteps of Christ the Re-deemer toward the final end that will abolish all history and establish redeemed mankind in the state of glory.

The state of beatitude is the sacred and final reality to which the first two states of cult are ordered. The eternal stability to which man tends, and in which, through the merits of Christ, he will be estab-lished body and soul, will succeed the provisional realities, shadows, and figures of this world. There, "In this state of the Blessed, nothing in regard to worship of God will be figurative; there will be naught but 'thanksgiving and voice of praise.'"[70] Thus, the Angelic Doctor cites Apocalypse (21:22): "I saw no temple in the city, for its temple is the Lord God the Almighty and the Lamb."

---

70. *ST* I–II, q. 103, a. 3.

3

Christ

God's Religious Man according to
St. Thomas Aquinas

The ceremonial precepts decreed by the Divine Legislator, though transitory and imperfect, regulated the religious life of his chosen people. Through these precepts he wished to preserve them from idolatry, while also prefiguring for them the mystery of salvation that was still to come. Following the lead of St. Thomas Aquinas, we now turn to the accomplishment of this mystery in its religious and cultic dimension. To the *corporeal cult* of Israel succeeds the *spiritual cult* of Christ. If we describe the cult of the New Testament as *spiritual* in comparison with the cult of the Old Law, it is not because it involves a purely interior cult without figures or images, for we already know that this sort of cult becomes possible only in the state of glory. On the contrary, "by His Passion [Christ] inaugurated the Rites of the Christian Religion."[1] With Christ humanity enters into a more perfect theological state and thereby into an economy of exterior rites grafted onto the redemptive sacrifice, into which Christ wills to bring the humanity he has redeemed.

In order to illustrate the specific nature and the supernatural

---

1. *ST* III, q. 62, a. 5.

quality of the "rites of the Christian religion," in this present study we will focus on the priestly function of the Incarnate Word on earth and on what Christ the Sovereign Priest continues to accomplish in heaven. Thomas's doctrine on the priesthood of Christ is contained entirely in question 22 of the *Teria pars* of the *Summa theologiae*, which is contained in the treatise on the Incarnation (q. 2–26) and more precisely in the section where he analyzes the "consequences" of the hypostatic union (q. 16–26). We will follow the outline of question 22, departing from it only to point out—generally within the context of the *Teria pars* and in the *Commentary on the Letter to the Hebrews*—where he develops certain themes only hinted at in this text.[2]

The first article defines the sacrifice of Christ as a kind of *mediation*. Beginning in the second article, our Doctor takes up the principal act of Christ's priesthood, namely sacrifice, asking whether Christ was at the same time the priest and the victim of his own sacrifice. In this regard, we will discuss the nature of the sacrifice of Christ on Calvary. Having considered the sacrifice of the cross, we will again take up the thread of question 22 with article 5: If the bloody oblation of his sacrifice has been accomplished once and for all on the cross, how does the victorious Christ, eternal High Priest, consummate his sacrifice from his place of glory? Finally, the sixth article dedicated to the relation between the priesthood of Christ and the priesthood "according to the order of Melchizedek" will permit us to discern the ritual economy of Christ's Church.

2. By dedicating a separate question to the priesthood of Christ, St. Thomas distinguishes himself from Peter Lombard and the whole body of his contemporaries who until then had made only occasional allusions to the notion. Already in an earlier work, *Commentary on the Letter to the Hebrews* (ch. 7, lect. 1), he had begun his thinking about the nature of the priesthood of Christ and demonstrated its superiority over the Levitic priesthood. Moreover, soon after the redaction of the first twenty-five questions of the *Tertia pars* around 1272–1273, St. Thomas gave an oral teaching on the Psalms at Naples, which was transcribed by a disciple as the *Commentary on the Psalms*. Albeit by way of allusion, this commentary offers "a sacramental vision of the function of the priesthood in the history of salvation" (Martin Morard, "Sacerdoce du Christ et sacerdoce des chrétiens dans le *Commentaire des psaumes* de saint Thomas d'Aquin," *Revue thomiste* 99, no. 1 [1999]: 140), with a particular insistence on the notion of spiritual cult.

THE PRIESTHOOD AND CHRIST'S MEDIATION

We must first consider the *mission* of the Word, sent into the world to reestablish the harmony between God and men that had been disrupted by sin. Jesus Christ brought this redemptive mission to its conclusion by the offering he made of himself on the cross in sacrifice to the Father. He reestablished harmony by rendering to God the homage of a perfect cult.

Was it fitting that Christ was a priest? Our response must have recourse to the category of *mediation*, for "the office proper to a priest is to be a mediator between God and the people."[3] In the words of the Apostle, Jesus Christ, who is God and man, has been established as the "one mediator between God and humankind."[4] But St. Thomas chooses to treat the priesthood of Christ in a separate question, distinct from the one he dedicates later to the notion of Christ's mediation (*ST* III, q. 26), a question that serves as a recapitulation of the whole treatise on the Incarnation. Aquinas's intention in question 22, therefore, is to explain the priestly dimension of Christ's mediation.

By virtue of the hypostatic union, Christ has been consecrated to God in a very special manner. Made holy by a substantial holiness, he is placed at the summit of creation, set up as the only mediator possible between God and men, whom he has received the mission to save, and whom he renders participants of his grace.[5] Though his mediatory function is certainly related to his role as king, prophet, and legislator,[6] he exercises it principally through his priesthood.

---

3. *ST* III, q. 22, a. 1.

4. 1 Tm 2:5, see *ST* III, q. 7, a.1, where St. Thomas cites the same passage apropos of the presence of habitual grace in Christ's soul.

5. See Gérard Remy, "Sacerdoce et médiation chez saint Thomas," *Revue thomiste* 99, no. 1 (1999): 109: "Meditation is founded in Christ's soul: his union to the Word disposes him to the maximum influx of divine grace, making him capable of union with God through knowledge and love. This relation with God is reflected in his role as mediator with the rest of mankind, for his role is to make the plenitude of his grace flow upon them."

6. See Thomas, *Commentary on the Letter to the Hebrews*, ch. 1, lect. 4: "He is our

Since it is a consequence of the hypostatic union, his priesthood must be understood in light of the fact that he is the Incarnate Word and so capable of reuniting the two extremes of God and man in his one person.[7] From this standpoint, the link between mediation and priesthood in Christ appears clearly; the prerogative of his priest-hood is rooted in the perfection of the grace of union. Distant from God by his nature as a man and distant from men by his dignity of grace and glory, "it belongs to [Christ], as man, to unite men to God, by communicating to men both precepts and gifts, and by offering satisfaction and prayers to God for men."[8]

Aquinas sums up the whole of Christ's mediation in two move-ments. The first movement is *descending* and situated in relation to men, consisting in the communication of "divine realities"—pre-cepts and gifts—to the people. The second movement is *ascending*, situated in relation to God. It consists in offering the prayers of the people and making satisfaction to God for sins through sacrificial offering. The exercise of Christ's priesthood is thus essential for the accomplishment of his redemptive mediation as expressed in this double movement. Mediation embraces priesthood, whose sacrifi-cial dimension it takes to itself. Mediation and priesthood meet on the same Christological ground, which is the excellence of Christ's humanity, an excellence that renders pleasing and efficacious the sacrifice that Jesus has received the mission to offer.[9]

---

king.... He is also a priest.... He was also a prophet." See also *ST* III, q. 22, a. 1, ad 3: "Christ, as being the Head of all, has the perfection of all graces. Wherefore, as to others, one is a lawgiver, another is a priest, another is a king; but all these concur in Christ, as the fount of all grace. Hence it is written (Is 33:22): 'The Lord is our Judge, the Lord is our law-giver, the Lord is our King: He will come and save us.'"

7. *ST* III, q. 26, a. 2. The *sed contra* cites St. Augustine: "Not because He is the Word, is Christ Mediator, since He Who is supremely immortal and supremely happy is far from us unhappy mortals; but He is Mediator, as man" (*City of God* 9.15).

8. *ST* III, q. 26, a. 2.

9. See Remy, "Sacerdoce et médiation chez saint Thomas," 108–9: "Priesthood and mediation are united because they share a common property: Christ's humanity. His priesthood is based necessarily on this anthropological foundation because He exercises it through an act—namely His expiatory sacrifice offered in view of the good things of

THE SACRIFICE OF CHRIST

A Priestly Action

For St. Thomas, the Incarnation of the Word is entirely ordered to his mission of redemption. The Word came into the world to satisfy for the sins of mankind. Without sin, the Incarnation would never have taken place.[10]

Christ exercises his mediatory function principally, therefore, in the exercise of his priesthood, and more precisely by offering himself in sacrifice. The effect of his priesthood, which is to say, the fruit of his self-oblation, is the remission of sins: "they are now justified by his grace as a gift, through the redemption that is in Christ Jesus, whom God put forward as a sacrifice of atonement by his blood, effective through faith."[11]

Thus, by the sacrificial offering of the Mediator, an offering of satisfaction acceptable to the Father, mankind is rejoined in friendship with God, and sanctifying grace is communicated to him. The grace of the head, which is the basis of the acceptability of his sacrifice, could not be communicated to his members without the offering of this sacrifice. Concomitantly, the sacrifice of Christ is the basis for the presence of grace in the souls of all those for whom he is offered in an efficacious manner. Sacrifice and reconciliation, cult and

---

salvation—that comes from human nature.... Though his definition through the union of these two terms—God and man—in the hypostatic union is not only legitimate but must even be taken for granted, for Thomas as for Augustine it is Christ's humanity that aligns most exactly with his role as mediator, because his humanity is both distant from God by its nature and thus close to man, and distant from us by 'its dignity in grace and glory,' and thus close to God (*ST* III, q. 26, a. 2). It is the very excellence of this humanity, endowed with these two perfections of grace and glory, that raises Christ to the rank of mediator in an absolute and untransmittable sense, just as it guarantees the superiority of his priesthood and the efficacy of his sacrifice in relation to mans's needs: namely the elimination of sins and the gifts of saving grace and glory."

10. See *ST* III, q. 1, a. 3: "Hence, since everywhere in the Sacred Scripture the sin of the first man is assigned as the reason of the Incarnation, it is more in accordance with this to say that the work of Incarnation was ordained by God as a remedy for sin; so that, had sin not existed, Incarnation would not have been."

11. Rom 3:24–25, cited in *ST* III, q. 22, a. 3.

sanctification go hand in hand, and the root of this great movement is the plenitude of grace received by the divine head.[12]

The acceptance of Christ's offering, the fact that it is efficacious, is what radically distinguishes the sacrifice of the New Law from the ineffective sacrifices of the Israelite cult, bodily shadows and figures of a reality that was yet unperceived.[13] The sacrifice of the Incarnate Word is indeed the sole propitiatory sacrifice for sins, the only one that can satisfy God's justice and by which men can be united to him.

In our analysis of the sacrificial act, we pointed out its orientation to satisfactory homage: a desire to be reconciled with angry gods in primitive and archaic religions, and a more perfect desire for purification manifested by the offering of "sacrifices for sins" in the Mosaic cult. Yet on account of the infinite offense done to God,[14] no

12. See *ST* III, q. 8, a. 1–2; *Commentary on the Gospel According to St. John*, at 1:8 ("full of grace and truth") and 1:10 ("and from his plenitude we have all received"). Jean-Pierre Torrell wrote apropos of *ST* III, q. 22, a. 1: "We must note the double direction—'descendant' and 'ascendant' (the first coming before the second in this article)—in which the sacerdotal mediation of Christ is exercised; it thus takes place in the great movement, also in two directions, by which the mediation of reconciliation is defined. The recent Latin theological tradition (since the 15th century) used to speak of the redemption accomplished by Christ the man as if the only thing that mattered was his merit, the ascending side of his mediation. The eastern tradition of the Church was more attentive to the descendant aspect, and spoke more amply of the salvation that was came about by the Word's coming into our world. Contemporary theologians have begun to give this aspect more attention. We should also point out that, prior to the exercise of his sacerdotal function and to everything Christ does in his graced humanity, there is the gift of God who is the first and already acting in his person. This is absolutely present and operative in Thomas: the gift of grace is the source of merit for free will, and of the charism for cultic action in service of the life of grace. Not only Christ the priest, but his ministers after him, thus appear as representatives of God among men, before being man's (representatives to God, and they only fulfill this latter function to the degree that they have been sacramentally enabled to do so." Jean-Pierre Torrell, *Le Verbe incarné*, vol. 3 (Paris: Cerf, 2002), 355.

13. See *ST* III, q. 47, a. 2, ad 1: "Yet because the Old Law was ended by Christ's death, according to His dying words, 'It is consummated' (John 19:30), it may be understood that by His suffering He fulfilled all the precepts of the Old Law.... Christ likewise by His Passion fulfilled the ceremonial precepts of the Law, which are chiefly ordained for sacrifices and oblations, in so far as all the ancient sacrifices were figures of that true sacrifice which the dying Christ offered for us."

14. See *ST* III, q. 1, a. 2, ad 2: "A sin committed against God has a kind of infinity

sacrifice offered by the hands of men, even those whose figurative value was determined by God, could be acceptable. None of man's homage could repair the insult done to the sovereign *right* of the creator and master of all things and so satisfy justice.

Satisfaction for sin must be in proportion to the gravity of the offense. So that this satisfaction would have an infinite efficacy, God, in his great mercy, sent the Word into the world in order to accomplish his will for man's salvation.[15] The God-Man offered himself as a sacrifice of propitiation for mankind, reconciling all things in his blood,[16] and so doing inaugurated the rite of the Christian religion.

Priest and Victim of His Sacrifice

The sacrifice of Christ is different from all the sacrifices of history in that the offerer is identical with the thing offered; Jesus is at the same time priest and victim of his own sacrifice. Set up as the unique mediator between God and man, he is thus the only possible priest, standing in for humanity in the priestly act of sacrifice. But before offering the sacrifice that will be perfectly acceptable, he also stands in for the victim.

In the Old Law, the animals the priests sacrificed had been chosen by God. They were licit, endowed with a certain purity and ritual "holiness." The "pure" victims of the Levitic sacrifices also prefigured the cult of the New Law, whose sacrifice contains a spiritual grace and is acceptable in itself.[17] This *spiritual* sacrifice is the priestly

---

from the infinity of the Divine majesty, because the greater the person we offend, the more grievous the offense."

15. See Thomas, *Commentary on the Letter to the Hebrews*, ch. 10, lect. 1: "Therefore, in the head of the book, i.e., in me, according to my divine nature, it is written of me, according to my human nature, I have come to do your will, i.e., this was foreordained that by Your grace I should do Your will, by offering Myself for the redemption of the human race."

16. See *ST* III, q. 1, a. 2, ad 2: "Hence for condign satisfaction it was necessary that the act of the one satisfying should have an infinite efficiency, as being of God and man."

17. See *ST* I-II, q. 102, a. 4, ad 3.

offering that the Savior makes of himself to the Father.[18] Only he can be the spiritual victim of his own sacrifice, the *pure oblation* spoken of by Malachai, henceforth offered throughout the world from the rising of the sun to its setting (cf. Mal 1:11).

Interior Sacrifice and Exterior Sacrifice

The sovereign Priest offers no other sacrifice than the supremely perfect one of which he is at the same time priest and victim. Herein lies the fundamental originality of the sacrifice of redemption. In order to better understand it, we must situate the act of Calvary in its nature as a *visible sign* of the spiritual and interior sacrifice of Christ.

Christ's *spiritual* sacrifice is the proper act of the priesthood of the New Covenant, and the sacramental sacrifice offered on the altar of the Church must represent and be ordered to it. The Angelic Doctor takes St. Augustine's definition as a point of departure for his argument: "Every visible sacrifice is a sacrament, that is, a sacred sign, of the invisible sacrifice" (*City of God* 10.5). Sacrifice does not reach God except in the form of a spiritual act. But the ritual act is the exterior object of the essential interior offering, therefore, "whatever is offered to God in order to raise man's spirit to Him, may be called a sacrifice."[19]

Christ's act of sacrifice resides principally in that interior act of the will by which he offered himself freely to the Father ever since his coming into the world. At the same moment of the Incarnation in which Christ was substantially constituted by the ineffable grace resulting from the hypostatic union, our High Priest was also substantially consecrated in heart and soul in the state of a holy victim.[20] The sacrifice of the cross is, therefore, the sacred exterior

18. See Thomas, *Commentary on the Letter to the Hebrews*, ch. 5, lect. 1: "He is called a priest because He offered Himself to God the Father."

19. *ST* III, q. 22, a. 2. See Torrell, *Le Christ en ses mystères*, 2:411–12: "Thanks to the Doctor of Hippo, the concept of sacrifice in the *Summa* takes on an almost undefined extension. Though it does not disappear entirely, the concrete act in which the sacrifice takes place becomes much less important than the soul's act of self-offering, i.e., his interior sacrifice."

20. See Augustin Barrois, "Le sacrifice du Christ au Calvaire," *Revue des sciences philosophiques et théologiques* 14, no. 2 (1925): 153: "From the moment of the Incarnation

sign of the perpetual interior offering of the Mediator. The spiritual sacrifice of Christ, therefore, consists in the homage that the Savior bore toward his Father by his adoration, prayers, and supplication in an unceasing manner throughout the whole course of his earthly life, a homage of filial love and obedience; according to Psalm 50:19, "the sacrifice acceptable to God is a broken spirit."

The Sacrifice in the Passion

But because Christ had assumed human nature, he had to signify and consummate his sacrifice of love and obedience in a manner proportionate to this nature; precisely what he accomplishes in his Passion. In keeping with our cultic standpoint, we will now turn our attention to the sacrificial act of Calvary as treated in the questions St. Thomas dedicated to the Passion of Christ (especially ST III, q. 48). The sacrifice of Christ must be both oblation and immolation. It requires the immolation of the offerer in order to satisfy for the sins of mankind. But the immolation is nothing more than the *sign* of the voluntary oblation of love and obedience that, as we have already claimed, constitutes the sacrifice.

Satisfaction and Immolation

Since Christ was holy in his very substance in virtue of the hypostatic union, each of his works on earth was also satisfying to the Father and thus meritorious for the salvation of men. If that is so, why was it necessary for the Savior's satisfaction to be accomplished by means of the sufferings of the Passion and for his interior sacrifice to be consummated in a bloody immolation?

The initial offering that Christ made of himself, and then perpetuated at each instant of his earthly life by dint of his infinite

---

Jesus is forever a victim, and he will obey to the point of death. In so doing, he does nothing more than develop the multiple aspects of a quality he possessed in plenitude in his mother's womb. The consummation of his sacrifice will be the visible corollary of his assumption of human nature, which remains prior in an absolute sense, and prepares the victim for Calvary." See also Barnabé Augier, "Le Sacrifice rédempteur," *Revue thomiste* 37 (1932): 406–7.

perfection, had already merited salvation for humanity. But according to the divine plan Christ had to be offered in sacrifice on the
cross even though all of his actions were meritorious and efficacious
in themselves and possessed sanctifying virtue for all men. In his justice and love for man, God required a plenary satisfaction for sin in
the person of the One who had been substituted for humanity: the
Incarnate Word, beloved Son of the Father.

The price of sin is death, a punishment God imposed after man
willed to set himself up as master of his own life. Therefore Jesus
would have addressed only a part of the debt contracted by man in
the offended justice of God if his humanity had undergone any punishment less than death. Thus it was appropriate for Christ's satisfaction to be as thoroughgoing as possible, so that, having assumed
our nature, Christ "could suffer for man in it what man himself deserved to suffer on account of his sin, and thus offer satisfaction on
man's behalf."[21]

The satisfaction the God-Man had to accomplish required, therefore, the bloody immolation and death on the cross. The Redeemer had to offer the Father his physical Passion, the only punishment
capable of rendering the victim equal to the standards of divine justice.[22] In virtue of the punishment suffered in the shedding of his
blood,[23] a pledge of infinite satisfaction,[24] man is once again *joined*
to God. By Christ and with Christ, it is now truly possible for him to
perform the sacred cult in an acceptable manner.

21. Thomas Aquinas, *Compendium of Theology*, I, ch. 226 (trans. Cyril Vollert,
in *Opuscula 1 : Treatises* [Green Bay, WI: Aquinas Institute, 2018], 187).
22. *ST* III, q. 48, a. 2: "He properly atones for an offense who offers something which
the offended one loves equally, or even more than he detested the offense."
23. See *ST* III, q. 48, a. 5: "Now Christ's blood or His bodily life, which 'is in the
blood,' is the price of our redemption, and that life He paid." See also Thomas, *Disputed
Questions on Truth*, q. 27, a. 4: "Christ's blood poured out for us had the ability to wash
away sins." (trans. Robert W. Schmidt, SJ, *Truth* [Chicago: Regnery, 1954], 333).
24. See *ST* III, q. 48, a. 6, ad 3: "Christ's Passion . . . , considered as being within
Christ's very flesh, acts by way of satisfaction." See also *ST* III, q. 48, a. 5.

The Passion's Mode of Causality

After considering the causality of the Passion in the mode of satisfaction, St. Thomas considers its causality in the mode of sacrifice (*ST* III, q. 48, a. 3). The *sed contra* invokes the authority of St. Paul: Christ "gave himself up for us, a fragrant offering and sacrifice to God" (Eph 5:2). We must, therefore, define the sacrifice of Calvary as that perfect act by which the Sovereign Priest *offers himself voluntarily* out of love for the Father and mankind as *a victim who is immolated* for the remission of sins. In this way he brings all of those for whom he offers himself into a communion of love with God.

Causality through Oblation

In its fullest sense sacrifice is more than satisfaction: "A sacrifice properly so called is something done for that honor which is properly due to God, in order to appease Him."[25] The consecration-immolation is not sufficient enough in itself; it becomes a sacrifice only if it proceeds from a free interior act of offering made to God. It is thus by offering himself voluntarily for mankind in his Passion that Christ fully accomplishes his priestly mission as the immolated victim of his own sacrifice.[26]

It is not precise to say that Christ allowed himself to be killed,[27] "but of His own free-will He exposed Himself to death, according to Isaiah 53:7: 'He was offered because it was His own will.' Thus He is

25. *ST* III, q. 48, a. 3.
26. See in *ST* III, q. 48, a. 3, the citation of St. Augustine (*City of God*, 10.6): "Christ offered Himself up for us in the Passion."
27. See *Quodlibetal Questions* I, q. 2, a. 2: "Nevertheless, Christ is not guilty of killing himself. For the body exists for the sake of the soul, not the other way around. Hence, the soul itself is harmed when an injury inflicted upon the body expels the souls from the body against the soul's natural desire (even if it happens not to be against the depraved will of those who commit suicide). But if the soul had the power to leave the body at will and to return again, then there would be no more guilt involve din leaving the body than there is in a resident leaving a house, although there would still be the guilt involved in evicting it against its will." *Thomas Aquinas's Quodlibetal Questions*, trans. Turner Nevitt and Brian Davies (Oxford: Oxford University Press, 2020), 186.

said to have offered Himself."[28] The death of Christ is distinguished essentially from ours in that Christ "did not die because of any necessity. He gave up His life by His power and His own will."[29] If he had willed it, Christ could have held his enemies in check "so that they would not have been eager to slay Him, or would have been powerless to do so."[30] In virtue of his union to the Divine Word in the unity of the same person, his soul had the power "of preserving His fleshly nature from the infliction of any injury." But he never made use of this power; since he "willed His corporeal nature to succumb to such injury, He is said to have laid down His life, or to have died voluntarily. Thus we can say that Christ was the indirect cause of his own death, in the sense that he did not prevent it, while his persecutors caused it directly."[31]

By offering himself voluntarily to die, Christ obeyed his Father's command. The will of the Father that sent him to the Passion was matched by the obedience of the Son when he offered himself as an oblation and fragrant victim (Eph 5:2) for man.[32] Because "obedience is worth more than sacrifice" (1 Sam 15:22), it was fitting that the sacrifice of Christ proceed from obedience.[33] Christ willed to submit to his Father's command, but he did this without prejudice to his freedom. For Christ as God "delivered Himself up to death by the same will and action as that by which the Father delivered Him up."[34] As man, "He died out of his will to suffer for man, which the

---

28. *ST* III, q. 22, a. 2, ad 1.

29. Thomas, *Compendium of Theology*, I, ch. 230 (trans. Vollert, 192). Explaining this special death of Jesus in relation to ours, St. Thomas says in the same place: "Whatever was natural in Christ as regards His human nature was completely subject to His will because of the power of His divinity, to which all nature is subject. Therefore Christ had it in His power that so long as He willed, His soul would remain united to His body, and that the instant He willed, the soul would depart from the body."

30. *ST* III, q. 47, a. 1.

31. *ST* III, q. 47, a. 1: "In this manner Christ's persecutors slew Him because they inflicted on Him what was a sufficient cause of death, and with the intention of slaying Him, and the effect followed, since death resulted from that cause."

32. *ST* III, q. 47, a. 3.

33. *ST* III, q. 47, a. 2.

34. *ST* III, q. 47, a. 3, ad 2.

Father had inspired in Him by the infusion of charity."[35] In this way there was no opposition between the Father when he gave up his Son to death and the Son who made himself the voluntary victim of his own sacrifice.[36]

Because Christ willed it, the act of his death "came from his exceeding charity,"[37] from a heart full of love. Out of love of the Father and for mankind, Christ paid the price of the fault through suffering. On account of the fact that he took it upon himself willingly, embracing the divine will, the pain he suffered was truly satisfactory for both the Father and for mankind. In fact, the offering Jesus lovingly made of himself was infinitely pleasing to the Father, and therefore caused the redemption of mankind. "And in like fashion Christ's voluntary suffering was such a good act that, because of its being found in human nature, God was appeased for every offense of the human race with regard to those who are made one with the crucified Christ."[38] St. Thomas strongly affirms that the will to establish communion between the redeemed soul and God is not only a constitutive element of the sacrifice but also its perfection.[39] He bases this claim on St. Augustine: "A true sacrifice is every good work done in order that we may cling to God in holy fellowship, yet referred to that consummation of happiness wherein we can be truly blessed."[40]

Thus by his voluntary oblation, made in love and obedience, Christ, the only one who has ever been a perfectly religious man

35. *ST* III, q. 47, a. 3, corp.

36. *ST* III, q. 47, a. 3, ad 2.

37. *ST* III, q. 48, a. 3; see also *ST* III, q. 47, a. 4, ad 2.

38. See *ST* III, q. 49, a. 4.

39. See Joseph de Sainte-Marie, "L'eucharistie, sacrement et sacrifice du Christ et de l'Eglise: Développements des perspectives thomistes," *Divinitas* 18 (1974): 251. The author highlights the fact that, in Christ's sacrifice, it is only through the voluntary offering made to God "that the life contained in the blood rises to God as toward its principle and end. It is also for this reason that the sacrifice culminates in communion, which results in the restoration of life to man, in the resurrection, which is not simply a return to a previous condition but an entry into a new condition of participation in the life that comes from God. Just as *death* was first a natural consequence of *sin* before being a *punishment*, the *resurrection* is a 'natural' consequence of *sacrifice* offered and accepted before it is a *reward* for merit."

40. Augustine, *City of God*, 10.6, cited in *ST* III, q. 48, a. 3.

toward the Father, has offered the one true sacrifice. He has raised up to God the homage and adoration that joins and subordinates men to God and has established them in the fellowship of his love, making them holy by his own holiness.

Causality through Immolation

Even if the primary reality in the act of sacrifice is the oblation, an interior act of love and obedience, nevertheless, the sacrifice of Christ was consummated on earth in an exterior and visible manner that was in conformity with the requirements of human nature and with the constitution of the sacrificial act itself. The sacred rite, or consecration, was his immolation. At Calvary Jesus consummates the sacrificial offering he had been making of himself ever since the moment of his conception in Mary's womb. Though every one of the actions of his life had manifested this interior offering, yet still it was on the cross, by offering this sacrifice of propitiation, that his offering reached its full completion.

We should not distinguish, however, two distinct moments in the offering of the sacrifice of Christ, namely an interior sacrifice begun in the first instant of the Incarnation, perfect and potent in itself, and an exterior sacrifice performed on Calvary that is related in some way to the initial offering. The sacrifice of Christ is one unique action, essentially constituted by the oblation that Jesus made of his life to God as a consecrated priest and victim from the moment of his Incarnation—and that he continues to represent on our altars and to offer in the state of glory as a *heavenly victim*. On earth, however, insofar as Jesus had not yet entered into his Passion, his sacrificial offering, though it was already accomplished from the point of view of formal perfection, remained imperfect and incomplete. It did not yet contain (except in its cause) the material perfection of its object, namely the positive disposition of the victim, at a particular moment, to the requirements of divine love and justice.[41]

41. See Barnabé Augier, "Le Sacrifice rédempteur," 418: "The Savior's will to offer himself relates to its object from the standpoint of its perfection; he desires it to be

Taken as a purely material fact, the exterior act of bloody immolation perpetrated by those who killed Christ added nothing to
his primordial interior act. The executioners did not make Our Lord
an immolated victim. By striking him and crucifying him, they did
nothing more than place him in the state of *passive immolation*. But
while they struck and crucified him, Christ submitted himself to his
Father in an act of love and obedience, shedding his blood on the
cross and committing his soul into the hands of one to whom he
freely offered himself. This voluntary submission to suffering constituted the priestly action of Calvary, the *active immolation*. It was
not the sufferings undergone that made the Passion a true sacrifice,
but rather the fact that Jesus suffered in charity.[42] The sufferings *consecrated* him as a victim only because he accepted them and they became part of his sacrifice only insofar as he embraced them.

It is thus in virtue of the interior and voluntary oblation manifested in it that the bloody immolation is constitutive of the redemptive sacrifice, which is at once oblation and immolation. The two aspects are complementary; the sacrifice of Calvary consists formally
in the oblation of the immolated victim, the shedding of blood ac-
quiring satisfactory power only in virtue of the offering that it expresses. The immolation of Christ on the cross is thus the effect and
the visible *sign* of the invisible and perpetual oblation of the Incarnate Word, along with the absolutely unique fact, in relation to other
sacrifices, that here the *sign* is a *reality*. Christ offers a sacrifice, and
what he offers is not an exterior *sign* of his adoration and submission

perfect and moves it toward its perfection. Therefore, his will to offer constitutes, along
with the will for satisfaction—which is intrinsic to the initial offering—and the passive
acquiescence of the body to death—which is extrinsic to the interior offering in its effective reality—a unique oblation, i.e. the offering to God of the redeeming sacrifice....
For whenever one power moves another, whenever one act informs another, the moved
power participates in the form of the motive power; the two acts constitute in some
manner one sole act, meriting one and the same name in all its parts, since matter and
form are indivisible. If this is the case, we must recognize that the sacrificial oblation of
Jesus Christ was only complete in every respect on Calvary, at the '*consummatum est*.'"

42. See *ST* III, q. 48, a. 3, ad 3: "Christ's Passion was indeed a malefice on His slayers'
part; but on His own it was the sacrifice of one suffering out of charity."

to the Father; rather, when he offers himself with his body and blood on the altar of the cross, the exterior *sign* of the oblation is the very body of the one who offers it.[43]

The oblation turns the immolation required by divine justice into a satisfaction made as an act of love for the Father in order to reestablish communion between God and man. As Fr. Joseph de Sainte-Marie has remarked, "even when it requires immolation, the essence of sacrifice remains the subordination of man to God. This subordination achieves its end in the communion of man with God in this act of *cultus* and adoration through the grace of God that man has received."[44]

THE CONSUMMATION OF THE SACRIFICE OF REDEMPTION IN ETERNITY

We now return to the order of exposition of question 22. The first effect of the priestly mediation exercised by Christ in his Passion was the remission of mankind's sins (a. 3). The exercise of his priesthood did not result in any effects for Christ, since he offered his priesthood not for himself but for man, so man could have access

---

43. Here we must call attention to a discussion about the nature of the sacrifice of the cross that took place after the publication of Fr. Maurice de la Taille's work *Mysterium fidei: De augustissimo corporis et sanguinis Christi sacrificio atque sacramento* (Paris: Gabriel Beauchesne, 1924). The author had attempted to find a physical, ritual action of oblation in the events of the Passion that corresponded precisely to the physical constitution of the sacrifice in its double dimension of offering and consecration-immolation. Thus he identified the ritual oblation with the Last Supper: this consisted in the offering of the material of the sacrifice before it was consecrated in the immolation. However attractive this hypothesis might be, he seems to go beyond the intentions of St. Thomas. It was criticized in its day by Thomists (see, among others, the cited articles of Frs. Augier and Barrois). When considering the sacred action of immolation, Aquinas, as we have seen, says only that Christ's interior sentiments made the immolation a true sacrifice. The sacrifice on Calvary was the consummation of the continual oblation that Christ, constituted as priest and victim ever since the Incarnation, made of himself to his Father. Thus, each of the actions of his life, the preaching of the Gospel, the words pronounced during his Passion, and all the circumstances of his death manifested sufficiently, and in a sensible manner, the principal, interior oblation of Our Savior.

44. De Sainte-Marie, "L'eucharistie, sacrement et sacrifice," 253.

to God.[45] Nevertheless, returning to the principal effects of the sacrifice of the cross in a systematic way later on (*ST* III, q. 49), our Doctor will affirm that the humiliations and sufferings of the Passion merited for Christ's humanity his glorious resurrection, his ascension into heaven, his sitting at the right hand of the Father, and his power to judge all flesh.[46]

Since Christ now reigns in glory, a treatise on the effects of the redemptive sacrifice must take into account the mode of their communication to man in history. The next logical step for Aquinas is thus to consider the eternal dimension of the priesthood of Jesus Christ (a. 5). Already in the *Commentary on the Letter to the Hebrews* he had written this very brief formula: "Christ's sacrifice, since He is God and man, has power to sanctify for ever."[47] Later on he will ask: Does Christ provide a "medicine by which all sicknesses can be cured even in the future"?[48] For there are men existing at all times, and they need to take advantage of the infinite merits of the redemptive sacrifice at the moment in history in which they find themselves. And by benefiting from it here below, they will be able to enter one day into the glory of eternity. Thus the covenant sealed in the blood of Christ has inaugurated a new age; it embraces the *saints* who are in history and the *blessed who dwell* in eternity.

When arguing that Christ's priesthood is eternal, Aquinas distinguishes two parts in the priestly office: the *oblation* and its *consummation*. The first was accomplished once for all on Calvary. But the *consummation* of the sacrifice is not yet finished.

45. *ST* III, q. 22, a. 4: "A priest is set between God and man. Now he needs someone between himself and God, who of himself cannot approach God; and such a one is subject to the priesthood by sharing in the effect thereof. But this cannot be said of Christ; for the Apostle says (Heb 7:25): 'Coming of Himself to God, always living to make intercession for us.' And therefore it is not fitting for Christ to be the recipient of the effect of His priesthood, but rather to communicate it to others."

46. *ST* III, q. 49, a. 6.

47. Thomas, *Commentary on the Letter to the Hebrews*, ch. 10, lect. 1. We find an echo of this formula in *ST* III, q. 22, a. 5, ad 2.

48. *ST* III, q. 49, a. 1, ad 3. See also *ST* III, q. 49, a. 4.

To make sense of this doctrine, found in article 5, we must keep in mind the plan of the *Tertia pars*. At the conclusion of the treatise on the life of Christ, just before the treatise on the sacraments, are the questions St. Thomas dedicated to Christ's resurrection (q. 53–56), ascension (q. 57), and sitting at the right hand of the Father in the heavenly homeland. For the Word, having gone out from the bosom of the Father to become incarnate and to offer himself in sacrifice here below, continues to offer the Father the homage of his cult in the state of glory, in his glorified humanity.

If we are able to say that Christ's sacrifice subsists eternally, it is first of all because his interior offering, made of love and obedience, is eternally tied to his humanity.[49] The immolation of Christ on the cross was not the final end of his sacrifice; it was only its exterior sign here below, its consummation on earth, the extreme means of its completion. It no more abolishes the perpetual oblation Jesus made of himself than it abolishes his identity as priest and victim. Jesus' whole soul was consecrated priest and victim for eternity, so that when he died on the cross he offered his inanimate body and blood along with his soul.

By fulfilling the figure of the High Priest of the Old Law (Lv 16:11), who entered once per year into the Holy of Holies with the blood of goats and oxen,[50] the Incarnate Word has taken possession of the Kingdom of Heaven after being offered on earth as a sacrifice of propitiation. His state of abasement in the Passion corresponds now to a state of exaltation. In the glory of eternity, Christ, "high

---

49. See Denis Chardonnens, "Eternité du sacerdoce du Christ et effet eschatologique de l'eucharistie," *Revue thomiste* 99, no. 1 (1999): 171. "A consummation of this nature involves a double cause: on one hand, the dignity of the life given by Christ in sacrifice, namely the life of God and the life of man; on another, the interior disposition of Christ, namely the loving obedience to the Father that, tied to the humanity of Christ, persists eternally."

50. *ST* III, q. 22, a. 5: "Christ entered into the Holy of Holies—that is, into heaven—and prepared the way for us, that we might enter by the virtue of His blood, which He shed for us on earth." See also the *Commentary on the Letter to the Hebrews*, ch. 4, lect. 3: "Christ through His own blood entered into the heavenly holy of holies. Hence, he says, 'who has passed through the heavens,' i.e., He entered by His own power."

priest of the good things that are to come,"[51] sitting at the right hand of the Father, continues to offer himself entirely in sacrifice, presenting the stigmata of his Passion in his glorified flesh to the Father.

On the other hand, the exercise of the eternal priesthood of Christ has a salvific effect for mankind because it obtains spiritual and eternal benefits for them.[52] For those for whom he sacrificed himself, the Savior procures reconciliation and divine life, begun in this life by the gift of grace and fully consummated in heaven. It is still in virtue of his sacred humanity, which exists *presently* in heaven and in the state of a heavenly victim for all eternity, that justification is given and grace distributed. For Jesus, in the glory of eternity, "always lives to make intercession [to the Father] for us" (Heb 7:25).[53] He completes his mediating role as advocate for humanity, of which he is the head, and in his glorious suppliant hands he holds the power and virtue to apply to his members the eternal benefits of his sacrifice.[54] The Sovereign Priest never ceases to work to unite all the

51. Heb 9:11. See *Commentary on the Letter to the Hebrews*, ch. 9, lect. 3: "There are two things to be considered in every testament: namely, the end promised in that testament, and the things handed down in it. But the goods promised in the Old Testament were temporal goods: 'If you be willing and will hearken to me, you shall eat the good things of the land' (Is 1:19). Therefore, the other was a high priest of temporal goods; But Christ is the high priest of heavenly goods: 'Rejoice and be glad, because your reward is great in heaven' (Mt 5:12). Therefore, He is a high priest of the good things to come, because by His high priesthood we are brought to goods to come: 'We shall be filled with the good things of your house' (Ps 64:6)."

52. See *ST* III, q. 22, a. 5: "The consummation of the sacrifice [consists] in this, that those for whom the sacrifice is offered, obtain the end of the sacrifice. Now the end of the sacrifice which Christ offered consisted not in temporal but in eternal good, which we obtain through His death, according to Hebrews 9:11: 'Christ is a high-priest of the good things to come'; for which reason the priesthood of Christ is said to be eternal."

53. See *Commentary on the Letter to the Hebrews*, ch. 7, lect. 4: "He interposes for us, first, His human nature, which He assumed for us by representing; secondly, His most holy soul's desire, which He had for our salvation and with which He intercedes for us."

54. See *ST* III, q. 57, a. 6: "As the high-priest under the Old Testament entered the holy place to stand before God for the people, so also Christ entered heaven "to make intercession for us," as is said in Hebrews 7:25. Because the very showing of Himself in the human nature which He took with Him to heaven is a pleading for us.... Being established in His heavenly seat as God and Lord, He sends down divine gifts upon men."

elect in his love: "It is by virtue of his priesthood that grace is given to us, by which our hearts are turned to God."[55]

Thus the eternity of the priesthood of Christ is the basis for the priestly mission of the Church and, therefore, of the sacramental mode by which, in the power of the Holy Spirit, the Church essentially accomplishes this mission. In this sense the doctrine concerning the eternal consummation of the sacrifice sheds light on the "theophanic" dimension of sacramental doctrine, a dimension that is essential for us if we are to understand the spirit of the liturgy.

FROM THE PRIESTHOOD OF CHRIST TO THE SACRAMENTS OF THE CHURCH

St. Thomas concludes the question on the priesthood of Christ by asking why it is said of Christ, according to the words of the Psalm, that he is "a priest forever according to the order of Melchizedek" (Ps 109:4). Our Doctor responds that the priesthood of the King of Salem, whose sacrifice consisted in the offering of bread and wine, was a figure of the excellence of the priesthood of Christ in a manner even more perfect than the Levitic priesthood after him would be. Of course, *as to the actual offering*, the priesthood of Melchizedek was a less expressive figure of the immolation of Calvary than the bloody sacrifice of the Mosaic Law. But with regard to *participation in this sacrifice and in its effects*, the sacrifice of Melchizedek announced the excellence of the priesthood of Christ in a more adequate manner, since it consisted precisely in the offering of bread and wine, the mode in which "in the New Law the true sacrifice of Christ is presented to the faithful under the form of bread and wine," and the unity of the Church, an effect of the sacrament of the Eucharist, is achieved.[56]

Thus the Angelic Doctor concludes the entire question on the priesthood of Christ by indicating, albeit in an indirect manner, the

55. *ST* III, q. 22, a. 3.
56. *ST* III, q. 22, a. 6, ad 2.

sacramental mode by which the Church, once the Lord has been raised into glory, continues the cult of Christ on earth and distributes the infinite benefits of the redemptive sacrifice through the gift of grace.

In the first theological state, the regime of grace in which the elect, "under the truth of faith,"[57] are *in via* towards eternity, Christ's priesthood continues to function in a manner proportionate to the condition of mankind. Here below, in the time of the Church, it is by the use of exterior and sensible signs,[58] the sacraments of faith, that the perfect cult of Christ and his members is rendered to the Father (*ascending* motion) and that the sanctification of souls is accomplished (*descending* motion).[59] Unlike the *corporal* cultic regime of ancient Israel, the sacraments are no longer limited to prefiguring a supernatural reality, but, as the sign of the bloody immolation they both represent and contain that supernatural reality, and they are the earthly means by which we are united to the sacred humanity of Christ, the sacrament of salvation, as we await the vision of God face-to-face in eternity.

Thus the ritual economy of the New Covenant in no way modifies either the necessity of offering sacrifice, which is connatural to man, or the physical nature of the sacrificial act. Moreover, as testified by the vocabulary of the *Letter to the Hebrews*, the sacral categories proper to the Hebrew religion—but also, as we have seen, to every religious expression in history—remain the same: temple, sanctuary, priest, sacrifice, victim, sacred action, and so on. But

---

57. See *ST* III, q. 53, a. 2: "The first [epoch for the saints] was under figures of the Law (*sub figura legis*); the second under the truth of faith (*sub veritate fidei*); while the third will be in the eternity of glory (*in aeternitate gloriae*), which Christ inaugurated by rising again."

58. See *ST* III, q. 8, a. 6, where St. Thomas asks whether it is proper to Christ to be the head of the Church: "The head influences the other members in two ways. First, by a certain intrinsic influence, in as much as motive and sensitive force flow from the head to the other members; secondly, by a certain exterior guidance, inasmuch as by sight and the senses, which are rooted in the head, man is guided in his exterior acts."

59. See *ST* III, q. 60, a. 5: "In the use of the sacraments two things may be considered, namely, the worship of God, and the sanctification of man."

they are transposed, assumed, and elevated by the person of Christ, "God's religious." In the sacramental order and liturgy of the Church, the exterior acts of cult have acquired a new dimension that allows them to signify grace and announce the glory to come.[60]

60. See A.-I. Mennessier, *Saint Thomas d'Aquin: L'homme chrétien* (Paris: Cerf, 1965), 123: "The fact remains that these cultic categories and all the ritual structures they imply are for us a normal expression of that religious reality *par excellence* that is salvation in Christ Jesus. Do we not spontaneously translate our understanding of God, and the aspirations that flow from it, into the basic language and actions of sacrifice—which supposes the social presence of the priest? As long as the age of faith and hope lasts, is it not by means of sensible rites, instituted by Christ himself, that new grace is communicated to us? St. Thomas thus makes room for this formulation of the Christian mystery. But his concern for theological understanding—and understanding pertains to the real—leads him to organize his treatise on the Savior not around Christ's *priesthood* but around the benefits of grace and union with God of which his priesthood is the source, and which are the reason for this religious formulation of the mystery of redemption.

4

The Sacraments
Signs of the Divine Cult

Our search to uncover a liturgical theology in the works of St. Thomas now turns to the most expressive and most powerful of exterior acts of cult found in salvation history: the sacraments of the Church, by means of which the saving actions of Christ the Sovereign Priest continue to work in the world. In the *Summa theologiae*, within the treatise on religion, in the *proemium* to question 89 of the *Secunda secundae*, the Angelic Doctor had decisively situated the study of the sacraments after Christology. It is fitting to treat the sacraments only after having considered the person, priestly mission, and life of the Incarnate Word, not only because "they take their efficacy from the Incarnate Word,"[1] but also because their structure—natural and supernatural, sensible and divine, exterior and interior—cannot be grasped except in relation to the human-divine structure of Jesus and thus of his Church. The order of teaching (*ordo disciplinae*) thus models itself rigorously on the order of salvation (*ordo salutis*).

1. *ST* III, q. 60, prologue.

THE *SUMMA THEOLOGIAE*'S TREATISE
ON THE SACRAMENTS IN GENERAL

The treatise on the sacraments in general (*ST* III, 60–65), redacted between 1272 and 1273, after St. Thomas's return from Paris to
Naples,[2] will be the main focus of these observations. It is not impossible that the lively discussions that were galvanizing the University of Paris between 1267 and 1272, concerning the positions of Siger
de Brabant on the ontological separation of the intellect, may have
had some influence on the thought of our Doctor, since the dispute
sparked by Siger's positions, because it pertained to the structure
of man and the unity of the human composite in its dual corporal
and spiritual dimensions, meant that there was something indirectly at stake for sacramentology. As we shall see, there is an analogy
between the unity of man, composed of body and soul, and the sacramental structure of matter and form. The controversy may thus
have nourished what in the following pages will be called the anthropological dimension of Thomas's sacramental theology, his very
marked insistence on "the complete coherence [of the sacrament]
with human reality."[3]

The doctrinal synthesis of the treatise on the sacraments in general is innovative with respect to the *Commentary on the Sentences*[4]
and the *Summa contra Gentiles*.[5] The treatise contains six questions

2. On this question, see Fernand van Steenberghen, *Le mouvement doctrinal du XI*ᵉ
*au XIV*ᵉ *siècle: Le XIII*ᵉ *siècle* (Paris: Bloud et Gay, 1951), 179–328, and Edouard-Henri
Weber, *L'homme en discussion à l'université de Paris en 1270* (Paris: Biblioteque thomiste,
1970).

3. Marie-Dominique Chenu, "Pour une anthropologie sacramentelle," 99. See also
Liam G. Walsh, "The Divine and the Human in St. Thomas' Theology of Sacraments," in
Pinto de Oliveira, *Ordo sapientiae et amoris*, 321–52, and Fernández Rodríguez, "Hombre
y sacramento en Santo Thomás," *Studi Tomistici* 44 (1991): 245–52.

4. In the *Sentences*, St. Thomas did not discuss the nature of sacraments in an organized way, but at four different moments, twice directly (*Commentary on the Sentences* IV,
d. 1, q. 1; d. 2, q. 1), and twice indirectly in relation to the sacrament of Baptism (*Commen-*
tary on the Sentences IV, d. 4, q. 1; d. 5, q. 1 and 2).

5. While the *Summa contra Gentiles* offered a copious meditation on the sacraments
in speciali (*SCG* IV, c. 59–78), the sacraments in general received only a brief discussion

(60–65). Question 60 deals with the essence and material cause of the sacrament. St. Thomas begins by showing that the sacrament is a sign (a. 1–3), then examines its constitutive elements (a. 4–8). In question 61, our Doctor examines the sacramental sign under the aspect of final cause, affirming the necessity of the sacramental sign for the salvation of man who is wounded by sin. Nevertheless, as he had already noted, there are two things to consider in the use of this sign: the worship of God (divine cult) and the sanctification of man.[6] For this reason the sacrament is the formal cause of a double effect. On the one hand, it causes grace as an instrumental cause (q. 62), and on the other, it imposes a character on the soul that deputes it to the cult of God (q. 63). Question 64 takes up the notion of instrumental cause, this time not considering the grace it produces but its nature as a formal cause working through the minister of the sacrament. After defining the sacrament, St. Thomas gives a real division and justifies its sevenfold nature (q. 65).

In choosing to define a sacrament as a "sign of a holy thing so far as it makes men holy," our Doctor has given priority, in the order of his exposition, to the aspect of sanctification. He reserves his analysis of the cultic dimension of sacrament for question 63, where he will consider the cult man renders to God as the effect of the soul's sanctification through divine grace. On one hand, the sacraments are the channels of Christ's grace, which they extend and communicate by virtue of the Holy Spirit. On the other, under the action of the same Spirit, they make present the eternal oblation Christ makes of himself to the Father, a cult without which man's sanctification is not possible. Because the sacraments of the Church continue and prolong in time the twofold mediation (ascendant and descendant) of Christ's priesthood, St. Thomas will firmly maintain this double

---

in three earlier chapters (c. 56–58). In the *Summa theologiae*, the elements of the four individual treatises of the *Commentary on the Sentences* have been reassembled in a systematic manner, while the ideas presented in the *Summa contra Gentiles* about the fittingness of the sacramental regime have been inserted into the larger context of a genuine treatise.

6. ST III, q. 60, a. 5: "*In usu sacramentorum duo possunt considerari, scilicet cultus divinus et sanctificatio hominis.*"

dimension of the sacraments throughout the whole study: sanctification and cult.

Since the object of our observations in what follows is the relation between sacrament and cult, we will not mention the sanctifying dimension except insofar as it clarifies our understanding of the
Angelic Doctor's liturgical theology.

As "sacraments of the faith," the sacramental signs share in the
realism of the redemptive Incarnation. In choosing to define the
sacrament through the notion of *sign*, "a sign of some sacred thing
pertaining to man,"[7] St. Thomas underlines the extent to which the
structure of the sacramental reality, composed of sensible realities[8]
and the verbal forms that determine these realities,[9] corresponds
to the mode of existence proper to man, for whom the sacraments
have been instituted.[10] But even further, by virtue of the Incarnation,
the structure of the sacrament is modeled on the structure of the
God-Man, the Instrument, *Mystery*, or *Sacrament* of salvation. Just
as the divinity elevated human nature in the person of the Word, just
so, in the sacrament, by divine power, the words elevate the sensible
realities, allowing them to signify the cult of God and the sanctification of man.[11]

7. *ST* III, q. 60, a. 2.

8. "It is part of man's nature to acquire knowledge of the intelligible from the sensible. But a sign is that by means of which one attains to the knowledge of something
else. Consequently, since the sacred things which are signified by the sacraments are the
spiritual and intelligible goods by means of which man is sanctified, it follows that the
sacramental signs consist in sensible things" (*ST* III, q. 60, a. 4).

9. "Now in all things composed of matter and form, the determining principle is on
the part of the form, which is as it were the end and terminus of the matter. Consequently for the being of a thing the need of a determinate form is prior to the need of determinate matter: for determinate matter is needed that it may be adapted to the determinate
form. Since, therefore, in the sacraments determinate sensible things are required, which
are as the sacramental matter, much more is there need in them of a determinate form of
words" (*ST* III, q. 60, a. 7).

10. See Hyacinthe-François Dondaine, "La définition des sacrements dans la
Somme théologique," *Revue des sciences philosophiques et théologiques* 31 (1947): 214–28.
Marie-Dominique Chenu notes: "the two words 'anthropology' and 'sacramental" are
inseparable from one another, not only methodologically ... but constitutively" ("Pour
une anthropologie sacramentelle," 87).

11. "For in the first place [the sacraments] can be considered in regard to the cause

As sensible signs adapted to man's condition, the sacraments of the New Law are first and foremost signs of divine action. Under the cultic regime of the Old Law, the "sacramental" signs did nothing more than announce or represent the mystery of Christ by way of anticipation. Though they were confessions of faith, spiritual acts, they were still not able to signify the divine cult and the sanctification of man in an efficacious manner, something that only Christ, as the instrumental cause of salvation, would be able to accomplish adequately.[12] The sacraments of the Church, on the other hand, in their nature as exterior signs and sacred actions, establish vital physical contact with the redemptive Passion. As an instrument conjoined to his divinity, the holy humanity of Christ continues its work on earth through the sacraments; by means of separate instrumental causes,[13] the sacraments tie the members of the Mystical Body to the holy humanity of their divine Head.[14] The sacraments extend into the time of the Church, our time, the work that Christ accomplished on the altar of the cross, a work that remains thereby forever sanctifying.

---

of sanctification, which is the Word incarnate: to Whom the sacraments have a certain conformity, in that the word is joined to the sensible sign, just as in the mystery of Incarnation the Word of God is united to sensible flesh" (*ST* III, q. 60, a. 6).

12. "The Fathers of old had faith in the future Passion of Christ, which, inasmuch as it was apprehended by the mind, was able to justify them. But we have faith in the past Passion of Christ, which is able to justify, also by the real use of sacramental things" (*ST* III, q. 62, a. 6, ad 1).

13. "The sacraments of the New Law are both causes and signs. Hence, too, is it that, to use the common expression, 'they effect what they signify.' From this it is clear that they perfectly fulfill the conditions of a sacrament; being ordained to something sacred, not only as a sign, but also as a cause" (*ST* III, q. 62, a. 1, ad 1). On *separate instrumental causality*, see *ST* III, q. 62, a. 5: "Now an instrument is twofold. the one, separate, as a stick, for instance; the other, united, as a hand. Moreover, the separate instrument is moved by means of the united instrument, as a stick by the hand. Now the principal efficient cause of grace is God Himself, in comparison with Whom Christ's humanity is as a united instrument, whereas the sacrament is as a separate instrument. Consequently, the saving power must needs be derived by the sacraments from Christ's Godhead through His humanity."

14. "Christ's Passion, although corporeal, has yet a spiritual effect from the Godhead united: and therefore it secures its efficacy by spiritual contact—namely, by faith and the sacraments of faith ..." (*ST* III, q. 48, a. 6, ad 2). See also *ST* III, q. 68, a. 8, ad 1.

THE CULTIC DIMENSION OF SACRAMENTALITY

There is a cultic action at the very root of the communication of the graces of salvation: the offering of the pure oblation of the Incarnate Word, priest and victim of his own sacrifice. The graces of salvation, the fruits of the acceptance of a perfect cult, are imparted to us through the sacramental sign, which is at one and the same time an act of cult and a sanctifying reality. This dual purpose of the sacraments is brought up more than once in the treatise on the sacraments in general.[15] The notion of the cultic finality of sacramentality, introduced in the *Commentary on the Sentences*, becomes in the *Summa theologiae* "the key motif in Aquinas's last sacramental symphony," as M. Turrini has remarked.[16] In the sacramental structure, *cult*, like the supernatural reality of *grace* and in close connection with it, becomes the object of a reflection that runs through the whole treatise on the sacraments. To his repeated affirmation of the sacraments' dual purpose, we must add the fact that the term *cultus* appears forty-one times in the course of the treatise (*cultus divinus, cultus Dei, cultus christianus*, etc.) and the term *ritus* eight times.

To our mind, this marked insistence testifies to the Angelic Doctor's growing interest in a "liturgical" point of view. Of course, the grand cultic themes of the *Commentary on the Letter to the Hebrews*, fruits of his teaching in Rome (1265–1268), in addition to orienting the priestly dimension of his Christology, also exercised a persistent influence on the evolution of his sacramental theology. In fact, the doctrine found in the treatise on the sacraments is the culmination of his reflections on cult in the previous treatises—on the Old Law, on the virtue of religion, on the Incarnate Word, and on the Passion

---

15. Thus apropos of the sacraments' relation to the Passion of Christ: "Now sacramental grace seems to be ordained principally to two things: namely, to take away the defects consequent on past sins ... and, further, to perfect the soul in things pertaining to Divine Worship in regard to the Christian Religion" (*ST* III, q. 62, a. 5). See also *ST* III, q. 63, a. 1 and 6; and *ST* III, q. 65, a. 1.

16. Mauro Turrini, *L'anthropologie sacramentelle de saint Thomas d'Aquin* (Paris: Institut Catholique de Paris et Université de Paris-Sorbonne, 1996), 108.

of Christ—treatises we have discussed in previous chapters. With regard to the treatises on the virtue of religion and on the Old Law, we considered the nature and exterior manifestations of *homo cultualis*, showing that man is religious by nature by the intention of the creative Wisdom. Man is gradually led, through Revelation, to the culmination of the mystery, but always in harmony with what is innate in him. Christ, Mediator between God and men, by rendering to the Father the homage of his sacrifice, has caused the remission of sins and the sanctification of men. In so doing, Aquinas says, "by His Passion He inaugurated the rites of the Christian Religion."[17] He has allowed the redeemed to take part in the only cult that pleases God, celebrated and rendered present here below by his Church, a cultic society. The cult of the Christian religion thus shares in the sanctifying efficacy of the cult of Christ. In the sacraments of the New Law, in keeping with what was accomplished in the Person of Christ, the ascending and descending movements of his mediation—cult and sanctification—are united and co-penetrating. The sacraments of faith are simultaneously *signs of sanctification* and *signs of cult*.

Sanctification and cult are made efficacious in the economy of sacramental signification. Christians practice this cult with the aid of visible signs: in the first place, the sacramental signs, in the second place, the liturgical signs that the Church has received the power and mission to institute. The sacraments and, in a lesser measure, the rites of the Church themselves are given the power to represent, reproduce, and contain the all-perfect cult of Christ in an efficacious manner. In order that they might perform them validly, Christ's faithful are deputed to the use of these signs by a spiritual *character* that renders them participants in the priesthood of Christ. The worshipping man of the New Law is thus not only the recipient of sacramental signs but even more, in virtue of the cultic dimension inherent in these signs, a subject of liturgical actions.[18]

17. *ST* III, q. 62, a. 5.
18. See Turrini, *L'anthropologie sacramentelle de saint Thomas d'Aquin*, 125: "The sacraments are thus charged with an anthropologically positive meaning; they can 'make

Faced with the *esse sacramentale*'s twin sanctifying and cultic dimensions, St. Thomas chose to give priority, in his order of exposition, to God's relation with man—that is, to the exclusive power God has to sanctify man by the gift of grace[19]—the "principal" effect of the sacrament. But the cultic dimension is not "secondary," except insofar as it has to do with man in his relations with God, that is, insofar as graced man is rendered capable of rising to God and professing his faith by means of sanctifying cultic signs; or put another way, the fact that this cult is acceptable depends on the sanctification man has acquired through the sacrifice of Christ. Correlatively, the gift of grace demands that sanctified man render God the perfect cult of which he is now capable as a member of Christ. This link between sanctification and cult certainly explains why, after the study on grace (*ST* III, q. 62), St. Thomas moves on to another effect of the sacrament, the sacramental character (*ST* III, q. 63), a study that will permit the Angelic Doctor to identify the relation between sanctification and cult more precisely.

CULT AND THE SACRAMENTAL CHARACTER

The *Summa theologiae*'s teaching on the sacramental character is a new and original step in relation to the teaching presented in the *Sentences*.[20] When the *Commentary on the Sentences* was written, the consensus opinion followed Augustinian tradition in holding

---

perfect,' rendering man a citizen of the new cultic age, a subject who manifests his sanctification by a cultic motion toward God. Thomas thus completes the discourse he began with the virtue of religion." Further, "the place given to the *homo cultualis* is much more than a concession: the theological payoff of Thomas's reflection comes from his interest in man and from the fact that he has posited a solid sacramental anthropology."

19. "Since, therefore, the sanctification of man is in the power of God Who sanctifies, it is not for man to decide what things should be used for his sanctification, but this should be determined by Divine institution" (*ST* III, q. 60, a. 5).

20. *Commentary on the Sentences* IV, d. 4, q. 1, a. 1–4. See also a brief study in the treatise *De articulis fidei et Ecclesiae sacramentis* and a few allusions in the *Commentary on the Letter to the Hebrews* (ch. 11, lect. 7) and the *Commentary on the Letter to the Romans* (ch. 7, lect. 1). The character receives no systematic treatment either in the *Compendium* or in the *Summa contra Gentiles*.

that the character was a special effect of the sacraments of Christian initiation,[21] and St. Thomas followed his scholastic contemporaries in viewing it as an exterior mark of grace, a "distinctive and configuring sign" proper to Baptism.[22] In this case, the word *sign* should not be understood in its strict sense, but in the sense of the relation of the character with the visible sacrament by which the character is received. But a better understanding of the Aristotelian categories allowed the Angelic Doctor, unlike his predecessors, to define the nature of character more precisely and thus to emphasize the primacy of its relation to cultic actions. Character in his definition is not a *habitus*, since the impression of the character is indifferent to the morality of the subject who receives it, but belongs rather to the second species of Aristotelian quality: the active potency. It is a supernatural potency, a dynamic reality that makes the recipient capable of actions in conformity with the state in which he has been constituted by the sacrament received. The sacramental character marks and deputes the subject to the act, that is, to effective participation in the activities that belong to the supernatural life, activities that our Doctor here identifies, possibly under the influence of Pseudo-Dionysius,[23] as hierarchical, or liturgical, activities. Hence: "This sign is nothing other than a certain power by which one is capable of hierarchical actions, which are ministrations and receptions of the sacraments, and of other things that pertain to the faithful."[24]

21. See Alexander of Hales, *In IV Sent.*, d. 6, q. 2; Albert the Great, *In IV Sent.*, d. 6, q. 3–9; Bonaventure, *In IV Sent.*, d. 6, q. 1.

22. "*Signum distinctivum et signum configurativum*" (Thomas, *Commentary on the Sentences* IV, d. 4, q. 1).

23. Like the rest of his contemporaries, St. Thomas attributes to Pseudo-Dionysius a definition of the sacramental character that was actually something read into his work by an anonymous author from the early thirteenth century in the second chapter of the *Ecclesiastical Hierarchy*, where there is a question about a "signation," probably chrismal. See Jean-Benoît d'Argenlieu, "Note sur deux définitions médiévales du caractère sacramentel," *Revue thomiste* 33 (1928): 271–75, and Bertrand-Marie Perrin, "Le caractère de la Confirmation chez saint Thomas," *Revue thomiste* 98, no. 2 (1998): 236–40.

24. Thomas Aquinas, *Commentary on the Sentences* IV, d. 4, q. 1, a. 1 (trans. Beth Mortensen, *Commentary on the Sentences*, Opera omnia 7 (Green Bay, WI: The Aquinas Institute, 2018), 156–57.

Therefore the character is the indelible, distinctive sign that renders access to sacred actions possible to the one marked by it. God gives efficacy to the spiritual actions of the subject in consideration of this distinction imprinted in the faculties of his soul. Though the primary contribution of the *Commentary on the Sentences* is the classification of the character as a *potentia*, nevertheless, even here we can detect that Thomas envisages the character from the point of view of its relation to cultic actions, even if the term *cult* does not appear in any of the four articles dedicated to the character. There is an implicit orientation toward the grand idea of the *Summa theologiae* in the idea of configuration through the sacramental character, which participates in the "Character of Christ," and thus in the actions of Christ the Priest.[25]

The *Summa theologiae* goes beyond these mere hints to make the cultic dimension explicit. His view is not the result of an examination of the character; on the contrary, the study and definition of the character proceed from his position on the cultic finality of the sacraments themselves. His doctrinal treatment of the character is not inserted *en passant* into the context of the particular case of Baptism, but occupies a whole question (*ST* III, q. 63) of the treatise on sacraments in general, and has the whole Christological horizon of the *Tertia pars* as its backdrop.

The Character: *Sign, Deputation,* and *Potency* in the Cultic Order

St. Thomas first asks about the existence of the sacramental character.[26] His point of departure is the double finality of the sacraments, and here he is concerned with the second of these finalities: "for the perfecting of the soul in things pertaining to the Divine worship according to the rite of the Christian life." But in order validly to perform the cultic actions that Christ has chosen and instituted, one

---

25. "By the character of Christ, one is configured to the actions of Christ" (*Commentary on the Sentences* IV, d. 4, q. 1, a. 1, ad 3).

26. *ST* III, q. 63, a. 1.

must be deputed by God. The idea of deputation is directly tied to the idea of consignation (*consignari*), related to the ancient practice of marking a soldier's body as a sign of his deputation to the armed service: "Since, therefore, by the sacraments men are deputed to a spiritual service pertaining to the worship of God, it follows that by their means the faithful receive a certain spiritual character."

In his attempt to express the nature of the character, St. Thomas presents it as a *sign*. *Signum distinctivum, signaculum, quaedam signatio* are the expressions he uses to specify the relation between the character and the sacrament. However, the imprinted character does not have the nature of sign in itself, but only by virtue of the sensible cause from which it proceeds.[27] As a fruit of the sacramental sign in its aspect of sanctification, the character itself is oriented toward producing the second aspect of the sacramental sign, which is the divine cult. Since the character is described as a sign insofar as what the character does resembles what is done by a sign in the proper sense, we can speak of character as producing only a "certain signification." Nevertheless, the use of the word "sign" here serves to connect the essential definition of the sacraments with their cultic dimension.

Reading question 63, article 1, we can see how much Thomas relies on the notion of *deputation* to cult through the sacraments—the verb *deputare* is used five times. Further, deputation is always linked to the notion of consignation: a man is marked with a seal because he is deputed to the spiritual service of the cult of God. Affirmed again and again throughout question 63, the relation of deputation to character will be the foundation for his reflection on the nature of the character.

This cultic deputation has an eschatological foundation. Because he is destined to the life of glory by the "seal of grace," the Christian in the present time—which is the first phase of eschatological time—is deputed by the character to sacred actions that signify the cult of Christ and announce the coming of the Kingdom.[28] This cor-

27. *ST* III, q. 63, a. 1, ad 2. See also *ST* III, q. 63, a. 2, ad 4.
28. *ST* III, q. 63, a. 1, ad 1.

respondence, elaborated in question 63, article 3, between the *signaculum gratiae*, which deputes and introduces one to the state of glory, and the sacramental character, which deputes one to the present rite of the Christian religion, must be put in relation with the idea of the eternal consummation of the sacrifice of Christ, or in other words with the cultic dimension of eternal life, which must ground our understanding of the earthly liturgy. Our Doctor will discuss this more explicitly later on, affirming that the character, along with its cultic finality, remains forever and indelibly in the soul.[29]

In question 63, article 2, continuing a reflection begun in the *Commentary on the Sentences*, St. Thomas claims that the character deputes man to the divine cult as a spiritual *potency*. To support his claim, he appeals to Pseudo-Dionysius,[30] for whom the divine cult consists in receiving and transmitting divine things. Aquinas remarks that in order to perform these two offices a potency is required: "to bestow something on others, active power is necessary; and in order to receive, we need a passive power. Consequently, a character signifies a certain spiritual power ordained unto things pertaining to the Divine worship."[31] As a potency, the character is a dynamic reality, entirely oriented to the production of determinate acts. But potencies are divided into two general types: passive and active. The Christian possesses a potency that is either *passive*, disposing him to

29. See *ST* III, q. 63, a. 5, corp. and ad 3: "Although external worship does not last after this life, yet its end remains. Consequently, after this life the character remains, both in the good as adding to their glory, and in the wicked as increasing their shame." However, as M. Turrini has observed: "While the idea of *deputation* tends to align the notions of glory and cult, as expressions of the same economy, nevertheless the distinction between grace—the condition for entry into the things to come—and the character—the capacity for cultic activity in the present—assures the presence of both of the two aspects in the Thomistic exposition, so that the weight of the eschatological perspective, which takes priority, does not stifle the cultic dimension" (*L'anthropologie sacramentelle de saint Thomas d'Aquin*, 464).

30. "God, by imprinting a kind of sign, grants a share of Himself to those that approach Him, by making them Godlike and communicators of Divine gifts." The text is taken from the second chapter of Pseudo-Dionysius's *Ecclesiastical Hierarchy*, which had already inspired Thomas's reflections in the *Commentary on the Sentences*.

31. *ST* III, q. 63, a. 2.

receive a motion, or *active*, ordering him to the act of transmission. The character thus consists in a certain spiritual potency, active in the case of the sacrament of Holy Orders, active in a certain manner in the sacrament of Confirmation,[32] and purely passive in Baptism.

The Angelic Doctor further specifies that the character is a potency in the order of *instrumentality*, similar to the spiritual virtue in the sacraments that operates under the motion of the principal agent. The seal of the character deputes the one who is marked by it to the cultic ministry: "to have a sacramental character belongs to God's ministers: and a minister is a kind of instrument, as the Philosopher says (Polit. 1.3)."[33] But what does "minister" mean here? Does it refer to ministers marked by the character of the sacrament of Holy Orders, who are the dispensers the Lord's sacraments? Or does St. Thomas consider all the baptized "ministers of God" in virtue of the consignation of the baptismal character that deputes every Christian to cultic functions? An examination of article 3, which treats the relation between the sacramental character and the character of Christ, will permit us to better understand the meaning of this assertion and therefore of the character's instrumentality.

The Character: Participation in the Priesthood of Christ

The *Summa* goes beyond the intuitions of the *Commentary on the Sentences* to define the sacramental character principally in relation to the "character of Christ," or in other words, as a participation in the priesthood of the mediator.

In the *Sed contra* of question 63, article 3, Thomas merely repeats the classical definition in currency with most of the Scholastic masters, that the character is "a distinctive mark printed in a man's rational soul by the eternal Character." He immediately observes that by "eternal Character" we must understand Christ: for Jesus is indeed, according to Hebrews 1:13, "the reflection of God's glory and the exact imprint" or character, as Thomas points out following the

---

32. "in a certain manner" = "*Quodammodo.*" See *ST* III, q. 63, a. 6.
33. *ST* III, q. 63, a. 2.

Gloss, "of God's very being." The sacramental character, therefore, must be situated in direct relation to and in immediate dependence on Christ.

In the body of the article, the link between the sacramental character and the character of Christ is linked directly to the doctrine of Christ's priesthood:

Now the whole rite of the Christian religion is derived from Christ's priesthood. Consequently, it is clear that the sacramental character is specially the character of Christ, to Whose character the faithful are likened by reason of the sacramental characters, which are nothing else than certain participations of Christ's Priesthood, flowing from Christ Himself.

The only cult conceivable in the Christian religion is one that refers to and depends on the cult of Christ the Sovereign Priest. The Mediator washed mankind from their sins and granted them the gift of grace precisely by offering himself in sacrifice to the Father, an offering commenced at the Incarnation and consummated on the altar of the cross. This act was the supreme exercise of Christ's priesthood. The sacramental cult of the Church is one reality with the cult of Christ. When the Church uses the sacraments of the faith, it is really Christ who, through the ministry of the Church, continues to exercise his priestly mediation, not only by sanctifying those who receive the sacraments, but also by rendering to the Father, in the unity of the Holy Spirit, the only cult that is acceptable to him. The subjects of the sacraments are admitted to participation in this same, unique cult of the Redeemer precisely through the gift of the character. Consequently, the cultic *potentia* granted to man, by which St. Thomas has just defined the character, derives from him who has the plenitude of spiritual priesthood, Christ the Sovereign Priest.[34]

34. We should remark that, though Thomas speaks about the *character Christi*, it is certainly not because he maintains the existence of a cultic potency in the Person of the Word. St. Thomas uses the expression here in the sense of the scholarly definition enunciated above, derived from the words of the Apostle, in which Christ is "the reflection of God's glory and the exact imprint of God's very being." Later on, when he reaffirms his notion of character-participation, he is more precise: "In a sacramental character Christ's faithful have a share in His Priesthood; in the sense that as Christ has the full power of

Only Christ has given the Father a cult that is perfect and complete. After his entry into glory, and as long as he continues to offer his Father the homage of his glorious humanity on the altar of the heavens, the faithful are granted to participate in his priesthood through the imprint of the sacramental character, permitted to unite themselves to the perfect, complete, and eternal cult of the Mediator.

In the ad 2 of question 63, article 3, the Angelic Doctor defines the precise status of the character in the sacramental organism. In the structure of the sacrament, the sacramental rite is only an exterior sign (*sacramentum tantum*), while the grace produced is the ultimate reality (*res tantum*). Nevertheless, the character in the three sacraments of Baptism, Confirmation, and Holy Orders, is both sign and grace, the intermediary and signifying reality designated by the school as *res et sacramentum*. With respect to grace, it is a *signum*, or *sacrament*, because it signifies and disposes for "adjuvant" sacramental grace and the other actual graces that are proper to the exercise of cult.[35] Nevertheless, due to "the purpose of the sacramental character properly speaking," it is also a *res* because it imprints a seal on the soul, a distinctive sign that deputes the faithful to acts of cult and configures them to the Sovereign Head.

For St. Thomas the character is both *participation* and *configuration*, a view that allows him to better define the relation established between Christ and the faithful by the character. Christ, the sovereign author and principal agent of cult, enrolls those whom he admits to collaborate with him in this cult, marking them with the seal of the head. By the seal of the character, the faithful are thus "configured" to Christ and participate in his cultic power in a manner more or less extensive according to the particular deputation linked

a spiritual priesthood, so His faithful are likened to Him by sharing a certain spiritual power with regard to the sacraments and to things pertaining to the Divine worship. For this reason it is unbecoming that Christ should have a character: but His Priesthood is compared to a character, as that which is complete and perfect is compared to some participation of itself" (*ST* III, q. 63, a. 5).

35. See P. Blázquez, "El carácter como disposición a la gracia sacramental según Santo Tomás," *Studium* 13 (Madrid): 321–35.

to the sacrament that they receive—Baptism, Confirmation, Holy Orders.[36]

In virtue of the potency they receive that configures them to the divine head, Christ's faithful participate in the cult of the Sovereign Priest himself. Thence it follows necessarily that the members are *instrumental* or *ministerial* causes of a cult whose cause and principal agent is Christ. Since the characters are, to use the words of our Doctor, "nothing else than certain participations of Christ's Priesthood, flowing from Christ Himself,"[37] they thus participate in the *effective* instrumental causality of Christ's holy humanity, whose exercise culminated in the priestly and cultic act of Calvary. As M. Turrini remarked, "cultic activity is no less instrumental than sanctification. The sanctifying movement that comes from God to man thus establishes the model that governs the cultic movement that rises from man to God; both unfold through instrumentality."[38]

The spiritual potency that the sacramental character gives to those on whom it is imprinted is, therefore, not at all an independent potency. It has been placed in the faithful soul by Christ the Sovereign Priest so that, in the words of Charles Journet, the soul may "dispose ministerially what Christ has disposed principally."[39] Possession of the sacramental character amounts to becoming a

36. "It is Christ Himself, the principal agent and supreme authority in all that relates to the divine cult, who decides on this ordering; and it is His sign, impressed on the human soul, that indicates by its special character what type and what sphere of priestly power the man signed with it participates in. At the same time, the sacramental instrument or rite that Christ uses to imprint his mark on the soul exercises its influence on the physiognomy of this mark, because through its reality as sign it indicates the type and the sphere of this participation and determines its limits through instrumental causality. Thus, when each sacrament imprints its character on the human soul, it causes through its rite the realization of a certain participation of man in the sacerdotal power of Christ. Thus, the man who receives all the sacraments that confer a character participates in some way in the plenitude of the sacerdotal power of Christ." Irénée Georges Łuczyński, "Le caractère sacramentel comme pouvoir instrumental selon saint Thomas d'Aquin," *Divus Thomas* 68, no. 1 (1965), 5.

37. *ST* III, q. 63, a. 3.

38. Turrini, *L'anthropologie sacramentelle de saint Thomas d'Aquin*, 476.

39. See Charles Journet, "Questions détachées sur la sacramentalité," *Vie spirituelle-supplément* 19 (1928): 121–50.

"minister of God," and to being so *per modum instrumenti*,[40] as an instrument of the principal agent, God. Thus constituted, the minister will effectively exercise the acts of cult that pertain to Christ.

Further, because the character is a participation in the eternal priesthood of Christ, its presence in the soul is permanent and indelible, since this participation lasts as long as his eternity.[41] The indelibility of the sacramental character is thus a consequence and requirement of participation in Christ's priesthood. In the mode of participation, the faithful soul is deputed in a stable and definitive manner to use the sacraments and everything related to the divine cult. Configuration to Christ is a sort of irrevocable "consecration" of the Christian to the dignity of a minister of God. This consecration is more perfect and durable than what is given to inanimate things like churches or altars,[42] not only because of the participated eternity of Christ's priesthood, but also from the fact of the incorruptibility of the soul itself.[43]

Finally, if grace is ordered to the enjoyment of glory, then the character, though it relates first of all to the cult of the present Church, also embraces the cult of the heavenly Jerusalem. In and through Christ, grace and character are linked and brought to fulfillment by the life of glory at the end of history.

Character and Grace

The notion of participation in Christ's priesthood allowed Thomas to affirm the cultic nature of the character. This same liturgical point of view will clarify the relation between the character and grace, treated indirectly in articles 4 and 5 of question 63.

---

40. *ST* III, q. 63, a. 2.

41. "Christ's Priesthood is eternal, according to Psalm 109:4: 'Thou art a priest for ever, according to the order of Melchisedech.' Consequently, every sanctification wrought by His Priesthood, is perpetual, enduring as long as the thing sanctified endures" (*ST* III, q. 63, a. 5).

42. *ST* III, q. 63, a. 5.

43. For "the subject of a character is the soul as to its intellective part, where faith resides … ; [thus] it is clear that, the intellect being perpetual and incorruptible, a character cannot be blotted out from the soul." (*ST* III, q. 63, a. 5).

The character's seal marks the soul in a way that enables it to receive and transmit things pertaining to the divine cult. Now the divine cult consists in certain acts to which the potencies of the soul are ordered, like essence to existence. Thus the subject of the character is one of the soul's potencies. While the character is grounded in a potency in the soul, grace pertains to the soul's essence: "Just as the essence of the soul, from which man has his natural life, is perfected by grace, from which the soul derives spiritual life; so the natural power of the soul is perfected by a spiritual power, which is a character."[44] Therefore grace pertains to the spiritual life, while the character perfects cultic actions: "a character disposes the soul directly and proximately to the fulfilling of things pertaining to Divine worship."[45]

But does grace have a place in the cultic dimension? If it does, what is its role in the liturgical domain, which is the special realm of the character?

Because cult cannot be accomplished suitably (*idonee*) without the help of grace, since, according to John 4:24, "they that adore" God "must adore Him in spirit and in truth," consequently, the Divine bounty bestows grace on those who receive the character, so that they may accomplish worthily (*digne*) the service to which they are deputed.[46]

This citation of the Gospel of St. John allows Aquinas to show what is radically new in the cult of the New Law. It is a cult acceptable to God, a cult penetrated with the grace of Christ, impregnated by theological faith that sanctifies the one who performs and participates in it. It is not that a man would not be able to exercise acts of cult if the grace of Christ the Head was lacking in his soul. Nevertheless, without grace, the cultic acts he performed would not be done suitably (*idonee*). Grace is given to the one marked with the seal of the character so that he may worthily (*digne*) perform the sacred functions.

44. *ST* III, q. 63, a. 4, ad 2.
45. *ST* III, q. 63, a. 4, ad 2, ad 1.
46. *ST* III, q. 63, a. 4, ad 2, ad 1.

Thus we see how St. Thomas emphasizes the importance of grace in order for the cultic act to be carried out worthily, even while he appreciates the objective validity of this act when it is performed through the instrumental causality of the character. But if the character assures the objective performance of the Christian cult, it is grace that assures its subjective performance. Grace permits one to perform *well* the cultic functions to which one is deputed, that is, to participate worthily in the cult of Christ.

In question 63, article 5, Thomas examines and compares the modality of the presence of grace and the character in the soul. Unlike the character, grace, though it is a realized form, stands in direct dependence on its subject, the free will, and thus can be lost: "Since the soul as long as it is a wayfarer is changeable in respect of the free-will, it results that grace is in the soul in a changeable manner." The character, on the other hand, because it is an instrument whose principal subject is God, is not dependent on the inconstancy of a free will, but participates in the stability and immutability of its source. In fact, the character's stability and immutability are assured "not from any perfection of its own, but from the perfection of Christ's priesthood, from which the character flows like an instrumental power." Thus the character confers on the soul the permanent capacity to become the instrument of Christ the Priest, or to perform acts of the divine cult, whether or not the soul is in a state of grace. Of course, if the soul does not possess God's grace, it will not perform the works of cult "worthily"; nevertheless, cult will survive by virtue of the sacramental character, an indelible participation in the priesthood of Christ.[47]

47. See Turrini, *L'anthropologie sacramentelle de saint Thomas d'Aquin*, 489–90: "Thomas's serious preoccupation with anthropology can be seen in the fact that he makes the deputation to cultic activity a great axis of sacramentality; he thoroughly defends man's capacity to exercise this function, even in the least favorable circumstances. While clearly admitting that acts of cult *sine auxilio gratiae* are an anomaly, and that, without the aid of the grace that God assures to the acting subjects, we would face a contradiction, Thomas defends the value and solid substance of the character. *Non propter sui perfectionem*: it would be an affront to grace to attribute to the character, a secondary effect of the sacraments, a quality that would put it before the principal effect. It is the

THE SACRAMENTAL CHARACTERS
AND THE EXERCISE OF CULT

St. Thomas's reflection on the character has allowed him to illustrate the second finality of the sacraments: "to perfect the soul in things pertaining to Divine Worship in regard to the Christian Religion."[48] His next question asks whether all the sacraments of the New Law imprint a character.[49] In other words, do all the sacraments dispose the soul in a direct and proximate manner to perform the divine cult?

Though all sacraments have the twofold purpose—to sanctify the soul and render homage to God—they are not all ordered directly to the divine cult. For example, the sacrament of Penance, because it relates principally to personal perfection, "does not afford man any advance in the Divine worship," but consists essentially in delivering man from sin and restoring him to God's grace. As we shall soon see, the cultic deputation caused by the character is independent from individual perfection of soul and is oriented to the edification and stability of the cultic society of the Church. The sacraments that confer a character, therefore (Baptism, Confirmation, and Holy Orders), are those that give the power to transmit or receive the other sacraments.

But the other sacraments are also ordered, if indirectly, to divine cult. Later on, when giving an account of the sevenfold nature of the sacraments, at the outset the Angelic Doctor affirms the cultic dimension of the whole ensemble of the sacraments and even puts their liturgical finality first in the order of exposition.[50] He always links the two aspects of sanctification and cult in his consideration of

---

perfection of Christ's priesthood, whose indelible seal the faithful bear, which prevents cult from exiting its Christic trajectory, even when it is not accompanied by grace because of the mutability of the human will."

48. *ST* III, q. 62, a. 5.

49. *ST* III, q. 63, a. 6.

50. *ST* III, q. 65, a. 1. See also the response to the third objection, where St. Thomas makes a serious dialectical effort to divide the sacramental organism following the three Dionysian hierarchical activities: *purgatio, illuminatio, perfectio.*

the sacraments, whether they perfect man personally or build up the Church—the "social community" in whose bosom Christ's faithful live. Thus even if Penance, Extreme Unction, and Marriage do not afford any advance in the divine cult, they are, nonetheless, ordered to it in an indirect manner, insofar as they are exterior acts of the worshipping man, for the reception and transmission of which the character marks him.

The cultic dimension is more pronounced in the three sacraments that imprint the character. They perfect the believer in his performance of cultic actions either *per modum agentis*, when they create sacred ministers; or *per modum recipientis*, when they create subjects of cultic actions:

It is the sacrament of order that pertains to the sacramental agents: for it is by this sacrament that men are deputed to confer sacraments on others: while the sacrament of Baptism pertains to the recipients, since it confers on man the power to receive the other sacraments of the Church; whence it is called the "door of the sacraments." In a way Confirmation also is ordained for the same purpose.... Consequently, these three sacraments imprint a character, namely, Baptism, Confirmation, and Order.[51]

Cult and the Sacrament of Holy Orders

The virtue of Christ's Passion working through the sacrament of Holy Orders confers the priestly character on the minister, an *active* participation in the priesthood of Christ that deputes the recipient to the public, present exercise of the divine cult—a cult that is sacramental and Eucharistic—and to transmission of the sacraments of the faith: "by [the sacrament of Holy Orders] man is made a perfecter of others."[52]

In the *Summa theologiae*, Aquinas's account of the sacramental economy relies on the analogy between spiritual and bodily life. Similarly, it is in virtue of the relation between the hierarchical priesthood and public service of the community, that is, the Church,

---

51. *ST* III, q. 63, a. 6.
52. *ST* III, q. 65, a. 2, ad 2.

that he justifies the existence of the sacrament of Holy Orders and assigns it its place in the sacramental organism.[53] The ministers are the agents and dispensers of the sacraments and of every reality that pertains to cultic administration. For this reason, immediately after pointing out the cultic dimension of the sacraments (*ST* III, 63), St. Thomas moves on in the next question to examine the exercise and conditions of *ministry*—that is, of the hierarchical priesthood—in transmitting the sacraments of faith—*sacramenta Ecclesiae*.[54]

In question 64, article 1, the Angelic Doctor begins by recalling that God, the principal agent from whom the interior effects of the sacraments derive, has set up certain instrumental causes that, when moved by him in the person of the ministers, simultaneously produce divine grace in the soul and render Christ's cult to the Father. Thus Christ works as the principal cause; the Church's role is only ministerial. The prayers that accompany the administration of the sacraments, like the devotion of the minister and the assistants, have no direct influence on the production of the sacrament's effect: "that which is the sacramental effect is impetrated not by the prayer of the Church or of the minister, but through the merit of Christ's Passion."[55]

Consequently, in administration of the sacraments, the Church's ministers' cultic action is the instrumental cause, separate and animate, of the principal cultic action performed by Christ in his Passion, in keeping with the mode of the production of grace, which is the cultic action's primary effect. Christ is the sovereign author of the sacraments insofar as he is God. Insofar as he is man, because his humanity is an instrument conjoined with his divinity, Christ "has

---

53. "In regard to the whole community, man is perfected ... by receiving power to rule the community and to exercise public acts: and corresponding to this in the spiritual life there is the sacrament of order, according to the saying of Hebrews 7:27, that priests offer sacrifices not for themselves only, but also for the people" (*ST* III, q. 65, a. 1). See also *ST* III, q. 65, a. 4, and *SCG* IV, c. 58.

54. See *ST* III, q. 60, prologue; q. 62, a. 1, sed contra; q. 62, a. 5; q. 63, a. 6; q. 64, a. 9, ad 3; and q. 65, a. 1.

55. *ST* III, q. 64, a. 1, ad 2.

a certain headship and efficiency in regard to extrinsic instruments, which are the ministers of the Church."[56] He is the principal minister of the sacraments, and the ministers of the Church are only extrinsic instruments of his sovereign and eternal priesthood.[57]

St. Thomas is concerned less with the personal worthiness of the minister than with his instrumentality and what we will call the ecclesiological character of his ministry. From the same standpoint, he moves on to ask about the minister's *intention* in sacramental action, then about the conditions required for that intention to be validly exercised (*ST* III, q. 64, a. 8–10). A close examination of these articles, which we cannot undertake at this time, would only confirm how completely our Doctor depends on the notion of instrumentality. By linking the minister's intention to Christ as the principal agent, and taking for granted that the Church's intention is always the same as Christ's,[58] Aquinas limits the role of the minister in order to highlight the ministeriality of the Church independent of the subjective faith of the minister. If the minister's intention conforms to the intention and faith of the Church, this intention is sufficient for the sacrament.

The Cultic Finality of Baptism and Confirmation

As a potency ordered to the realities of the divine cult, the baptismal character bestows on every believer the capacity to receive divine things, that is, the power to receive the other sacraments of the Church: "whence [Baptism] is called the door of the sacraments."[59] As a passive potency, the baptismal character is no less than a particular participation in the priesthood of Christ insofar as it permits the Christian marked by Christ's seal to render God the cult that is due and acceptable to Him. The Christian believer becomes a cultic person by virtue of his configuration to the *homo cultualis* par

56. *ST* III, q. 64, a. 3.
57. See *ST* III, q. 64, a. 5.
58. See *ST* III, q. 64, a. 10, ad 1.
59. *ST* III, q. 63, a. 6.

excellence. Thereby, he participates in the cult of the divine head and of the mystical body of which he is a member.

Reception of the sacrament of Baptism is a profession of the recipient's faith and thus a first exterior act of cult, since the divine cult is "a protestation of faith expressed by exterior signs."[60] The baptismal character, therefore, deputes the believer to a liturgical participation that may be called *active* on the condition that we remain mindful of the distinction between the baptismal priesthood and the hierarchical or ministerial priesthood.[61] In a certain sense every believer can be called a minister of cult, since "to have a sacramental character belongs to God's ministers."[62] Nevertheless, the minister in question here is not one who is oriented to the production and transmission of sacred realities, principally the sacraments, but one who has *access* to them: "the recipients are those who approach the sacraments."[63] More precisely, it is the faithful's sufficient participation in and proportionate access to the priestly cult that Christ, through the hierarchic ministry of the Church, gives to the Father in his name and in the name of all those who have been configured to him by Baptism.[64]

In this light the sacrament of Confirmation appears as a true

60. *ST* III, q. 63, a. 4, ad 3.

61. Following Pseudo-Dionysius, the Angelic Doctor says that "in hierarchical actions we must consider the agents, the recipients and the actions. The agents are the ministers of the Church; and to these the sacrament of order belongs. The recipients are those who approach the sacraments: and these are brought into being by Matrimony" (*ST* III, q. 65, a. 1, ad 3).

62. *ST* III, q. 63, a. 2. See also *Commentary on the Sentences* IV, d. 13, q. 1, a. 1, ad 1: "Every good person is said to be a priest mystically, because he offers himself as a mystical sacrifice to God, namely, a living victim to God."

63. "*Recipientes autem sunt illi qui ad sacramenta accedunt*" (*ST* III, q. 65, a. 1, ad 3).

64. The baptismal character "is thus seen as a consecration of the Christian in all his religious activity, a general deputation for all the cultic acts of the Christian life: a very broad deputation, because every act accomplished under the motion of the virtue of religion with the formal intention of honoring God becomes a cultic act. The baptismal character can thus come into play in all the acts that belong to the common priesthood of the faithful, and in particular in acts of confessing the faith, even though it is not specifically ordered to these as is the character of Confirmation. But the baptismal character comes into play in a privileged way in acts of sacramental participation, both in its passive aspect, permitting the reception of sacramental effects, and in its active aspect,

completion and extension of Baptism.[65] Drawing an analogy with bodily growth toward perfection, Thomas shows how Confirmation corresponds, in the supernatural order, to "growth whereby a man is brought to perfect size and strength."[66] As Aquinas will say more amply in the treatise on the sacraments in particular, in question 72, the character conferred in Confirmation enables the believer in Christ to confess more perfectly and more openly the faith he received in Baptism. The character of Confirmation perfects what was already *active* in the baptismal character.[67] As the profession of faith becomes more perfect, the believer grows in his practice of the sacraments of the faith and of the divine cult, which is itself already a *protestatio fidei*, as we have said. Nevertheless, the character of Confirmation confers only a deputation to receive the sacraments; in no way does it give the power to transmit them.[68] The believer's participation in the priesthood and cult of Christ remains the same as that given by the baptismal character—*per modum recipientis*; it is merely perfected and reinforced.[69]

---

permitting a manifestation of faith objectively representative of the offering of Christ, in the sacramental cult." Perrin, "Le caractère de la Confirmation chez saint Thomas," 262.

65. See *ST* III, q. 65, a. 4: "*Nam confirmatio perficit baptismum quodammodo.*"

66. *ST* III, q. 65, a. 1.

67. See *ST* III, q. 72, a. 5, ad 2.

68. Thus when the Angelic Doctor says of the sacraments of Holy Order and Confirmation that both "depute the faithful of Christ to certain special duties" (*ST* III, q. 65, a. 3, ad 2), i.e., to an active function, it is important to distinguish the two active powers in question. The first orders to the transmission of the sacraments *in persona Christi* for the building up of the Church; the second is oriented to the confession of faith, not only personally, but also publicly and solemnly."

69. St. Thomas sees "the character of Confirmation as an extension of the baptismal character considered in its active aspect. Confirmation's character permits one to manifest the Christian faith in more powerful actions more representative of Christ's oblation than the actions of confessing the faith. It assures a stronger identification of the Christian with Christ, a better objective ordering of the acts of his witness in relation to the witness given by Christ to the truth, a greater sacrificial expressivity of his acts (even to the point of martyrdom) capable of touching his neighbors more profoundly. Thus his active role is exercised in a way that permits him to better give glory to God and to have a deeper impact on others: not in the mode of doctrinal teaching or dispensation of the sacraments, but in the mode of a witness, working for their edification. In the same order of cultic manifestation of the faith (the aspect of continuity with Baptism), the character of Confirmation thus appears as a perfection of the baptismal character (the aspect of change). This is well expressed by the notion of growth, which integrates

Only the character of the sacrament of Holy Orders can configure a believer to the priesthood of Christ the head in an active way.
Therein lies the great importance St. Thomas gives the sacrament
of Holy Orders. In the *Summa*, as Fr. Gy has remarked, Holy Orders occupies the central place in the arrangement of the sacramental characters, the latter being defined principally by their relation to
the priesthood of Christ[70]—that is, in relation to the Eucharistic sacrifice, the heart of the liturgy and of the life of the Church. We must,
nevertheless, observe that for Thomas, the fact of being deputed to
approach and receive the sacraments constitutes a genuine cultic status and thus a real participation in the cult of Christ according to
the subordinate mode inherent in the character received. Thus the
Church's liturgy is not the work of *agentes alone*, of those who are
deputed to ministerial celebration of the Eucharistic sacrifice; it also
includes the *recipientes*, everyone who approaches it and participates.

---

the two aspects. We could specify this perfection by seeing in the character of Confirmation a reinforcement and cultic specification of the baptismal character. It is a reinforcement because the confirmed can manifest the faith of the Church in more powerful actions more representative of the total self-oblation of Christ: acts of confession of
faith. It is a specification, because the character of Confirmation is specially ordered to
these acts of defense and propagation of the faith; which is not the case for the baptismal
character, which does not include this specific orientation" (Perrin, "Le caractère de la
Confirmation chez saint Thomas," 260–61).

70. "Probably under the influence of his commentary on Hebrews, Thomas modified the balance among the sacramental characters, which he henceforth centers on
Order and no longer on Baptism. This displacement, well known by historians of sacramental doctrine, goes hand in hand with two others: one in the direction of priesthood,
the other in what is related to the manner in which the sacramental characters are articulated with salvation history. One the one hand, Thomas insists more on the priesthood
of Christ.... As for the *in persona Christi*, ... in the *Tertia Pars* the expression, which was
previously formulated by St. Thomas with several variants and nuances, and without an
absolute technical meaning, and which was used at the time in Biblical typology and
liturgical and sacramental theology, goes beyond the theological context of the words of
consecration and attaches to the sacerdotal ministry as such. On the other, St. Thomas
understands the sacramental characters in a novel way: for him, they are no longer defined like the ancient *sphragis* of which they are the successors, as eschatological marks,
but as cultic and sacramental power in the realm of the Church Militant." Pierre-Marie
Gy, "Avancées du traité de l'Eucharistie de saint Thomas dans la *Somme* par rapport aux
Sentences," *Revue des sciences philosophiques et théologiques* 77, no. 2 (1993), 223–24.

5

The Eucharistic Sacrifice

Sacrament of Christ's Passion

In the previous chapter, we expounded St. Thomas's doctrine of the sacramental character as found in the *Summa*'s treatise on the sacraments in general.[1] There he defined the character as a genuine participation in the power to honor God given to those stamped by it. Because of the Fall, only the Incarnate Word possesses this power by right; only he can offer the worship that is acceptable to God. Only through being configured to Christ, therefore, in a more or less plenary manner by the three sacramental characters can man present himself before God as a worshipping subject, that is, as a participant in the worship of Christ.

We have seen that Christ's worship consists essentially in the sacrificial oblation he made of himself to the Father from the first instant of his conception, and which he consummated in a bloody manner on the altar of the cross for man's salvation. In heaven, in his glorified humanity, he continues to present one and the same oblation to the Father, while here below it is represented and contained each day in the Eucharistic sacrifice.

The hierarchical priesthood and the baptismal priesthood are

1. *ST* III, q. 60–65.

ordered to the offering of this sacrifice, which is Christ and his Church's act of worship *par excellence*. While the sacraments of Baptism and Confirmation provide subjects for this worship (*per modum recipientis*), and the sacrament of Holy Orders appoints its ministers (*per modum ipsius actionis*): "the Eucharist belongs to the Divine worship, for the Divine worship consists principally therein, so far as it is the sacrifice of the Church."[2]

The sacrament of the Eucharist is, therefore, a cultic action, the highest form of worship, the "sacrifice of the Church." This sacrifice is defined by the sacrament and contained in it; the sacrament of the Eucharist is the *sign* or *representation* of the sacrifice of Christ that the Church has received the mission to celebrate and perpetuate. In this chapter, we shall explain and analyze this perspective, this sacrificial liturgy of the Church, as the Angelic Doctor understands it. We will begin by tracing the outlines of a Eucharistic theology in the treatise on the sacraments in general, and then proceed to analyze the only article that St. Thomas dedicated specifically to the theology of sacrifice in the treatise on the Eucharist.[3] This method is fitting because, before approaching Thomas's *Expositio missae*[4] in the appendixes, it is necessary first to lay out his fundamental doctrine of Eucharistic sacrifice—a doctrine that is preliminary to every explanation of the prayers and ceremonies of the Mass.

THE MOST IMPORTANT OF ALL THE SACRAMENTS

Precisely due to its perfection, the sacrament of the Eucharist does not imprint a character. Being, in the words of Pseudo-Dionysius, "the end and consummation of all the sacraments,"[5] this sacrament does not order man to do or receive any other supernatural reality

2. *ST* III, q. 63, a. 6.
3. *ST* III, q. 83, a. 1.
4. *ST* III, q. 83, a. 4–5.
5. Pseudo-Dionysius, *Ecclesiastical Hierarchy*, c. 3. (Translation by the English Dominicans).

in the sacramental order: "it contains within itself Christ, in Whom there is not the character, but the very plenitude of the priesthood."[6]

St. Thomas develops this theme in question 65. After establishing that there are seven sacraments (a. 1) and distinguishing their internal order (a. 2), our Doctor dedicates article 3 entirely to showing that the Eucharist is "the most important and most perfect of all the sacraments." The three reasons he adduces, standing at the end of the whole treatise on the sacraments in general, will show how the two dimensions of the sacramental reality—sanctification and worship—are joined in a perfect unity.

The Eucharist Contains Christ Himself Substantially

Aquinas first takes up sanctification, arguing that the Eucharist is the most important sacrament because of what it contains, namely "because it contains Christ Himself substantially," unlike the other sacraments, which "contain a certain instrumental power which is a share of Christ's power."[7]

While the other sacraments contain sanctity in a transitive and imperfect way, producing it in the soul through the exercise of their instrumental causality, the sacrament of the Eucharist contains the plenitude of sanctity in substance. Now each sacrament signifies the grace it procures in a threefold manner: it is "a reminder of the past, i.e. the passion of Christ; and an indication of that which is effected in us by Christ's passion, i.e. grace; and a prognostic, that is, a foretelling of future glory."[8] Because it contains sanctity in the plenitude of its source, the Eucharist manifests this threefold signification proper to every sacrament in a most excellent manner, fully expressing what belongs to each of these three levels: Passion, grace, and glory. For the past, this sacrament commemorates and represents the sacrifice made on Calvary—as we shall discuss later. For the

---

6. *ST* III, q. 63, a. 6. See also *ST* III, q. 65, a. 3, ad 3.

7. *ST* III, q. 65, a. 3. See also Thomas, *Commentary on the Sentences* (IV, d. 8, q. 1, a. 1, ad 3) and *Disputed Questions on Truth* (q. 27, a. 4).

8. *ST* III, q. 60, a. 3.

present, this sacrament confers grace on Christ's members, unites them intimately to their divine head, and thus constitutes on earth the perfective sign of the unity of the Church.[9] Finally, the Eucharist prefigures a reality still to come, the state of glory promised to those who live and persevere in grace. Thus when the Christian participates in the Eucharist and receives this sacrament, his soul is united with Christ in a unique way. There is a substantial encounter of the creature with his Lord sacrificed on the altar and given as food under the Eucharistic species. The soul receives life and strength,[10] is filled with grace, and guided toward glory.[11]

The Eucharist is the End of All the Other Sacraments

St. Thomas has the primacy of the sacrament of the Eucharist flow from "the relation of the sacraments to one another. For all the other sacraments seem to be ordained to this one as to their end."[12] He organizes the seven sacraments coherently around the Eucharist. From our cultic perspective, we can content ourselves to point out the Eucharistic orientation of the three sacraments of character: the end of Holy Orders is the consecration of the Eucharist, the end of Baptism is reception of it, while by Confirmation "a man is perfected, so as not to fear withdrawing himself from this sacrament."[13]

Having considered the place Aquinas assigns to the sacrament of Holy Orders in the organization of the sacramental characters and

---

9. See *ST* III, q. 73, a. 4.

10. See *ST* III, q. 65, a. 1.

11. Thomas expresses the same idea in the antiphon *O sacrum convivium* of Second Vespers for the Office of the Blessed Sacrament: "O sacred banquet! in which Christ is received, the memory of his Passion is renewed, the mind is filled with grace, and a pledge of future glory to us is given." The doctrine of the threefold signification of the Eucharist—as a memorial of the Passion, a sign of the Church's unity, and a pledge of future glory—permits us to identify the place and importance of this sacrament in salvation history "at the convergence of all the main lines of the integral Paschal Mystery, which lies at the heart of the economy of salvation. But the anchor-point for this three-leveled signification is found in the consideration of the Eucharist as a memorial of the Passion" (Chardonnens, "Éternité du sacerdoce du Christ et effet eschatologique de l'eucharistie," 166).

12. *ST* III, q. 65, a. 3.

13. *ST* III, q. 65, a. 3.

thus in the economy of worship, we shall focus on the relation between Holy Orders and the Eucharist. The Angelic Doctor defines the priestly office in terms of the Eucharist. The priestly office looks first of all to the perfection of the community,[14] since the edification and the good of the whole Church is found in the offering of the Eucharistic sacrifice and in communion in the Body of the Lord. In the former case, "priests offer sacrifices not for themselves only, but also for the people"[15]; in the latter, "the common spiritual good of the whole Church is contained substantially in the sacrament itself of the Eucharist."[16]

The *Summa*'s general teaching on the sacraments extends the often-cited formulae from the fourth book of Thomas's *Commentary on the Sentences*: "A priest has two acts: one principally toward the true body of Christ, and the other, secondary one, toward the mystical body of Christ."[17] And again "A priest has two acts: one principal act, namely, to consecrate the true body of Christ; and another secondary act, namely, to prepare the people for the reception of this sacrament."[18] Here we must understand "secondary" in the sense that the administration of the other sacraments depends and proceeds from the sacrificial consecration of the most august sacrament of them all, which contains the author of grace and represents the act of Calvary. Since grace descends from the divine head to the members of the mystical body, every sacramental act that confers and strengthens grace depends on the sacramental act accomplished on the real Body of the same divine head.

The reflections of Henri de Lubac in his study of the relation between the *Corpus verum* and the *Corpus mysticum* are well known;[19]

14. *ST* III, q. 65, a. 1.
15. *ST* III, q. 65, a. 1.
16. *ST* III, q. 65, a. 3, ad 1.
17. Thomas, *Commentary on the Sentences* IV, d. 24, q. 1, a. 3, sol. 2, ad 1. Translated by Beth Mortensen, *Commentary on the Sentences*, Opera omnia 8 (Green Bay, WI: Aquinas Institute, 2018), 605.
18. Thomas, *Commentary on the Sentences* IV, d. 24, q. 3, a. 2 (trans. Mortensen, 8:629).
19. Henri de Lubac, *Corpus Mysticum: The Eucharist and the Church in the Middle Ages*, trans. Gemma Simmonds, Richard Price, and Christopher Stephens (Notre Dame, IN: University of Notre Dame Press, 2006).

among them is this beautiful formula: "The Church makes the Eucharist, but the Eucharist also makes the Church."[20] Likewise, according to the teaching of Aquinas, if all the sacraments flow from the Passion of Christ and by this fact exercise a certain efficient and formal causality on the Church,[21] then the Eucharist can justly be called "the heart of the Church,"[22] insofar as it communicates capital grace in all the abundance that was poured out over the altar of the cross, and insofar as it brings the faithful soul into intimate union with its Lord. The administration of the other sacraments, the cultic structure, and even the ministry of preaching prepare, to a greater or lesser extent, for the representation of the sacrifice of Christ and for the reception of the Eucharistic gifts. Indeed, all holy and sacred realities tend to the sacramental celebration of the sacrifice that is the basis of all sanctity and thus of the unity of Christ and His Church.

The Most Perfect Sacramental Rite

Finally, St. Thomas illustrates the superiority of the Eucharist over all the other sacraments on the basis of liturgical practice. He points out, with Pseudo-Dionysius,[23] that the administration of nearly all the sacraments culminates in the Eucharist: "thus those who have been ordained receive Holy Communion, as also do those who have been baptized, if they be adults."[24]

This remark, among others, offers noteworthy material for an evaluation of St. Thomas's sacramental doctrine.[25] It is based on the ceremonial practice and liturgical-doctrinal conceptions Thomas

20. Henri de Lubac, *The Splendor of the Church*, trans. Michael Mason (San Francisco: Ignatius, 1986), 127–61.

21. *ST* III, q. 64, a. 2, ad 3.

22. Martin Morard, "L'eucharistie, clé de voûte de l'organisme sacramentel chez saint Thomas d'Aquin," *Revue thomiste* 95 (1995), 246: "Comparable to the beating of the heart, [the Eucharist] assures the permanent circulation of Christic and Christ-conforming charity in the Mystical Body, a movement that draws all men to Christ and causes the currents of his own love to flow out upon them."

23. Pseudo-Dionysius, *Ecclesiastical Hierarchy*, ch. 3.

24. *ST* III, q. 65, a. 3.

25. See Gy, "La documentation sacramentaire de Thomas d'Aquin," 425–31.

himself experienced. Thus, for example, he thought that the sacrament of Holy Orders was conferred during the presentation of the sacrificial material to the ordained by the words: "Receive the power to offer sacrifice to God and to celebrate the Mass both for the living and for the dead."[26] For St. Thomas the practice of sacramental con-celebration, not wide-spread in the thirteenth century, was further evidence of the Eucharistic orientation of the sacrament of Holy Orders,[27] to say nothing of the marked tendency of Gothic liturgy to conceive the Mass as a "representation" of salvation history.[28]

THE EUCHARISTIC SACRIFICE: A *REPRESENTATIVE IMAGE* OF CHRIST'S PASSION

"Insofar as it is the sacrifice of the Church," the Eucharist is the act of worship *par excellence*. The sacrifice of Christ, the cultic act at the source of every divine gift given to men, is contained and signified in the Eucharist, the most important and most perfect of the sacraments of the Church. The celebration of this sacrament, entrusted to the hierarchical priesthood of the Church, is, in the order of sacramental sign, "a representative image" of the sacrifice of Calvary. Such is the claim of St. Thomas in the first article of question 83, precisely where he intends to give an account of the sacrificial character of the Eucharistic celebration.

Sacrifice and *Sacrament* in the Treatise on the Eucharist

This article (*ST* III, q. 83, a. 1) introduces the question of the rite of the sacrament of the Eucharist. It is the culminating question of the whole treatise on the Eucharist.

---

26. See Thomas, *Commentary on the Sentences* IV, d. 24, q. 1, a. 2, ad 2; *SCG* IV, ch. 74.

27. See *ST* III, q. 82, a. 2.

28. In the Gothic period, according to Joseph Jungmann, "the Mass [was] understood as a dramatic presentation of an action in the divine economy, especially of the suffering, death and resurrection of Christ, beginning with the longings and sighs of the patriarchs and prophets and concluding with our Saviour's ascension into heaven." Jungmann, *The Mass of the Roman Rite: Its Origins and Development* (*Missarum Sollemnia*), vol. 1 (Notre Dame, IN: Ave Maria Press, 2012), 103–27, at 109.

Since the most august of all the sacraments is confected through sacramental "representation" of the unique sacrifice of Calvary, the doctrine of the Eucharistic sacrifice must be the pinnacle of the Eucharistic edifice constructed in the previous questions. His commentary on the Eucharistic action in the following articles, especially in 4 and 5, logically can come only at the end of the treatise, so that it may make use of the acquired doctrinal material to clarify particular liturgical practice by appeal to various points of doctrine. On this sound foundation, his analysis of the rite is able to unite the doctrinal and spiritual senses in a manner similar to the method of Scripture commentary.

It is very surprising that Aquinas dedicated only this single first article of question 83 to the "nature of the sacrifice of the Mass," as if to make a mere appendix of a point that would become the object of a heated controversy in the sixteenth century. Nonetheless, our review of the Thomistic doctrine on sacrifice has already shown the great importance our Doctor attaches to the sacrificial act, which he places at the center and summit of the acts of worship. In his eyes sacrifice is in fact the most eminent and most expressive of the acts of worship, to the point that he ranks it among the acts of the moral virtue of religion; describes its various manifestations in the ceremonial precepts of the Old Law; and most of all contemplates it, no longer in figures but in all the truth of its consummation by the divine Word, on the altar of the cross. Moreover, in the study of Christian sacramentality, we are convinced with St. Thomas that:

by His Passion Christ inaugurated the Rites of the Christian Religion by offering "Himself—an oblation and a sacrifice to God" (Ephesians 5:2). Wherefore it is manifest that the sacraments of the Church derive their power specially from Christ's Passion, the virtue of which is in a manner united to us by our receiving the sacraments."[29]

If the various sacraments of the Church signify and dispense, in a manner proportionate to each, the multiple effects, merits, and sat-

29. *ST* III, q. 62, a. 5.

isfactions of the redemptive Passion, for its part, the Eucharist contains the whole undivided virtue of the redeeming sacrifice that it represents *in sacramento*.

Further, we note that the exposition of the treatise on the Eucharist[30] is not neatly divided between the Eucharist as *sacrifice*—a cultic action—and the Eucharist as *sacrament*—a sanctifying reality, unlike what was generally the case in the post-Tridentine period. This methodical distinction was unknown to our Doctor and to his predecessors and contemporaries. Aquinas affirms rather the simultaneous presence of the two realities "sacrament and sacrifice" in the Eucharist: "This sacrament is both a sacrifice and a sacrament";[31] "this sacrament is not only a sacrament, but also a sacrifice."[32] He is clear that the Eucharist "has the nature of a sacrifice inasmuch as it is offered up, and it has the nature of a sacrament inasmuch as it is received."[33]

The Eucharist is both realities. Sacrifice pertains to the cultic dimension, while what is more specially designated by the term "sacrament" refers to the sanctifying reality that is signified. The sacrifice is contained in the sacrament; it is represented there through the sign of an immolation in the successive consecration of bread and wine. Without this immolation, the sanctification that it signifies—namely spiritual eating along with all its effects of grace—would not be contained or communicated. To be both sacrifice and sacrament: that is the sacramental identity proper to and constitutive of the Eucharist.[34]

30. *ST* III, q. 73–83.
31. *ST* III, q. 79, a. 5.
32. *ST* III, q. 79, a. 7.
33. *ST* III, q. 79, a. 5. St. Thomas continues: "And therefore it has the effect of a sacrament in the recipient, and the effect of a sacrifice in the offerer, or in them for whom it is offered." In several places, St. Thomas points out the production of the effects of the sacrifice of the Passion in the Eucharist (see *ST* III, q. 79, a. 1; a. 2, ad 1 and 2; a. 3; a. 6).
34. See Thierry-Dominique Humbrecht: "L'eucharistie, 'représentation' du sacrifice du Christ, selon saint Thomas," *Revue thomiste* 98, no. 3 (1998), 355–86, at 378, who remarks: "this double identity of sacrifice and sacrament is itself the sacrament in its totality. In other words, the fact that the Eucharist is a sacrifice 'in addition' to being a sacrament is precisely what constitutes its properly *sacramental* identity. St. Thomas's claim is of primary

It is thus by keeping ever before our minds the simultaneity and concomitance of the two dimensions, sacrifice and sacrament, cult and sanctification, that we must now undertake an attentive reading of the *Summa theologiae*'s treatise on the Eucharist. We could also point out the many allusions, found in the questions preceding those about the "rite of this sacrament," to a theology of Eucharistic sacrifice, scattered indications for which Aquinas offers a synthesis in the first article of question 83.[35] But that would take us beyond the limits imposed by our study, and we will limit ourselves here to several useful citations for a better understanding of the article we have to examine.

In the first place, the Eucharistic sacrifice brings to completion the sacrificial figures of the Old Testament. These latter were nothing

---

importance because it solves a number of false problems in advance. This double identity of the Eucharist, or rather this two-tiered identity (a sacrament that is also a sacrifice) often leads people to separate the sacrificial level from the simple sacramental level, with which it seems to be heterogenous. Sacrifice seems to exceed the sacramental domain, obliging it to take on a non-sacramental, more 'realist' consistency, if you will, so that it may be honored in all its profundity (with the related question of the real presence). But such a move forgets Thomas's clear affirmation that this sacrament, which is also a sacrifice, is only truly this sacrament because it is both at once, and that this double level constitutes its proper sacramental identity. If the sacrament of the Eucharist is not a sacrifice, then it cannot be the sacrament of charity. And if this sacrifice is not a true sacrament (present under the sacramental modality of signs) it is longer the actualization of the virtue of Christ's sacrifice, and in the final analysis is nothing at all." According to P.-M. Gy, the "pivotal" distinction between the Eucharist as sacrament and the Eucharist as sacrifice in St. Thomas "corresponds closely, though implicitly, to St. Justin's fundamental distinction between the Eucharist as action and the Eucharist as holy thing. This distinction appears for the first time in the *Commentary on the Sentences* (IV, d. 12, q. 2, a. 2, ad 4). Its importance grows in the *Summa*, without affecting the structure of the treatise" (Gy, "Avancées du traité de l'eucharistie de saint Thomas dans la Somme par rapport aux *Sentences*," 227.

35. See Aimon-Marie Roguet, "Le sacrifice eucharistique," in *L'Eucharistie*, vol. 2 of *Somme théologique*, by Thomas Aquinas (Paris: Revue des Jeunes, 1967), 377–91, at 378: "Despite appearances, St. Thomas's thought is much more synthetic than analytic. Many articles in the *Summa* are less explorations of new terrain than pauses to reconsider the terrain he has already passed through. The article in question should not be considered in isolation, as an exposition that has value in itself. It is a sort of crystallization of a doctrine that lay just below the surface and frequently broke into the light throughout the treatise on the Eucharist. On a rapid re-reading of all the questions already treated, we will notice that the notions he considers here in themselves were there previously, spread throughout the earlier material, in the form of postulates or preliminary evidence."

more than shadows of good things to come (Heb 10:1), shadows of the true and unique sacrifice of the cross. The sacrifice of the New Covenant instituted by Christ "should have something more, namely, should contain Christ Himself crucified, not merely in signification or figure, but also in very truth."[36]

We find more than one example of a reading of the Eucharistic sacrifice that one might call liturgical—apart from his literal and mystical exposition in the other five articles of question 83. Our Doctor is looking for "representative" signs of the Passion in the great ritual signs of this sacrifice's celebration: the use of bread and wine as sacrificial material,[37] the fraction,[38] and even the immixture of water.[39]

But the Eucharistic sacrifice takes place essentially through the double consecration: "Our Lord's Passion is represented in the very consecration of this sacrament, in which the body ought not to be consecrated without the blood."[40] Further, St. Thomas comes back several times to the necessity of the separate consecration of the two species, but with a pronounced insistence on the consecration of the blood as especially representative of the redeeming sacrifice.[41] The importance of the rite of consecration applies, of course, to the words that accompany it. But the discussion of their essential role for the validity of the sacrifice isolates them, in scholastic fashion, from their liturgical context.[42]

---

36. *ST* III. q. 75, a. 1.
37. *ST* III, q. 74, a. 1.
38. See *ST* III, q. 77, a. 7.
39. See *ST* III, q. 74, a. 6.
40. *ST* III, q. 80, a. 12, ad 3.
41. *ST* III, q. 76, a. 2, ad 1: "Although the whole Christ is under each species, yet it is not without purpose [that they are distinguished]. For in the first place this serves to represent Christ's Passion, in which the blood was separated from the body; hence in the form for the consecration of the blood mention is made of its shedding."
42. *ST* III, q. 78, a. 1, ad 4: "It must be held that if the priest were to pronounce only the aforesaid words with the intention of consecrating this sacrament, this sacrament would be valid because the intention would cause these words to be understood as spoken in the person of Christ, even though the words were pronounced without those that precede." On the subject of this doctrine among the Scholastics, see Jean Gouillard,

Finally, since the Eucharistic sacrifice is "the memorial of Christ's Passion ... given by way of food,"[43] and "the cross made His flesh adapted for eating, inasmuch as this sacrament represents Christ's Passion,"[44] it is necessary that the priest who offers the sacrifice participate in it fully by receiving the precious gifts that are offered and consecrated. Reception of the sacrament, like external participation in the sacrifice, signifies one's union with the interior sacrifice.[45] Nevertheless, Aquinas insists, the reason for the celebration of the Eucharistic sacrifice is not primarily to enable the faithful's participation in the Eucharist, but rather pertains "chiefly to God to Whom the sacrifice of this sacrament is offered by consecrating."[46]

Is Christ Immolated in This Sacrament?

The citations we have provided above make sufficiently clear that the sacrificial character of the Mass is always present in St. Thomas's mind when he is considering the Eucharist. Now the first article of question 83 will offer a synthesis of his teaching on this point, forming a necessary introduction, as we have said, to any liturgical commentary.

---

introduction to *Explication de la divine liturgie* [Commentary on the Divine Liturgy], by Nicholas Cabasilas (Paris: Cerf, 1967), 9–46, at 35: "We cannot reproach Cabasilas for not separating the words of Institution from the epiclesis. The most ancient witnesses of the tradition, and before them a long series of Fathers, had acted in the same manner, both as regards these words and as regards the Eucharistic prayer as a whole. The form of Beranger's oath—'per mysterium sacrae *orationis* et verba nostri redemptoris'—only echoes the nearly unanimous sentiment of the centuries. The Scholastics innovated by claiming that the words of Institution were valid (though not licit) apart from any liturgical context, and good disciples of St. Thomas now agree that the Angelic Doctor fell into a formalism that is foreign to the thought of the Fathers. A Byzantine of the fourteenth century who drew his theology of the Eucharist from the liturgy could not but rebel against such a method." See also Gy, *La liturgie dans l'histoire*, 217–19, and "La documentation sacramentaire de Thomas d'Aquin," 427–28.

43. *ST* III, q. 80, a. 10, ad 2.

44. *ST* III, q. 81, a. 3, ad 1.

45. *ST* III, q. 82, a. 4: "The Eucharist is not only a sacrament, but also a sacrifice. Now whoever offers sacrifice must be a sharer in the sacrifice, because the outward sacrifice he offers is a sign of the inner sacrifice whereby he offers himself to God.... Hence by partaking of the sacrifice he shows that the inner one is likewise his."

46. *ST* III, q. 82, a. 10.

The title of the article clearly enunciates the doctrine at stake: Whether the sacrament of the Eucharist contains the sacrifice of Christ. In other words, it is a matter of finding, "in the celebration of this mystery,"[47]—which is to say, in the act of "confecting" this sacrament—the sacrificial offering of Christ. Does the act of the priest at the altar, essentially the double consecration that he performs there *in persona Christi*,[48] consist in the immolation of Christ on the cross as priest and victim of his own sacrifice? Note that St. Thomas here retains the term *immolation* to take account of the external and "representative" dimension of Calvary—the bloody immolation is itself the visible sign of Christ's interior oblation of love and obedience.

The two first objections deny the presence of an immolation in the Eucharist, arguing for the unique character of Christ's immolation on Calvary.[49] Sacramental immolation is denied insofar as it would seem to constitute a second immolation, numerically distinct from Calvary. We can already see that the only way to hold to the presence of sacramental immolation will be to identify it with the immolation on Calvary, in a mode that is yet to be defined. The third objection raises a difficulty based on the identity of the priest and the victim in Christ's sacrifice: at Mass the priest cannot be the victim he sacrifices. "Therefore, the celebration of this sacrament is not a sacrifice of Christ."

In the *Respondeo*, St. Thomas opposes the objectors with the authority of Augustine, who ties the immolation accomplished once on Calvary to the immolation that happens every day in the sacrament.[50] In the body of the article, Aquinas responds that "the cele-

---

47. Thomas uses this wording in the heading of q. 83; see ST III, q. 83.

48. See *ST* III, q. 22, a. 6; q. 78, a. 1; q. 82, a. 1.

49. *ST* III, q. 83, a. 1. The first objection cites a passage from the Letter to the Hebrews (10:14): "Christ by one oblation hath perfected for ever them that are sanctified." Since the oblation of Christ consisted in his immolation, it cannot be renewed "in the celebration of this sacrament." The second objection centers on the fact that Christ's immolation was accomplished on the cross. But in the sacrament of the Eucharist, Christ is not crucified. Therefore he is not immolated there.

50. *ST* III, q. 83, a. 1: "*Sed contra est quod Augustinus dicit, in* Libro Sententiarum Prosperi: *Semel immolatus est in semetipso Christus, et tamen quotidie immolatur in sacramento.*"

bration of this sacrament is called a sacrifice for two reasons." The first reason is related to the idea of "representation," or more precisely of a "representative image," of the Passion of Christ. The second reason, subordinate to the first, involves the application of the fruits of the Passion.

"Imago repraesentativa"

The first reason is formulated in the following manner:

First, because, as Augustine says (Ad Simplician. ii), "the images of things are called by the names of the things whereof they are the images; as when we look upon a picture or a fresco, we say, 'This is Cicero and that is Sallust.'" But, as was said above (III:79:1), the celebration of this sacrament is an image representing (*imago repraesentativa*) Christ's Passion, which is His true sacrifice (*vera immolatio*). Accordingly the celebration of this sacrament is called Christ's sacrifice.

The argument is surprising, even disconcerting. Is the Eucharistic sacrifice no more than a simple image referring to the exemplary sacrifice of the Passion, as a picture "represents" Cicero or Sallust? To understand the reason presented here and to adequately grasp its importance, we must study what St. Thomas means by "representative image." If we forego this inquiry, there is a serious risk that his response will seem "insufficient,"[51] a preliminary answer requiring clarification by other notions based only more or less on the Thomistic text. These supposed "other notions," have given rise to the various theories about "the essence of the sacrifice of the Mass."

The courses of Fr. von Gunten have,[52] in the wake of Dom Voni-

---

51. Such is, for example, the opinion of Cardinal Journet: "This response is meant to give a preliminary justification of certain Patristic texts.... But for St. Thomas this is not a sufficient response: the image of a true sacrifice is not itself a sacrifice. If it were, we could also say that the figures of the Old Testament, i.e., the immolation of the Paschal lamb, were already immolations of Christ" (Charles Journet, *La Messe, presence du sacrifice de la croix* [Bruges: Desclée De Brouwer, 1957], 111–12). See also Joseph de Sainte-Marie, "L'Eucharistie, sacrement et sacrifice du Christ et de l'Eglise," 416.

52. I am referring to an oral course by Professor Andreas F. von Gunten, *L'Eucaristia come sacrificio secondo San Tommaso e il Concilio di Trento*, given at the Pontifical University of St. Thomas Aquinas (the Angelicum), Rome, 1995. Fr. von Gunten is the editor of

er's study,[53] placed us in direct contact with the text of St. Thomas. Following von Gunten, we think that the notion of "representation" is sufficiently strong to account for the presence of sacrifice in the sacrament of the Eucharist.[54] But we must try to understand it as it is, without making it depend on Dom Casel's mystical conceptions.[55] In our account, to sacramentally "represent" will mean to "make present" the immolation of Calvary in an immediate and contemporary manner.

What then did St. Thomas mean by "representative image"? In the first place, what was the generally accepted meaning of the verb *repraesentare*? According to a recent study by Fr. Humbrecht,[56]

Cajetan's opusculum, dated 1525, *Instructio nuntii circa errores libelli de cena Domini, sive de erroribus contingentibus in eucharistiae sacramento*, Rome, 1962.

53. Anscar Vonier, *A Key to the Doctrine of the Eucharist* (Buckfast: Assumption Press, 2013).

54. See also A. M. Roguet: "There is no need to cast about for a solution other than the one Thomas gives. One has only to read him and grasp all the significance of notions that current teaching has falsified or impoverished, notably those of sacrifice, representation or memorial, and sacrament. Following him, one will be spared from adding to the long catalogue of still-born theories that have encumbered, not aided, the progress of theology" ("Le sacrifice eucharistique," 378). See also R. Tremblay, "Le Mystère de la messe," *Angelicum* 36, no. 2 (1959): 184–202; Marie Vincent Leroy, "Un traité de Cajetan sur la messe," in de Oliveria, *Ordo sapientiae et amoris*, 469–86; and especially Humbrecht: "L'eucharistie, 'représentation' du sacrifice du Christ, selon saint Thomas," 355–86.

55. See Odo Casel, "The Meaning of the Mystery," in *The Mystery of Christian Worship, and Other Writings*, ed. Burkhard Neunheuser, trans. I. T. Hale (Westminster, MD: The Newman Press, 1962), 101: "Through participation in the mysteries we enter into the image and so reach the archetype. Thus, the Mass not only represents the death of Christ and communicates to us the effects of his sacrifice; it is an active image of the Pasch of Christ, and makes us immediate members of what once took place in and upon him. It is therefore within the power of the Mass to bring us into the same temporal dimension with the saving deeds of Christ, and to place us in their immediate presence." The so-called "Caselian" interpretation of St. Thomas's doctrine was criticized by M. Matthijs, among others, in "'Mysteriengegenwart' secundum St. Thomam," *Angelicum* 34, no. 4 (1957), 393–99. See also Antonio Piolanti, *Il mistero eucaristico* (Rome: Libreria Editrice Vaticana, 1983), 455–66.

56. Humbrecht: "L'eucharistie, 'représentation' du sacrifice du Christ, selon saint Thomas." Before Humbrecht, R. Tremblay ("Le Mystère de la messe") showed that for Aquinas the verb *repraesentare* "means not to make present but *figurare, recolere, commemorare, designare, significare*." Consequently, we need not understand the derivative *repraesentatio* a refer to a new presence but rather, Tremblay concludes, as a synonym of "*figuralis repraesentatio, figura, imago, exemplum, memoria, memoriale, commemoratio,*

whose excellent treatment we follow here, the various uses of *repraesentare* can be reduced to three definitions: similitude—in the sense of formal resemblance—signification, and exemplary causality. In the case of the Eucharist, the idea of *repraesentatio*, which Aquinas receives from St. Augustine by way of Peter Lombard's *Sentences*,[57] pertains mostly to signification, without necessarily excluding the notion of a sign that represents causality.

Following the letter of the Thomistic argument, we find that the "celebration of this sacrament" is "an image representing Christ's Passion" which is "His true sacrifice." The notions "immolation-truth" seem to be set against the notions "celebration-image." But is the celebration of the Eucharistic sacrifice nothing more than an image, a simple figure of Calvary's immolation, like the sacrifices of the Old Covenant in which "Christ was also immolated" in a certain manner, as Thomas later remarks?[58]

It is precisely the notion of representation, or more exactly of *representative image* that allows us to establish the relation between the cross and the Eucharistic sacrifice, and that also constitutes the demonstration of the article's claim. In Aquinas's language, and particularly in the theology of worship that he develops in his *Commentary on the Letter to the Hebrews*, the *image* of the New Law is the successor to the *shadow* of the Old Law, with respect to the representation of future goods:

The Old Law is related to [future] goods as a shadow represents in general, and as to the nature of the species; an image, however, does so in particular and as to the nature of the individual, and specifically.... Hence, the New Law is called the law of love. Hence, it is called an image, because it has an expressed likeness to the goods to come.[59]

---

significatio, signum and *sacramentum rememorativum*, or *commemorativum*" ("Le Mystère de la messe," 192).

57. See Peter Lombard, *Sentences*, IV, d. 12.

58. *ST* III, q. 83, a. 1, at the end of the *corpus*: "It is true to say that Christ was sacrificed, even in the figures of the Old Testament: hence it is stated in the Apocalypse (13:8): 'Whose names are not written in the Book of Life of the Lamb, which was slain from the beginning of the world.'"

59. Thomas, *Commentary on the Letter to the Hebrews*, ch. 10, lect. 1.

Analogously, in the case of the Eucharistic sacrifice, the image is a formal resemblance, that is to say a similitude that tends to become identical with the Passion that it represents and signifies. "Representative image of the Passion of Christ" therefore indicates that in the Eucharist the unique immolation of Calvary is much more than signified; it means that *it is revealed and manifested in it through the mode of the sacramental immolation,* which exists for no other reason than to represent it.[60] Thus the sacramental immolation and the immolation of Calvary that it *commemorates* are but a single immolation in a unity of order. The victim is one and the same, only the mode of immolation differs: bloody on Calvary, unbloodly on the altar according to the rite instituted during the Last Supper.[61]

In the three responses to the objections, St. Thomas points out this same express similitude of the representative image with the manifested reality. Appealing to the authority of St. Ambrose, the Angelic Doctor first emphasizes the identity of the sacrificial offering of Calvary with that of the Church in the Eucharistic sacrifice: "There is but one victim and not many victims, because Christ was

60. On this point, see Cajetan: "The un-bloody manner of immolating was not instituted as a distinct manner of immolating, but solely insofar as it refers to the bloody victim on the cross. When one thing exists only for another, then they both make one thing (*ubi unum nonnisi propter alterum, ibi unum dumtaxat est*). Therefore, it follows that, properly speaking, we cannot claim that in the New Testament there are two sacrifices, or two victims, oblations, immolations, or whatever other name one might use to designate them, based on the fact that there is one bloody victim—Christ on the cross—and one unbloody victim—Christ on the altar. Rather, there is only one victim offered once on the cross and persisting (*perseverantem*) in the mode of immolation through its daily repetition in the Eucharist as instituted by Christ" (quoted by M.-V. Leroy, "Un traité de Cajetan sur la messe," 477.

61. See Cajetan: "The former manner of immolation was unique, substantial, original, and bloody insofar as it is in his proper species (*in propria specie*: in its natural condition) that he poured out his blood on the cross through the breaking of his body, whereas the latter manner of immolation, which is daily, external, and adventitious, is unbloody because it represents Christ's offering on the cross in an immolative manner (*immolatitio modo*: through the mode of immolation) under the species of bread and wine. That is why the bloody victim and the unbloody victim of the New Testament is one in what regards the reality that is offered, even though there is a difference in the mode of offering" (quoted by M.-V. Le-Roy, "Un traité de Cajetan sur la messe", 476—77. See Council of Trent, Session 12, 1 and 2.

offered but once: and this latter sacrifice is the pattern of the former."[62] The similitude extends to both the priest who offers the victim and the altar on which the victim is immolated. With regard to
the altar, "just as the celebration of this sacrament is an image representing Christ's Passion, so the altar is representative of the cross itself, upon which Christ was sacrificed in His proper species."[63] As for
the priestly function, the priest of the New Law, because he participates in the priesthood of Christ, "fountain-head of the entire priesthood," "works in His person"[64]: "the priest also bears Christ's image,
in Whose person and by Whose power he pronounces the words of
consecration."[65] Christ, the Sovereign Priest, is thus the principal actor on the altar. As the words of the consecration attest, the succes-
sions of ministers who consecrate the body and blood of Christ in
time do so in the name of One Who is himself offered as a victim,
and the virtue of whose sacrifice lasts eternally.[66] "And so," St. Thomas concludes, "in a measure, [at the altar] the priest and victim are
one and the same."

Participation in the Fruit of the Immolation

The second reason advanced in favor of the sacramental immolation
concerns "the effect of His Passion." St. Thomas cites the Secret prayer
of the ninth Sunday after Pentecost: "Whenever the commemoration

---

62. *ST* III, q. 83, a. 1, ad 1. The citation from St. Ambrose is taken from Gratian's
Decretals (de cons. D. 2 c. 53).

63. *ST* III, q. 83, a. 1, ad 2. Note the particular sacrality that is acquired in the cultic
economy of the New Law by the objects of cult destined in some manner for the celebration of the sacraments, and especially for the celebration of the greatest of them all.

64. *ST* III, q. 22, a. 4.

65. *ST* III, q. 83, a. 1, ad 3.

66. See Cajetan: "Do some say that it is unfitting to affirm that Christ's sacrifice in
the New Testament requires a succession of ministers, because this would seem to make
Christ's sacrifice insufficient? We respond that it is one thing to affirm a distinct victim
requiring a succession of priests, and another to affirm the persistence of the victim offered on the cross requiring a succession of ministers. The first case would not befit the
state of the New Testament; the second is perfected in accord with it, in that the one
victim, once offered, remains constantly in force" (quoted by M.-V. Leroy, "Un traité de
Cajetan sur la messe," 482).

of this sacrifice is celebrated, the work of our redemption is enact-ed."[67] Because Christ is immolated in this sacrament, those for whom the Eucharistic sacrifice is offered are allowed to participate in the ef-fects of his happy Passion: namely the remission of sins, an increase in charity, and the assurance of glory.[68] This participation comes about in a very particular way through access to the *sacrum convivi-um*, participation in Our Lord's table, a sacred banquet in which the immolated victim offers his glorified and immortal body as food. Ac-cess to the table, to the gift of Jesus Christ as food, is possible only through his immolation as represented in the sacrament. Incidental-ly, we should point out the futility—to say the least—of the modern opposition between the notion of Eucharist as sacrifice and Eucharist as banquet (in the primary and Thomistic sense of the term); often enough the same opposition is assumed by defenders of the sacrificial nature of the Eucharist.

In the sacrifice of the Mass—a "representative image" of the sac-rifice of Calvary—the perpetual virtue of the Passion continues to accomplish the salvation of the human race in an entirely special manner. In fact, though the virtue of the Passion works in all the sacraments; the sacrament of the Eucharist is distinct from the oth-ers in that, more than signifying a supernatural reality, "the Eucha-rist contains something which is sacred absolutely, namely, Christ's own body."[69]

---

67. "*Quoties huius hostiae commemoratio celebratur, opus nostrae redemptionis exer-cetur,*" Secret of the Mass for the ninth Sunday after Pentecost in the missal *secundum consuetudinem romanae curiae* (thirteenth century): see van Dijk, *The Ordinal of the Papal Court from Innocent III to Boniface VIII*; Marie Pierre Ellebracht, *Remarks on the Vocabu-lary of the Ancient Orations in the Missale Romanum* (Nijmegen: Dekker & Van de Vegt, 1963), 76; Gy, "La documentation sacramentaire de Thomas d'Aquin," 430.

68. See *ST* III, q. 49, a. 3, ad 3. This relationship of dependence between the *fruc-tus redemptionis* and the *memoria passionis* contained in the Eucharist is clearly affirmed also —besides in the antiphon *O sacrum convivium*—in the first oration for the Mass of Corpus Christi. The other two orations develop the themes of ecclesial unity, which is signified in the Eucharist, and the eschatological fruition that is prefigured. On the triple division of the fruits of the Eucharist, see also *ST* III, q. 73, a. 4.

69. *ST* III, q. 73, a. 1, ad 3. See *ST* III, q. 79, a. 2, and also the *Commentary on the Letter to the Hebrews*, ch. 10, lect. 1.

The object of the Eucharistic sacrifice, which is a true sacrament containing the priest and the victim, is to apply the infinite merits of his offering for the benefit of mankind in all times,[70] perpetuating the salvific efficacy of the sacrifice of which it is the commemoration and memorial. In this sacrament, therefore, participation in the fruits of the Passion is subordinated to participation in the unique immolation represented in it, such that if it were not represented there, then access to the benefits of the redemption would be blocked. As for participation in the fruit of the Passion, St. Thomas says, "it is proper to this sacrament for Christ to be sacrificed in its celebration."[71]

Thus it is clear that the second reason St. Thomas invokes is, in fact, directly dependant on the doctrine of representation just formulated;[72] it is because the Eucharist represents the sacrifice of Christ on Calvary in the mode of sacramental immolation that the Eucharist applies the fruits of redemption. In the words of Fr. Humbrecht, the representation of the redemptive Passion:

does not lie primarily in the modality of the sacrament (in its forms and in the sacramental species), but rather in the *virtue* of the sacrament itself, which places the notion of representation in clear relation to the effective causality of the Passion, and not only to its signification.[73]

70. Charles Journet wrote: "Christ wants now and until the end of the world, just as he wanted on the cross, that the rays of his bloody cross should touch and redeem every moment of time by their contact" (*La Messe, présence du sacrifice de la croix*, 112–13).

71. *ST* III, q. 83, a. 1, at the end of the corpus.

72. See Humbrecht: "Manifestly, then, there is one mode of representation proper to the Eucharist, but one that takes account both of the fact that the one immolation of Christ is represented in its celebration, and that because of this we are made participants in the effects of this salvific immolation, since the sacramental immolation itself participates in the virtue of the immolation of Calvary. The *duplex ratio* of St. Thomas is thus only one reason, seen in terms of its cause and in terms of its effects" ("L'eucharistie, 'représentation' du sacrifice du Christ, selon saint Thomas," 371). For C. Journet, on the contrary, this second reason is the "proper response" to the question of immolation in the Eucharistic sacrifice: "Thus, Christ is immolated at the Mass because the Mass brings us the effect of his Passion, actualizes it for us, makes us participants in its fruits, and accomplishes each time the work of our redemption.... Where Christ's Passion is truly present, Christ's immolation is truly present. St. Thomas gives a direct answer to the direct question he posed" (*La Messe, presence du sacrifice de la croix*, 112).

73. Humbrecht, "L'eucharistie, 'représentation' du sacrifice du Christ, selon saint Thomas," 373.

The notion of sign alone cannot account for the sacramental reality unless it is joined with the notion of causality, which enables the sacrament to participate, as a separate instrument, in the instrumental causality of Christ's holy humanity. "The sacraments of the New Law are both cause and signs":[74] the sign is genuine only because it participates in the causality of Christ, which is to say, the redemptive virtue of his sacrifice. Therefore it is instrumental causality, "the middle term linking what represents to that which is represented,"[75] that allows the sacramental sign to truly represent the sacrifice of Christ and, at the same time, to produce the fruit of the Passion in the souls of believers.

Now is the appropriate time to point out the deep significance of the Thomistic definition of the sacrament. In fact, as Fr. Gy very acutely remarked, the definition of sacrament *in genere signi* should be understood "not as the displacement of signification by causality but as the reorientation of sign toward the sacrament's cause, Christ, rather than to its effect of grace."[76] Moreover, Fr. Gy writes that in the *Summa theologiae*, the sacrament, "before being the sign of a sacramental effect, is the sign of its cause, namely Christ (the Priest) acting in the sacrament."[77] It is the sign of Christ, we would add, offering to the Father *in sacramento* the perpetual homage of his sacrifice of love and obedience, and thus communicating to men the fruits of this same redeeming sacrifice.

THE EUCHARISTIC SACRIFICE: SALVATION HISTORY AND THE HEAVENLY LITURGY

Our study of the ritual economy of the Old Law pointed out the allegorical reading Thomas gives to the various sacrifices of the first Law,

74. *ST* III, q. 62, a. 1, ad 1.

75. Humbrecht, "L'eucharistie, 'représentation' du sacrifice du Christ, selon saint Thomas," 380.

76. Gy, "Divergences de théologie sacramentaire autour de saint Thomas," 427n9.

77. Gy, "Avancées du traité de l'eucharistie de saint Thomas dans la Somme par rapport aux *Sentences*," 223.

especially in the *ST*'s treatise on the Old Law. In one way or another, all were images *prefiguring* the redeeming sacrifice. He recalls this at the end of the corpus of the article we have just studied:[78] with regard to the mode of representation, "it is true to say that Christ was sacrificed even in the figures of the Old Testament."[79] The Eucharistic sacrifice is, in common with the figures, the image of the redemptive Passion. Nevertheless, it differs from them as an image that is no longer *figurative* but *commemorative* of the redemptive Passion, the central event of salvation history, whose virtue lasts eternally.

The ancient sacrifices announced and prefigured the event of the cross. The former did not have the capacity to represent the Passion, the efficient cause of a salvation that was still to come. But once the Passion came, the redeeming sacrifice could be represented efficaciously in a sacramental mode: Christ immolated—*Christus passus*—is henceforth really contained in the sacrament. Consequently, by what it represents and contains, as the sacramental celebration of the Lord's death,[80] the Eucharistic sacrifice, radically unlike the sacrifice of the Old Covenant, is endowed with a salvific efficacy that belongs to none other.

Here and now, in the time of the Church, every member of Christ participates in the sacrificial offering of the head through the cultic deputation he receives in Baptism. Regenerated and washed in the water and blood, the Christian is united to the sacrifice of the God-Man, makes the feelings of Christ, the Sovereign Priest, his own, offers the divine victim to the Father and, under the motion of the Spirit, is offered with the mediator. This union is the heart of the liturgical life of the Church. By the offering of the Eucharistic sacrifice and communion with the precious gifts, the body and blood of the Redeemer offered and given, the faithful Christian comes into

78. *ST* III, q. 83, a. 1.

79. See also the sequence *Lauda Sion* in the Mass of Corpus Christi: "In old types foresignified; / In the manna Heav'n-supplied, / Isaac, and the Paschal Lamb" (Translation Fr. Caswall).

80. *ST* III, q. 83, a. 1, end of the corpus, speaking about the effects of the Passion: "It is proper to this sacrament for Christ to be sacrificed in its celebration."

possession of the treasure and "mystery of faith." He benefits from the fruits of the blessed Passion: he receives grace (the *form of* his sanctification) in abundance; he is united to Christ, who gathers him into the unity of the Church;[81] and he finds a prefiguration and assurance of future glory.

We have also seen that, for St. Thomas, the sacrifice of Christ has an eternal consummation due to the eternity of his priesthood. This consummation consists in the communication of the spiritual fruits of the sacrifice to all those for whom Christ was immolated. Because these fruits are eternal goods, we may properly speak about the eternal consummation of the redeeming sacrifice.[82] On one hand, the elect of the earth benefit now, until the end of time, from the benefits of the redeeming sacrifice represented in the sacrament of the altar; on the other, the perpetual virtue of the same sacrifice is the principle of the glorification of the saints in the glory of heaven.

In this life, on the Church's altar, the oblation-immolation of the Savior accomplished on Calvary is "renewed" not in the sense that Christ continues to suffer,[83] but insofar as the perpetual virtue of the redeeming Passion continues to be at work in the mode of sacramental immolation. So in glory, the perpetual virtue of Christ's sacrifice continues to work, though the Incarnate Word has lost nothing of his character as priest and host of his own sacrifice of love and obedience. For by his incarnation, Christ has been made the priest and victim of his own sacrifice for eternity: "Christ's passion and death are not to be repeated, yet the virtue of that Victim endures forever."[84]

The Eucharistic sacrifice celebrated in time by the ministry of the Church is thus the sacramental representation or commemoration of a past oblation accomplished once and for all on Calvary's altar, but one whose virtue lasts eternally. Nonetheless, because the Christ

---

81. See *ST* III, q. 73, a. 4.
82. *ST* III, q. 22, a. 5.
83. See Thomas, *Commentary on the Sentences* IV, d. 12, expositio textus.
84. *ST* III, q. 22, a. 5, ad 2.

who is there immolated and given as food is the glorified Christ, and because eating the sacrament is ordered to the enjoyment of heaven,[85] the Eucharistic sacrifice is the sacramental celebration of an eschatological mystery,[86] namely participation, under a veil, under sensible signs, in the liturgy of heaven.[87]

There Christ, "high priest of the good things to come" (Heb 9:11), like the high priest who entered the Holy of Holies each year, does not cease to intercede for men by offering to his Father the homage of his unique sacrifice, clearing the way for mankind to enter through the virtue of his blood, which he shed,[88] dispensing to them the infinite merits acquired on the cross. It is important to note, however, that Christ's oblation in heaven does not substitute some new kind of heavenly sacrifice for the oblation of Calvary. The *heavenly victim* is no more distinct from the cross than the Eucharistic oblation is; it is one and the same unique sacrifice of the cross, accomplished on Calvary, commemorated on the altar, and consummated in heaven.

In heaven, Christ confirms the oblation of Calvary by an eternal act, "his unceasing intercession and mediation in favor of what he willed on the cross."[89] On the altar the same unique intercession

---

85. See *ST* III, q. 80, a. 2, ad 1: "The receiving of Christ under this sacrament is ordained to the enjoyment of heaven, as to its end, in the same way as the angels enjoy it."

86. See Charles Journet, *La Messe, présence du sacrifice de la croix*, 78: "Insofar as it was announced in the Mosaic Law and present even in the law of nature, the Christian Pasch, the Supper, the Mass, is a *Messianic mystery*. In turn, insofar as it announces what is to come and, under the veil of symbols, gives a share in the plenitude and inebriation of heaven, it is an *eschatological mystery*. It has been established on the threshold of the world's last age, staining the river of time with Christ's blood until it breaks into eternity."

87. See *ST* III, q. 61, a. 4, ad 1; *ST* I-II, q. 103, a. 3.

88. *ST* III, q. 22, a. 5.

89. Journet, *La Messe, présence du sacrifice de la croix*, 89–90: In this sense, "the priesthood of Christ is eternal: *it ratifies* and *progressively brings out the value of the unique sacrifice of the cross, whose inexhaustible virtue is therefore eternal* ... in heaven [Christ] continues to desire our salvation in precisely the same way he desired it once and for all by the act of his Passion and death, and he is made present at Mass in precisely the same way. Of course, he comes there in his state of glory, not, however, to impress us with his glory, but to 'proclaim his death,' to actualize the unique act of redemption. He comes there *with* his redeeming act. Between his glory and our sin he interposes his bloody cross."

of Christ is represented in the sacramental mode, and its fruits are dispensed. Cajetan penned an illuminating reflection on this point, provoked by the necessity of responding to the Lutheran doctrine:

Just as Christ entered into heaven through his own blood, remaining a priest forever to intercede in our favor, so he remains with us in the mode of immolation through the Eucharist, in order to intercede for us. Just as the sufficiency and sovereign efficacy of the sacrifice offered on the wood of the cross does not exclude Christ's dwelling in heaven to intercede for us, so it does not exclude his dwelling with us in the mode of immolation to intercede for us. Just as the continual intercession of Christ for us in heaven does not detract from the unique intercession of Christ's death, so, for an even stronger reason, Christ's remaining in the mode of immolation in order to intercede for us and make us participants in the remission of sins accomplished on the altar of the cross does not detract from it.[90]

Thus by reason of the eternal duration of his priesthood, Christ is and remains the mediator of the absolute gift that God makes of himself *in praesenti et in futuro*. His sacrificial oblation accomplished on earth in his immolation on Calvary embraces time and eternity. On earth, because it perpetuates the salvific efficacy of the unique redeeming sacrifice, the Eucharist communicates to mankind in history the benefits of salvation. In heaven, the victorious Christ in his glorified humanity presents to the Father the sacrificial act that is the principle of saints' glory and the intercession *par excellence* for the men that are still to be saved.

Nevertheless, at the end of history, at the moment when all things will have been "recapitulated" in Christ and the number of the elect attained, the offering of the sacrifice of propitiation on earth will cease and there will no longer be material altars or temples. All that remains is for the elect to be led to the blessed end by Christ himself.[91] They will possess the perfect union and beloved vision of which the sacrament of the Eucharist, "the last historical phase of

---

90. Cajetan, quoted by M. V. Le-Roy, "Un traité de Cajetan sur la messe," 483–84.
91. *ST* III, q. 22, a. 5, ad 1.

our return to God in Christ, the High Priest of the good things to come,"[92] is only the pledge and figure.[93]

Once the union of all the elect with God, the last end for which Christ offered and continues to offer his satisfaction, has been accomplished in glory,[94] what will become of Christ's oblation in its eternal consummation? Because from the first moment of the Incarnation the sacrifice of Christ, sacrifice of love and obedience, was entirely impregnated, according to the words of Isaiah (51:3), "with thanksgiving and the voice of praise," Christ the priest and victim for eternity will always continue to offer the Father the spiritual sacrifice of thanksgiving and praise, as it is said in Psalm 49:23: "*Sacrificium laudis honorificabit me.*"[95] Thus, in the final analysis, the es-

---

92. Denis Chardonnens, "Eternité du sacerdoce du Christ et effet eschatologique de l'eucharistie," 179–80: "The connection between the eternity of Christ's priesthood and the eschatological effect of the Eucharist sheds light on the place of this sacrament in the larger plan of the economy of salvation. It must always be considered in this context in order for us to appreciate its significance and efficacy. The Eucharist is the last historical phase of our return to God in Christ, the High Priest of the good things to come, and an anticipation of eternal life. Thus we uncover in the Thomistic doctrine of the Eucharist an eschatological conception of the human person in the Church, the whole of which is called to a consummation in glory."

93. See Humbrecht, "L'eucharistie, 'représentation' du sacrifice du Christ, selon saint Thomas," 382: "In this sense, the sacrament of the Eucharist is both much and little: much by reason of its end and its informing action, which is growth in charity; little, because of its sacramental modality, which is really no more than sacramental. We do not (yet) possess Christ in his proper aspect, which is not the first or only way of possessing him either. Thus the Eucharist, a representation true and proper of the sacrifice of Christ on Calvary, is itself only a figure."

94. See, in *ST* III, q. 22, a. 5, the third reason that man requires the sacrifice of Christ: "*ad hoc quod spiritus hominis perfecte Deo uniatur: quod maxime erit in gloria.*"

95. See Thomas, *Commentary on the Letter to the Hebrews*, ch. 3, lect. 1 and. Martin Morard, "Sacerdoce du Christ et sacerdoce des chrétiens dans le *Commentaire des psaumes* de saint Thomas d'Aquin," 133–34: "The *Commentary on the Psalms* links … priesthood and interior sacrifice; it makes the act by which Christ offers himself through love the proper act of the priesthood of the New Covenant, and particularly highlights its cultic role in the order of praise. From these points of view, the priestly action of Christ comes into play, certainly, in the corporeal sacrifice of the cross and in the sacramental sacrifice of the Mass. But it doesn't stop there. From the Eucharist 'follows a threefold spiritual effect: namely, sufficiency, praise, and life' (*Super Ps.* 21:22). The sacrament of the altar, the *Super Psalmos* continues, causes a reorientation of the soul toward God, who leads us to offer, not a ceremonial worship, but the interior worship of true adorers."

chatological dimension allows us to link Thomas's doctrine with the deeper meaning of the term *eucharistia*, which according to the patristic tradition is both an *action*, or sacrifice of thanksgiving, and a *holy thing*, or the sacrament of the Eucharistic gifts.[96]

96. See Gy, "La documentation sacramentaire de Thomas d'Aquin," 427–28.

Conclusion

———:———

We began this study with an analysis of the *Summa theologiae*'s treatise on the moral virtue of religion, presenting St. Thomas Aquinas's arguments on the necessity of external acts of worship. For the Angelic Doctor, these are full-fledged acts of the debt of religion connatural to religious man, formally due because of his corporeal dimension. However, because in man bodily realities are ordered to the moral and spiritual dimension, the external acts of worship are owed to God only in a secondary capacity, as *signs* that provoke, excite, and manifest the principal, interior religion made up of acts of devotion and prayer.[1]

We have noted a whole hierarchy of external acts of worship: gestures of adoration, vocal prayer, oblations, sacrifices, and so forth, examining the various meanings contained under these multiple acts. Among these, Aquinas emphasizes the preeminence of sacrifice, noting its connaturality, defining its exclusively latreutical nature,[2] and analyzing its inner structure. Moreover, to the sacrificial offering and to the other public acts of religious homage rendered in the name of human society are ordered not only ministers, but also

1. *ST* II-II, q. 81, a. 7: "In the Divine worship it is necessary to make use of corporeal things, that man's mind may be aroused thereby, as by signs, to the spiritual acts by means of which he is united to God."

2. *ST* II-II, q. 85, a. 2: "Just as to God alone ought we to offer spiritual sacrifice, so too ought we to offer outward sacrifices to Him alone."

places and objects separated from profane use, established in a state of "cultic sanctity"—the *sacred*—through rites of consecration. .

These first analyses embraced only the moral duty of the religion, considering the cultic manifestations connatural to religious man and disregarding the cultic regimes of salvation history. However, as the numerous allusions in the treatise to Church practice prove, St. Thomas obviously did not intend to subtract the acts of the virtue of religion from the cultic economy of revelation. Rather he progressed according to a logical order, choosing to highlight first the work of creative Wisdom in human reason.

We have also seen that St. Thomas's observations, bolstered by reasonings drawn from Aristotelian metaphysics, have not been contradicted by contemporary research in religious anthropology. In other words, beyond the superstitious practices and various deformations that have emerged in the history of religions, one finds the permanent values and manifestations of the moral virtue of religion, which sin could not annihilate. This recognition makes it possible to grant the various sacrifices of this history their own religious consistency; they announce and prepare, albeit in an imperfect way, the offering of the redemptive sacrifice.

Consequently, the manifestation and communication of God's plan of salvation in history cannot modify nor shake the anthropological foundations of the acts of the virtue of religion, but rather strengthen and elevate them. After studying the anthropological foundations of cultic practices, the second part presented a much more developed study of the cultic economy of the *ordo temporis*, of salvation history in its two great phases: the Old Law, with its figurative and imperfect worship; then the New Law, whose worship is the superabundant and sanctifying worship of the mediator, Jesus Christ, continued and communicated by his Church in the celebration of the sacraments of faith—in expectation of the third and final phase, the eternal life of which the sacraments are the pledge.[3]

3. See *ST* I-II, q. 106, a. 4, ad 1: "There is a threefold state of mankind; the first was under the Old Law; the second is that of the New Law; the third will take place not in

In manifesting himself to Abraham, then in revealing himself to the Hebrew people through the gift of the Law to Moses, God commanded his chosen ones in each instance to perform external acts of worship, especially to offer sacrifices. He also instituted "sacraments" such as circumcision, the Paschal Lamb, and priestly consecration, among others. However, unlike the natural sacrifices and sacraments, the sacrifices and sacraments of the Old Testament added to the religious intention of latreutic homage proper to the virtue of religion a new meaning, one entirely relative to the Mystery of Christ, which they announce and represent. They even allowed men to establish, by faith, a certain contact with Christ. Although they did not satisfy the debt of worship, which sinful man cannot pay, and although they are therefore not capable of procuring sanctification, they were nevertheless already signs and declarations of the faith that justifies. For under the Old Law the religious man was saved by faith manifested in worship. In the first phase of salvation history, external worship was already related to supernatural faith and hope, not only insofar as they relate to heavenly goods, but also insofar as they relate to the Way by which they are reached: Christ the High Priest, the Author of Sanctification.

The fruit of the Law is Christ and along with him the whole new economy, which he came to seal by offering himself as a sacrifice on the cross.[4] The person of the Incarnate Word enlightens the cultic economy of the two Testaments: "Christ is the fountain-head of the entire priesthood," says Aquinas, "for the priest of the Old Law was a figure of Him; while the priest of the New Law works in His person."[5] Around Christ, the center of history, the various states of divine worship corresponding to the successive stages of the communication of the mystery of salvation are progressively defined.

---

this life, but in heaven. But as the first state is figurative and imperfect in comparison with the state of the Gospel; so is the present state figurative and imperfect in comparison with the heavenly state, with the advent of which the present state will be done away."

4. *ST* I-II, q. 102, a. 6, ad 5: "The Fruit of the Law, i.e., Christ, was to be offered to God."

5. *ST* III, q. 22, a. 4.

The figure, the "corporeal" cult—of itself incapable of being accepted and procuring sanctification—is succeeded by the perfect cult of
Christ, the Redeemer.

St. Thomas considers Christ's priesthood to be a consequence of
the hypostatic union. The holy humanity of Christ, the conjoint instrument of his divinity, was consecrated to render perfect and *spiritual* worship to God. Constituted as a priest from the first moment
of the Incarnation, Christ, "Mediator of God and men,"[6] never
ceased during his entire earthly life to render to the Father the homage of his worship of thanksgiving and praise. Because he had united himself to human nature, Christ's worship had to be both interior
and exterior. Here below, Jesus offered himself to the Father at every
moment by an interior act of love and obedience, as a sacrifice for
the salvation of men. However, freely adhering to the Father's will,
he willed his interior sacrifice to be signified, manifested, and consummated by the bloody oblation of Calvary. There, on the altar of
the cross, he made himself both priest and victim of his sacrifice, offering his holy humanity to divine Justice as a propitiatory host for
mankind. Thus he brought up to the Father the only acceptable sacrifice and, because this tribute of adoration was accepted, brought
down upon men the benefits of redemption.

From his seat in heaven, Christ, a priest for all eternity, consummates in his glorified humanity the homage of his sacrifice, whose
virtue remains eternal.[7] In the same way, on earth, in the era of the
Church, it is due only to a real link with the now-glorious humanity
of Christ, eternal instrument of his divinity, that the divine cult inaugurated in his Passion can be celebrated,[8] and that the grace of the
divine adoption merited on the cross can be granted to us.[9]

---

6. 1 Tm 2:5.

7. *ST* III, q. 22, a. 5, ad 2: "Although Christ's passion and death are not to be repeated,
yet the virtue of that Victim endures forever."

8. *ST* III, q. 62, a. 5: "By His Passion He inaugurated the Rites of the Christian Religion by offering 'Himself—an oblation and a sacrifice to God' (Eph 5:2)."

9. *ST* III, q. 57, a. 6: "Christ entered heaven 'to make intercession for us,' as is said
in Hebrews 7:25, because the very showing of Himself in the human nature which He

Therefore, the sacramental signs, "sacraments of faith" instituted by Christ, espouse the realism of the redemptive Incarnation. In the *Summa theologiae*, St. Thomas defines the sacrament as a "[sensible] *sign* of a holy thing so far as it makes men holy,"[10] thus underlining the extent to which the structure of the sacramental reality—composed of sensible things and the words that determine them, that is, of matter and of form—corresponds to the mode of being proper to the human being for whose use the sacraments were instituted. On this point, M.-D. Chenu wrote, "the two words 'anthropology' and 'sacramental' are inseparable from each other not only in terms of methods ... but constitutively."[11] Even more, the structure of the sacrament is modeled on that of the Incarnate Word, the Instrument of Salvation. Indeed, just as in the Person of the Word the divinity has elevated human nature, so in the sacraments the words elevate the sensible realities, giving them the power to signify the worship of God and the sanctification of men.[12]

As sensible signs adapted to the human condition, the New Law's sacraments are, above all, signs of divine action, whereas the sacramental signs of the Old Covenant only announced or represented by anticipation the mystery of Christ. Although they were a protestation of faith, an act of the soul, they could not, as far as sacred actions and external means were concerned, signify in an effective way the divine cult and the sanctification of men, which only Christ, the instrumental cause of salvation, could accomplish.[13] As for the sacraments of the Church, or the sacraments of faith, they

---

took with Him to heaven is a pleading for us, so that for the very reason that God so exalted human nature in Christ, He may take pity on them for whom the Son of God took human nature."

10. *ST* III, q. 60, a. 2.

11. Chenu, "Pour une anthropologie sacramentelle," 87.

12. *ST* III, q. 60, a. 5: "In the use of the sacraments two things may be considered, namely, the worship of God, and the sanctification of man."

13. *ST* III, q. 62, a. 6, ad 1: "The Fathers of old had faith in the future Passion of Christ, which, inasmuch as it was apprehended by the mind, was able to justify them. But we have faith in the past Passion of Christ, which is able to justify also by the real use of sacramental things."

establish a physical contact with the redemptive Passion according to their identity as sacred signs and actions.[14] Through the sacraments, the holy humanity of Christ, conjoined instrument of the divinity, continues to operate here below: as separate instrumental causes, the sacramental signs link men to the divine Head's holy humanity. By celebrating the Mediator's worship and communicating the graces of salvation, they prolong in time the work Christ accomplished on the cross.

The Eucharist is the greatest and most perfect of the sacraments. To the Eucharist, whose proper and constitutive sacramental identity is to be both sacrifice and sacrament,[15] all the other sacraments are ordered as to their end.[16] The Eucharist does more than signify grace; it contains its Author and, consequently, the common spiritual good of the whole Church.[17] It represents the Passion of Christ, fills the soul with an abundance of grace, and promises future goods.[18]

We have shown how strongly St. Thomas insists on the cultic dimension of the sacraments—affirming it repeatedly throughout the treatise on the sacraments in general—and how he links it inseparably to their sacramental dimension. The sacramental sign is modeled on the saving work of the Incarnate Word. In the sacraments, we see exercised the twofold mediation, ascending and descending, of Christ's priesthood. They send up a perfect cult that is acceptable to God and then, on account of this acceptance, they cause the grace

14. *ST* III, q. 48, a. 6, ad 2: "Christ's Passion, although corporeal, has yet a spiritual effect from the Godhead united: and therefore it secures its efficacy by spiritual contact—namely, by faith and the sacraments of faith."

15. *ST* III, q. 79, a. 5: "This sacrament is both a sacrifice and a sacrament. it has the nature of a sacrifice inasmuch as it is offered up; and it has the nature of a sacrament inasmuch as it is received."

16. *ST* III, q. 65, a. 3: "[That the sacrament of the Eucharist is the greatest of all the sacraments] is made clear by considering the relation of the sacraments to one another. For all the other sacraments seem to be ordained to this one as to their end."

17. *ST* III, q. 65, a. 3, ad 1: "The common spiritual good of the whole Church is contained substantially in the sacrament itself of the Eucharist." See also *ST* III, q. 79, a. 1, corp. and ad 1.

18. See the antiphon *O sacrum convivium* for Second Vespers of the Feast of Corpus Christi.

of sanctification to descend upon all those for whom and in whose name the redemptive sacrifice is offered. What was accomplished in Christ, the instrument of salvation, is fulfilled in the sacrament. The two opposite but inseparable poles of the religious bond between God and man come together: divine worship and the sanctification of man.

In the *Summa*, the cultic dimension of sacramentality—which is often passed over too quickly—is developed in a particular way in relation to the sacramental character. The Angelic Doctor defines it both as a spiritual power ordered to divine worship and as a participation in Christ's priesthood. The character, which resides in the soul's intellectual power where faith has its seat, is "ordained unto things pertaining to the Divine worship; which is a protestation of faith expressed by exterior signs."[19] By receiving this power, according to a manner proper to each of the three characters, Christ's members marked with the seal of the character are deputed to the acts of worship of the Christian religion, whose "whole rite . . . is derived from Christ's priesthood."[20] They are thus made participants in Christ's priestly function as instrumental causes of a cult whose unique and principal priest is Christ.

Moreover, since it is in virtue of their relationship to Christ's priesthood that Aquinas defines the sacramental characters, the character of Holy Orders consequently occupies a chief place. The only one of the three characters that configures its recipient in an active way to Christ's priesthood in its fullness, it is the basis for the hierarchical constitution of the Church,[21] which is constructed around the offering of the Eucharistic sacrifice.[22]

19. *ST* III, q. 63, a. 4, ad 3.

20. *ST* III, q. 63, a. 3.

21. See Charles Journet, *The Church of the Word Incarnate*, vol. 1 (New York: Sheed & Ward, 1955), 50: "The power of order is merely the highest realization, reserved to the hierarchy, of a more general and very mysterious power, the sacramental power [*pouvoir cultuel*], whose two lower realizations, the one conferred by the power of Baptism and the other by the sacrament of Confirmation, are the common heritage of all the faithful, and put their stamp upon and inwardly penetrate the whole life of the Church as she now is."

22. *ST* III, q. 64 , a. 2, ad 3: "The apostles and their successors are God's vicars in

If the sacramental character consists in a participation in Christ's priesthood and gives men the power to honor God "according to the rite of the Christian religion," it grants them to participate in a more or less active way in the Redeemer's cultic action *par excellence*: the Eucharistic sacrifice, which, because of the eternal virtue of the unique sacrifice of the cross, is the representative image of Christ's Passion.

At the altar, the one who sacrificed himself once and for all on Calvary sacrifices himself every day in the sacrament—while "exalted above the heavens"[23] our High Priest "always lives to make intercession for us,"[24] consummating his priestly mediation in glory. Just as the *heavenly host* does not consist in a new sacrifice under glorious signs, the Mass is not some sort of sacrifice of a sacramental nature that replaces the oblation of Calvary. On the contrary, the concept of representative image must be understood as a formal resemblance of the altar to the cross, that is to say, a similarity in essence that tends to become identity with the Passion represented and signified, so that the sacramental immolation becomes one with the immolation of Calvary that it commemorates.[25] This is the profound meaning of the Pauline definition of the Eucharistic action: "proclaiming the Lord's death until he comes."[26]

Furthermore, the Eucharist, the sacrifice and sacrament of the body and blood of our Lord, is at the same time a "representative image" of the Passion and a "sacred banquet," or, in the sense that these expressions have in the patristic tradition, an "action" and a "holy thing." Because it represents the sacrifice of Christ in his Passion and contains the most perfect worship by which divine Justice has been appeased in regard to every offense, the Eucharist applies the

---

governing the Church which is built on faith and the sacraments of faith.... On the contrary, the Church is said [Glos. Lombardi, super *Rom.* 5:14] to be built up with the sacraments 'which flowed from the side of Christ while hanging on the cross.'"

23. Heb 7:26.

24. Heb 7:25.

25. *ST* III, q. 83, a. 1: "*Celebratio autem huius sacramenti ... imago est quaedam repraesentativa passionis Christi, quae est vera immolatio.*"

26. 1 Cor 11:26.

benefits and fruits of the redemption to mankind in the age of the
Church. Through the sacramental mystery of the redemptive immolation and by communion with the precious Eucharistic gifts, God
receives all honor and glory, reconciles man with himself, fills man
with grace, and gives him the pledge of future glory.

But the sacramental sign really represents the redemptive sacrifice and effectively produces the fruit of the Passion only because
it participates in the instrumental causality of Christ, the holy humanity of Christ contained in it substantially.[27] In the *Summa*, as
Fr. Pierre-Marie Gy has pointed out, the sign is oriented toward the
cause of the sacrament.[28] In other words, the sacramental sign is a
sign of its Cause, namely Christ, the Sovereign Priest, who, acting in
the sacrament, renders to the Father the cult that alone is acceptable
and sanctifies men. This observation applies to all the sacraments,
insofar as each one signifies and contains in its own way the redemptive Passion[29] in its double cultic and sanctifying dimension, and
insofar as all converge toward the Eucharist as towards their center
and their end.

It is, therefore, mainly in view of celebrating and participating
in the Eucharistic sacrifice that the redeemed are incorporated into
Christ by the sacramental characters and, consequently, that the
Church, the mystical Body of Christ, a holy nation, a cultic society,
is constituted and its hierarchy built up. The Bride of Christ has received the power and mission to continue Christ's priestly work in
time. She accomplishes this mission by celebrating and dispensing
the benefits of a cult of which Christ the Priest is the principal actor,
her role being purely ministerial.

This is why the Church's liturgy, instead of being considered as

---

27. *ST* III, q. 65, a. 3: "[The sacrament of the Eucharist] contains Christ Himself
substantially: whereas the other sacraments contain a certain instrumental power which
is a share of Christ's power."

28. Gy, "Divergences de théologie sacramentaire autour de saint Thomas," 427n9.

29. *ST* III, q. 60, a. 3: "A sacrament is a sign that is both a reminder of the past, i.e. the
passion of Christ; and an indication of that which is effected in us by Christ's passion,
i.e. grace."

the set of rites, prayers, symbols, and so on, by which the Church publicly renders God the worship due to him—which it also is, but in a secondary manner—must be defined in terms of its continuity with the exercise of the mediation of Christ's priesthood. The liturgy is the worship of Christ and, with him and through him, the integral and public worship of the Mystical Body, according to Pius XII's definition.[30] It consists in the exercise of the priestly function of Christ, as the Second Vatican Council specifies, in its twofold ascending and descending dimension, that is to say, cultic and sanctifying.[31]

As is well known, this profound view of the Christian liturgy, common to the patristic tradition and the Middle Ages, and so present, as we have seen, in the Angelic Doctor's doctrine of salvation

---

30. Pius XII, Encyclical Letter *Mediator Dei* (November 20, 1947), 20: "The sacred liturgy is, consequently, the public worship which our Redeemer as Head of the Church renders to the Father, as well as the worship which the community of the faithful renders to its Founder, and through Him to the heavenly Father. It is, in short, the worship rendered by the Mystical Body of Christ in the entirety of its Head and members."

31. Vatican Council II, Constitution *Sacrosanctum Concilium* (December 4, 1963), 7: "Rightly, then, the liturgy is considered as an exercise of the priestly office of Jesus Christ. In the liturgy the sanctification of the man is signified by signs perceptible to the senses, and is effected in a way which corresponds with each of these signs; in the liturgy the whole public worship is performed by the Mystical Body of Jesus Christ, that is, by the Head and His members." See Liam G. Walsh, "Liturgy in the Theology of St. Thomas," *The Thomist* 38 (1974): 557–83, at 571: "Definitions of liturgy in terms of the priesthood of Christ have, in fact, been offered by many authors side by side with or as part of their cult and sign definitions. The concept has found favour in official teaching. *Mediator Dei* uses it, although not as its principal definition of the liturgy. Vatican II makes it the starting-point of its definition and deduces its judgement about the objective value and efficacy of the liturgy from it. In both these documents the link between the priestly work of Christ and the liturgical activity of the Church is made by means of the head-member relationship within the mystical body. It is this relationship that allows one to see acts of the Church as acts of Christ and conversely find the priestly act of Christ realized in liturgical signs." Further, still according to Walsh: "The encyclical *Mediator Dei* defined the liturgy solely in terms of cult. There is no mention of sign, nor does the idea get much prominence anywhere in the encyclical. Sanctification is not included in the definition, although it is dealt with elsewhere in the text. The corresponding passage of Vatican II, *Sacrosanctum Concilium*, shows a definite development. The double movement of liturgy is explicitly recognized, and the notion of sign is introduced. The Council says explicitly that sanctification is done through signs" ("Liturgy in the Theology of St. Thomas," 568).

history, and still so alive in the Eastern Church, began to be partly neglected in the Latin world at the end of the Middle Ages. To explain this phenomenon, one must grasp, on the one hand, the influence of a conception of worship that was more ceremonial than mystagogic, linked to the development of the court ceremonial characteristic of the papal liturgy of the Avignon period;[32] and, on the other hand, that—no doubt as a kind of "subconscious" reaction—the *devotio moderna* led to the manifestation of a less collective, more intimate, and "devotional" way of participating and uniting with the sacred functions of the Church. From the second half of the nineteenth century to the present day, reflection that is focused on the nature of the liturgy has led to several definitions of the Magisterium[33] and has made it possible, thanks to a renewed knowledge of the patristic tradition, biblical exegesis, the manuscript sources of the liturgical books of the Latin tradition, and the like, to

32. See Marc Dykmans, *Le cérémonial papal de la fin du Moyen Age à la Renaissance*, vol. 25, *De Rome en Avignon ou le Cérémonial de Jacques Stefaneschi*, and vol. 26, *Les textes avignonnais jusqu'à la fin du Grand Schisme d'Occident* (Rome: Bibliothèque de l'Institut Historique Belge de Rome, 1981–1983).

33. Besides the two definitions of Pius XII and Vatican II, see also *Catechism of the Catholic Church*, 1070, 1084, 1111, 1124: "Christ's work in the liturgy is sacramental: because his mystery of salvation is made present there by the power of his Holy Spirit; because his Body, which is the Church, is like a sacrament (sign and instrument) in which the Holy Spirit dispenses the mystery of salvation; and because through her liturgical actions the pilgrim Church already participates, as by a foretaste, in the heavenly liturgy" (1111). Fr. Antolín González Fuente, in "La teologia nella liturgia e la liturgia nella teologia in san Tommaso d'Aquino," *Angelicum* 74 (1997): 359–417 and 551–601, remarks that the Catechism of the Catholic Church introduces the Holy Spirit's efficient causality into the notion of liturgy. Fr. González Fuente proposes a complete definition of liturgy by way of the four causes: "The liturgy as defined through the four causes would be described as follows: in its formal cause, namely the principal reality that it contains, its essence is 'liturgy,' the continuation, exercise, or actual presence of the priesthood (mediation) of Christ; in its material cause, or the visible 'place' where it is contained, it is constituted by the sum of the liturgical celebrations of the assemblies of the Church; in its efficient cause, it consists of the power, the 'virtue,' or the efficacy of the Holy Spirit; in its final cause, because it is directed to the glorification of God and the sanctification of men, it is a sanctification that redounds in turn to the glorification of God. In short, the liturgy is the continuation of Christ's priesthood in the sacrament of the Church's cult through the power of the Holy Spirit for the glory of God and the sanctification of men" ("La teologia nella liturgia e la liturgia nella teologia," 363).

recover the full meaning of worship. Thanks to this, we can now integrate the inseparable "ritual" dimension of the Church's cult to its proper place.

Since it is at the same time the cult of Christ and the cult of the Church, Christian cult comprises two levels of "rituality" in its celebration. The first is of divine institution and has to do with the substance or necessity of the sacramental cult; the second depends on ecclesiastical institution and has to do with the public or solemn celebration of this cult.[34]

In the first place, there is a fundamental rituality determined by Christ when he instituted the sacraments. For St. Thomas, a sacrament is by its essence a cultic action, in other words, a rite. Thus, at the Last Supper, Jesus instituted the rite of the Eucharist by pronouncing words of sacrificial consecration over the two materials of bread and wine. When he inaugurated the "spiritual cult," Christ gave the cultic dimension a fundamental place, proportionate to man's religious nature, in such a way that he made the ordinary production of grace possible only by way of cultic and sensible means.

Recall that in the treatise on the virtue of religion, St. Thomas first enumerated the sacraments among the external acts of worship "in which men do something divine,"[35] but referred their study to the historical framework of the *Tertia pars*. In sacramental institution, as in the Person of the Word, there is a meeting between humanity and divinity, between man's religious efforts and the divine act, and between the "natural" sacrifice of religious man and the redemptive sacrifice that assumes and accomplishes all sacrifice.[36]

---

34. *ST* III, q. 64, a. 2, ad 1: "Human institutions observed in the sacraments are not essential to the sacrament; but belong to the solemnity which is added to the sacraments in order to arouse devotion and reverence in the recipients."

35. *ST* II-II, q. 89, prologue.

36. See I. Mennessier, *Saint Thomas d'Aquin: L'homme chrétien*, 194: "The lowly journey by which man is led from the depths of the ages to go before his God and offer him in homage the good things he has received from him, *finds, in the Eucharist, its point of access to the Eternal.* The Christian community gathers to offer God its praise and the offering that expresses that praise. Mankind's sacrifice, which has been assumed into the sacrament and become the sacrifice of the Church, leads, as it were, to the Savior's

Man's religious relationship to God is thus restored as God gratu-itously allows man to offer him a cult that truly proceeds from the sanctified creature, and, because it is at the same time the cult of Christ and the cult of men incorporated into him in the Church, is an acceptable cult.

But there remains a second type of rituality about whose im-portance and role errors have frequently arisen in the course of the ages, whether overemphasizing it through "rubricism" or neglect-ing it in the name of a sort of spiritualism. Let us note that the rites of the Church, insofar as we distinguish them here from the rites of divine institution, do not in themselves constitute the liturgy—for the latter is above all the celebration of Christ's acts—but rather they surround the sacramental gestures of Christ and are integrated with them. Thus, in the celebration of the Eucharistic sacrifice, the prayers and rites of the Church express the intention of the mem-bers of the Mystical Body who offer themselves with Christ in a sin-gle sacrifice. The prayers, the rites, and the various consecrations and blessings—things that because of their relation to the sacraments have been referred to above under the generic term of *sacramen-tals*—express devotion and reverence, that is to say, the *religion* and sacrifice of the Church. They manifest in the eyes of men the truths signified by the sacraments and they participate in their own way in the sanctifying efficacy of the Redeemer's worship.[37]

---

unique sacrifice. Through the Eucharist, the sacrament of the Head's unity with its mem-bers, becomes tied *to the unique salvific value* of Calvary. Through sign and in the reality of its incorporation into Christ, the community of the faithful goes beyond the rite and enters into the great ascending movement of Jesus's eternal priesthood."

37. *ST* III, q. 66, a. 10: "all the other things which the Church observes in the bap-tismal rite, belong rather to a certain solemnity of the sacrament. And these, indeed, are used in conjunction with the sacrament for three reasons. First, in order to arouse the devotion of the faithful, and their reverence for the sacrament.... Secondly, for the instruction of the faithful.... And in this way by means of the sacramental ceremonies they are either instructed, or urged to seek the signification of such-like sensible signs. And consequently, since, besides the principal sacramental effect, other things should be known about Baptism, it was fitting that these also should be represented by some outward signs. Thirdly, because the power of the devil is restrained, by prayers, blessings, and the like, from hindering the sacramental effect."

Since "the worship of God pertains to man as referred to God,"[38] in the Church's cult, the whole system of cultic acts that belong to the virtue of religion—whose anthropological foundations we underlined in the first chapter—are elevated to the supernatural order. In the economy of the law of grace, man renders God valid worship only by reason of the sanctification that God works in him. As part of this sanctification, the gift of sacramental characters confers a deputation to the acts of a supernatural religion. For the natural seed of the virtue of religion is not capable of causing acts proportionate to the supernatural end that has been acquired for man through the cross. That requires God to bring into being, by divine production or *infusion*, a habit that is "to the theological virtues what the moral and intellectual virtues are to the natural principles of virtue."[39] While keeping its proper object—the reverence and service of God—the infused virtue of religion depends on and tends to a holiness of grace, and proceeds from and is ordered to supernatural charity.

Consequently, in the Church's liturgical worship one finds the psychological mechanism proper to the virtue of religion, and with it the whole structure of the *sacred*, but henceforth natural religion is situated on the supernatural plane of the infused virtue of religion. Thus, the prayers and the rites of the Church express the devotion and reverence driven by theological charity and tend to render to the divine Majesty a justice that is full of love. But furthermore, because the *spiritual* cult is related to the theological virtues, its external rites themselves become sanctifying. Around the sacramental signs received from the Lord, the prayers and ceremonies of the Church, which prepare, manifest, or prolong the sacramental efficacy, are also, though to a lesser degree, instruments of grace, while the various consecrations of places and objects of worship acquire a value relative to the cult of the supernaturalized soul.[40] Moreover,

38. *ST* III, q. 60, a. 5.

39. *ST* I-II, q. 63, a. 3.

40. See I. Mennessier, "Les réalités sacrées dans le culte chrétien," *Revue des sciences philosophiques et théologiques* 20, no. 2 (1931): 276–86, at 281–82: "The expression 'spiritual' cult thus designates the capacity of our rites to efficaciously produce the supernatural

because the liturgy is essentially a continuation of the exercise of Christ's priesthood, the various rites and sacred realities of Christian worship often carry a symbolism relating to the Mystery of Christ, representing some event in Christ's life—especially his Passion—or announcing the future glory of which the sacraments constitute the pledge.

Like the sacraments to which they all relate in some way, the rites of the Church are therefore intermediate realities that belong to that "in-between time of the Church which stretches between the two mysteries—which, in the end, are one—of the Passover and the Parousia of the Lord, in order to join the Alpha of the former to the Omega of the latter."[41] This is why the Christian liturgy, as borne out by the euchological literature and by the sources and history of cult, has always been stamped with the twofold mark of Christ's cross and Christ's glory, with one or the other perspective being emphasized more or less intensely. This double mark is exemplified in the Eucharistic sacrifice, which is not only an image of the redemptive Passion, but also, as the prayer of the Roman *anamnesis* affirms, a celebration of the whole Mystery of Salvation, that is, of the redemptive sacrifice in its eternal consummation: *"necnon et ab inferis resurrectionis, sed et in coelos gloriosae ascensionis."*

The Church's liturgy is a great poem of signs situated at the meeting point between time and eternity, and tending in its celebration of the sacrament of the Lord's death to manifest what is beyond the veil, namely the liturgy of celestial glory, the last stage of the cultic economy.[42] At the same time a liturgy of memorial, messianic liturgy,

---

life in our souls. It is not a synonym for interior cult. We are still talking about exterior rites, those that have this mysterious property of containing—in a sacramental mode, which we can define in terms of instrumental causality, one of the most mysterious of concepts—the supernatural grace that allows the soul to perform a perfect interior worship in true union with God."

41. Congar, "Le sens de l'économie salutaire dans la théologie de saint Thomas d'Aquin," 107.

42. Here we cite the opinion of Fr. Marie-Dominique Chenu, "Pour une anthropologie sacramentelle," 99: "Rather than St. Gregory the Great's myth according to which God created man to replace the fallen angels and to imitate the angelic liturgy, I prefer

liturgy of the promise, and theophanic or eschatological liturgy, its external acts are proportioned to the faith and to the intermediate condition of the Church, in the expectation of the full manifestation of the divine Mystery *in aeternitate gloriae*, where "nothing in regard to worship of God will be figurative; there will be naught but 'thanksgiving and voice of praise' (Isaiah 51:3)."[43] Thus, following in the footsteps of St. Thomas, we have progressively risen up to the spiritual cult *par excellence*, the cult of eternity of which the liturgy of the Church is the eschatological sign. Situated between the past event of Calvary and the promised eternity, the various ritual forms and traditions of the Church, both Eastern and Western, each translate, with their own genius, the liturgical dilemma that subsists between the cross and glory.[44]

After our investigation of the fundamental principles of Aquinas's liturgical theology, we are in a place to ask ourselves about the relevance today of the liturgical doctrine he expounds. Aquinas started from the observation that the external acts of cult, as acts of the virtue of religion connatural to man, are necessary and formally due, as external signs of the more primary interior religion. This observation, linked to an analysis of the various cultic forms and sacred realities of the "religious phenomenon," is the established view of contemporary religious anthropology. In our opinion, the Christian mind should be able to look past the various deformations and superstitious practices to recognize the work of creative wisdom and, consequently, the reality of a religious dimension that the economy

---

the cosmic liturgy in which matter plays a role because it is assumed by spirit. I need matter for creation to enter into play in the liturgy, instead of being left on the sidelines. Rituality implies this, and worship in spirit will be fully spiritual only when matter is included, not eliminated."

43. *ST* I-II, q. 103, a. 3.

44. See Ratzinger, *The Spirit of the Liturgy*, 50: "Christian liturgy is a liturgy of promise fulfilled, of a quest, the religious quest of human history, reaching its goal. But it remains a liturgy of hope. It, too, bears within it the mark of impermanence. The new Temple, not made by human hands, does exist, but it is also still under construction. The great gesture of embrace emanating from the Crucified has not yet reached its goal; it has only just begun. Christian liturgy is liturgy on the way, a liturgy of pilgrimage toward the transfiguration of the world, which will only take place when God is 'all in all.'"

of Salvation has not destroyed but progressively raised to the supernatural order. Thus, the natural acts of the virtue of religion were introduced at first to represent the mystery of Christ still to come. In the economy of the New Law, these natural acts of religion are raised to the supernatural order and become acts of the infused virtue of religion, driven by theological charity, with this radical difference: that the cult they signify receives divine approval and becomes an instrument of sanctification.

Fundamentally, therefore, the Redemption concerns not so much man himself, whose nature is not annihilated by grace, as the relationship, that is, the religious bond, of man to God. The Christian remains a man, a man who is no longer merely a creature but an adopted son of the Father, a new man washed in the blood of Christ, recreated by the outpouring of the Holy Spirit, whose worship is assumed by the Divine Word and participates in the instrumentality of his holy humanity. The presence of Christ the Head in the cult of the Church—which is the new humanity, the society of the redeemed—is what essentially constitutes the liturgy. Our analysis of St. Thomas's sacramental doctrine has allowed us to highlight this fundamental concept by which the Magisterium of the Church has defined the liturgy, especially on the occasion of the Second Vatican Council, insisting on Christian cult's double dimension of worship and sanctification.

Aquinas gave a fundamental place to the external worship of the Church insofar as it signifies here below, according to the instrumental mode, a religion of supernatural quality. But because this religion is entirely relative to the faithful's knowledge and love of God, it follows that these acts are temporary and transitory because they are subordinated to the spiritual end, the possession of the Kingdom that will succeed the regime of the present Church. In this sense, if St. Thomas's religious and sacramental doctrine gives the external acts of worship all the importance that is due to them, his teaching on the various states of worship throughout salvation history allows them to be seen in their proper, eschatological perspective.

However, St. Thomas does not offer a complete theology of the liturgy—if only because he did not treat the topic in a systematic way. To construct one, the points of fundamental liturgy that we have identified here would need to be supplemented and framed within an ecclesiological doctrine that sets out what is meant by prayer and worship performed *in persona Ecclesiae*. Similarly, the mission of the Holy Spirit at work in the sacraments must be more clearly highlighted. It is known, however, that St. Thomas did not write treatises on pneumatology and ecclesiology—treatises that in today's theology rightly follow the study of Christology. On the other hand, an in-depth study of his doctrine of the last ends, with which the *Summa theologiae* was to have culminated, might better establish the theophanic or eschatological dimension of cult, so rooted in the liturgical doctrine of the Christian East, and thus might specify more precisely the notion of the eternal consummation of Christ's sacrifice.

Regarding the nature of sacraments, if one leans too heavily into the distinction between the sacrament's divinely instituted *substantia* and the ecclesially instituted liturgical *solemnitas*, one runs the risk of reducing the liturgical celebration to a purely accessory role and damaging the unity of the sacrament, which is an indivisible act of Christ and the Church. To avoid this pitfall, it seemed necessary to us to situate the study of the sacramental reality after the treatise on the virtue of religion—which gave the external act of worship its anthropological and moral dimension—and the treatise on the Old Law—where we considered the elements of the priestly people's cultic system as prolegomena to the divine action.

Finally, our sketch of St. Thomas Aquinas's liturgical theology must of course be supplemented by a study of the role and the various meanings that our Doctor assigns to the rites of the Church in the treatise on the sacraments in particular of the *Summa theologiae*, but also in the other works—such as the *Commentary on the Sentences* and the *Summa contra Gentiles*—in which the Angelic Doctor sometimes tries his hand at "liturgical commentary." Such a project, besides involving an abundance of material, would still require the knowledge and critical eye of the historian of cult. Even if much of Aquinas's liturgical commentary could prove to be outdated and not very credible as a result of his lack of historical documentation and the influence of allegorical conceptions typical of the Middle Ages, there is no doubt that the examination still to be undertaken will allow for a more accurate view of the Angelic Doctor's cultic theology.

For those interested in the history of worship, these few Thomistic notes on fundamental liturgy are an opportunity to gauge the doctrinal weight and, therefore, spiritual role that the thirteenth century and the "Gothic period" more generally accorded to the external acts of worship, especially to the celebration of the sacraments centered on the Eucharistic sacrifice. The Angelic Doctor's theological reflections focused on the liturgical practice of his time, which he tried to explain. He thereby furnished it with a strong doctrinal foundation. To a certain extent, his doctrinal speculation was dependent on contemporary liturgical practice; as such, it sometimes goes astray by giving certain rites a decisive importance that a more accurate understanding of the history of worship and doctrine must deny them.

But St. Thomas's cultic theology was not tied exclusively to received usage. We believe that it had a real influence on liturgical concepts and on several ritual practices determined in the period immediately following Aquinas's death. At the end of the thirteenth century, William Durandus, who became bishop of Mende around 1285, after a long career in Italy, wrote the *Pontifical*, which was to become the bishop's book for the administration of the sacraments and sacramentals for more than six centuries. In this book, whose considerable historical and doctrinal importance has been demonstrated by Monsignor Michel Andrieu, one observes the spiritual foundations and order of the whole of medieval society at the precise moment when "the edifice of sacramental theology had been built up and arranged, with all its divisions and dependencies."[45] For the

---

45. Michel Andrieu, *Le pontifical de Guillaume Durand*, by William Durandus, xiv.

historian of worship, whose work straddles the borders of history and theology, Durandus's *Pontifical* is a golden opportunity to note the reciprocal influences between doctrinal works and liturgical texts.

St. Thomas's sacramental theology, the high point of the entire medieval sacramental edifice, emphasized the preeminence of the Eucharistic sacrifice, the sacramental representation of the Lord's Passion, and underlined the orientation of the other sacraments to the celebration of the sacrifice of the altar. He made all other cultic realities, such as consecrations, blessings, and so on, revolve around the sacramental celebration of the Lord's actions. At a time when the "institutional apparatus" of the Church and canonical science were themselves in full efflorescence, Aquinas made the whole organization of the Church depend on the sacramental order. He gave an account of Church hierarchy in terms of the gift of sacramental characters, and explained the various degrees of the priesthood in terms of the service of the altar and the administration of the sacraments.[46]

Thus the cultic theology of St. Thomas Aquinas explained and illustrated in a superior way the fundamental line of thought common to the whole of the Middle Ages, namely that "the mysteric was the Church's essential element,"[47] and the liturgy is "the center of the present Church."[48]

---

46. See Thomas, *Commentary on the Sentences* IV, d. 24, q. 2, a. 1, qa. 2; *SCG* IV, ch. 75.

47. Gy, "Evangélisation et sacrements au moyen âge," in *La liturgie dans l'histoire*, 151–63, at 163: "At a historical moment in which the institutional apparatus of the Church was in full development, the need was rightly felt to make a distinction between the Church's mysteric and organizational elements, establishing the latter in relation to the former. The Middle Ages may very well have overdeveloped the institutional at the expense of the mysteric, but they never ceased to believe that the mysteric was the Church's essential element, to which all her children should have access."

48. Journet, *The Church of the Word Incarnate*, 1:50.

Appendix I

The *Expositio missae* of the *Summa theologiae* (III, q. 83, a. 4–5), Part 1

In the *Summa theologiae*, it is at the end of the treatise on the Eucharist, in question 83, that St. Thomas Aquinas considers the liturgical celebration of the sacrament.[1] In article 1, the most well known of the question, he begins by proving that the rite of the Eucharist, or the sacrifice of the Mass, is "an image representing Christ's Passion, which is his true sacrifice."[2] The sacrifice of Calvary is represented at the altar according to the sacramental economy: by means of cultic

---

1. See A.-M. Roguet, "Note explicative 52 [Q. 83, Prologue]," in *Somme théologique*, by Thomas Aquinas, vol. 2., *L'Eucharistie* (Paris: Desclée, 1967), 316: "At first blush, this question might look like a sort of catchall in which Thomas dispatches a few stray questions that remained unaddressed: first the great theological problem concerning the essence of the Eucharistic sacrifice (art. 1) and then a certain number of questions variously combining liturgical mystagogy and canonical or rubrical prescriptions, these last especially in art. 2 and 6. In actual fact, question 83 is quite unified. From beginning to end it deals with the Eucharist in its celebration. Moreover, the whole second part of the treatise considers the dynamism of the Eucharist: the effects of its action, which are above all products of Holy Communion, and then the minister of this action. Now it takes up the concrete process of this action, and inside the treatise on the Eucharist we have a treatise on the Mass, insofar as we can speak of the Mass and the Eucharist being distinct. The first article governs those that follow: by this celebration the sacrifice of the cross is represented; such is the principle that will serve to explain the various ritual prescriptions."

2. On the notion of "representation" and its application to the rite of Eucharistic sacrifice, see Humbrecht, "L'Eucharistie, 'representation' du sacrifice du Christ, selon saint Thomas," 355–86.

signs, some of them essential and of divine institution, others added by the Church out of reverence for the sacrament.[3] Like a number of previous and contemporary theologians, the Angelic Doctor
does not disdain to enter into detail regarding liturgical rites and
observances. Two long articles nestled within the *Summa* constitute
a sort of *expositio Missae*: article 4, in which our Doctor asks whether "the words that accompany this sacrament are fittingly assigned,"
and article 5, where he examines "whether the rites performed in
the celebration of this sacrament are becoming."

As they are articles of a "liturgical" nature written by a theologian, they have attracted very slight attention from theologians and
liturgists. The former have often seen them as a sort of appendix
piece, an exercise rendered obligatory by the medieval penchant for
the "mysteric." The latter have found it to be too far removed from
the "patristic ideal of the liturgy." We point out the already-dated
studies of Damasus Winzen and Pierre-Thomas Dehau,[4] and the
notes to A.-M. Roguet's French translation, after which nothing has
followed more recently than several pages from Enrico Mazza's *The
Celebration of the Eucharist*. Despite his evident interest and precise
exposition, E. Mazza sees nothing more in the liturgical passages of
Aquinas than a digest of allegorizing ritualism and Eucharistic realism.[5] For his part, Pierre-Marie Gy, without touching on Thomas's
expositio missae directly, has offered valuable remarks in several

3. See *ST* III, q. 64, a. 2, ad. 1.

4. See D. Winzen, *Das Geheimnis der Eucharistie*, in *Die deutsche Thomas-Ausgabe*,
vol. 30 (Salzburg: Pustet, 1938), and Pierre-Thomas Dehau, "La structure liturgique de
la messe d'après saint Thomas d'Aquin," La Clarté-Dieu 7 (Lyon: Éditions de l'Abeille,
1943).

5. See Enrico Mazza, *The Celebration of the Eucharist: The Origin of the Rite and the
Development of Its Interpretation* (Collegeville, MN: Liturgical Press, 1999), 199–214. —
We would like to point out, however, the attention given to the Thomistic *expositio missae* by David Berger in his *Thomas Aquinas and the Liturgy* (Naples, FL: Sapientia Press,
2005), as well as by Catherine Pickstock in her "Thomas Aquinas and the Quest for the
Eucharist," *Modern Theology* 15, no. 2 (April 1999), 158–80. Contrary to E. Mazza, D. Berger is a defender, even an apologist for Thomas's use of allegorical commentary—even the
most exaggerated (Berger, *Thomas Aquinas and the Liturgy*, 37–41); as for C. Pickstock,
an Anglican theologian, she perceives in the unfolding of the liturgical rite as Thomas

articles about the connection between Eucharistic theology and liturgy in Aquinas.[6] In addition to Fr. Gy's helpful articles, we must also point out an unpublished dissertation of Niels K. Rasmussen entitled, "Saint Thomas et les rites de la messe: Étude historique sur la *Somme Théologique* IIIa Pars, q. 83, aa. 4 et 5."[7]

An interdisciplinary study standing at the frontier between history and theology, Rasmussen's dissertation, which remains singular, indicates the path we must follow. On the one hand, articles 4 and 5 of question 83 suppose a theology of cult as elaborated throughout the *Summa*, including the treatise on the Eucharist; the question we shall discuss is, what can we observe about the role and value of liturgical signs in this theology of cult? On the other hand, these articles belong, as we have already mentioned, to the genre of the *expositio missae*, which is a type of exegetical treatise on the prayers and rites of the Mass that one might call the Western counterpart to the commentaries and mystagogical catecheses of the Eastern tradition. While it is true that Thomas's commentary is modeled on a program of liturgical celebration that follows the general outline of the historical Roman Mass, nevertheless his outlook is rather that of a mystagogue than of a historian of cult. In analyzing the prayers and rites, Aquinas often privileges the *spiritual* or *allegorical* sense, sometimes to the detriment of the *historical* or *literal* sense of the liturgy. It appears necessary, therefore, to precede our study of the commentary with a study of the method of the medieval *expositio missae*. To what extent was recourse to the spiritual sense of the liturgy considered

---

describes it (*ST* III, q. 83, a. 4), a veritable pedagogy of *desire* for the Eucharistic presence (Pickstock, "Thomas Aquinas and the Quest for the Eucharist," 168–73).

6. See Gy, "Prière eucharistique et paroles de la consécration selon les théologiens de Pierre Lombard à Saint Thomas," in *La liturgie dans l'histoire*, 211–21; "Avancées du traité de l'Eucharistie de saint Thomas dans la *Somme* par rapport aux *Sentences*," 219–28; "Divergences de théologie sacramentaire autour de saint Thomas," 425–33; "La documentation sacramentaire de Thomas d'Aquin," 425–31; etc.

7. N. K. Rasmussen's dissertation was written in 1963 at Saulchoir, under the direction of Fr. P.-M. Gy, to obtain a lectureship in theology. A dactylograph example is currently conserved at the Bibliothèque du Saulchoir (couvent Saint-Jacques, Paris).

legitimate? Can there be a balance between the two ways of reading the rites of the Church: one historical, the other spiritual and
theological? Having posed the problem, we follow Thomas's analyses. Some general remarks on the various actors in the Eucharistic
celebration as well as the gestures frequently repeated in it will also
be useful to guide our reading of the article's commentary on the Eucharistic celebration.

SACRAMENTS, LITURGICAL SIGNS, SACRAMENTALS

"In the use of the sacraments two things may be considered, namely
the worship of God and the sanctification of man."[8] Aquinas's affirmation, throughout the treatise on the sacraments in general, of the
cultic dimension of the sacraments (the term *cultus* appears there
forty-one times, and *rite*, eight times) testifies to his growing interest in the "liturgical" perspective and forms a sort of culmination
of his reflections on worship contained in the previous treatises—
in particular the treatises on the Old Law and the virtue of religion
in the *Secunda pars* and, in the *Tertia pars*, on the Incarnate Word
and the Passion of Christ.[9]

It is "by his Passion [that] Christ inaugurated the rites of the
Christian religion."[10] Everything derives from his priesthood:[11]
priests and faithful are rendered participants in and associated to the
priestly function of the divine Head through the instrumental causes
of a cult of which Christ is the sole pontiff. Nonetheless, the divine

8. *ST* III, q. 60, a. 5.
9. The great cultic themes of the *Commentary on the Letter to the Hebrews*, developed
during his Roman teaching days in the years 1265–1268, besides orienting the sacerdotal
dimension of his Christology, certainly contributed to the evolution of St. Thomas's sacramental theology in a cultic direction, as seen in the redaction of the *Tertia pars*, which
is dated around 1271–1273.
10. *ST* III, q. 62, a. 5.
11. See *ST* III, q. 63, a. 3: "Now the whole rite of the Christian religion is derived
from Christ's priesthood."

cult continues to be celebrated in a manner proportionate to the condition of the religious man in this life, which is to say, in an economy of sensible signs that are henceforth granted a supernatural efficacy. Signs of the divine action whose celebration is confided to the Church, the sacraments represent, reproduce, and contain in an efficacious manner the perfect cult of the Redeemer. The religious man of the New Law of grace is deputed to the use of these signs. Rendered a participant in the priesthood of Christ, the religious man in the New Law is not only the recipient of sacramental signs, but further, in virtue of the cultic dimension inherent in these signs, a subject of liturgical actions.[12]

Thus the liturgy of the Church essentially consists in celebrating the sacramental signs that her divine Head has entrusted to her. In so doing, the Church, in virtue of the power that she has received from the Lord and in accord with her nature as a religious society, hierarchical and sacral, provides for the *solemn* celebration of the sacraments, surrounding them with liturgical signs that prepare, manifest, and extend the riches enclosed in the essential rite.[13] The term *solemnity* should not be understood as an accidental matter of decorum that one can lightly dispense with, nor something that may usefully be downplayed in the pursuit of authentic devotion. If it is secondary, it is so in relation to the *substance*, to that which, being instituted by Christ, is essential and primary and of absolute necessity for there to be a sacrament. Secondary is not a synonym for superfluous. Rather it corresponds here, in the wake of the treatise on religion, to the subordination of exterior acts to interior cult—acts

---

12. See Turrini, *L'anthropologie sacramentelle de saint Thomas d'Aquin*, 109: "The sacraments are thus charged with an anthropologically positive meaning; they can "make perfect," rendering man a citizen of the new cultic age, a subject who manifests his sanctification by a cultic motion toward God. Thomas thus completes the discourse he began with the virtue of religion."

13. See *ST* III, q. 64, a. 2, ad 1: "Human institutions observed in the sacraments are not essential to the sacrament; but belong to the solemnity which is added to the sacraments in order to arouse devotion and reverence in the recipients. But those things that are essential to the sacrament, are instituted by Christ Himself, Who is God and man."

both necessary and due, as they are proportioned to the nature of religious man and ordained to stimulate and express the cult of the spirit.[14]

Since religious man belongs by nature to a society that is also naturally cultic, acts of cult must be conducted in a public manner, which is to say, solemnly. It is the social and public dimension of cult that principally accounts for liturgical solemnity; thus, under the law of grace it is in the Church, the cultic society born of Christ, that we find the reasons for the solemnity of Christian cult. Of course, the necessity of secondary liturgical signs is not absolute as regards the production of the substance of the sacrament; nevertheless, the prayers and rites "contribute to the solemnity with which they are surrounded in order to excite the devotion and respect of those who receive them."[15] They have been instituted by reason of the *solemnity* inherent in the Church-society's cult. As a hierarchical and public society constituted by sacramental elements, the Church must ensure that the perennial memorial of the Lord is celebrated in a solemn manner, which is to say in proportion to her constitution. Not only is liturgical solemnity fitting for the Church, but, more than that, it is the supreme manifestation of her being and her structure: the Church is never more herself, manifesting the whole truth of her constitution and the mystery of her hierarchy, than when she solemnly celebrates the Eucharistic sacrifice. This observation, which seems to us to explain the purpose of the ceremonial dimension of

---

14. See *ST* II-II, q. 81, a. 7; q. 84, a. 2.

15. *ST* III, q. 64, a. 2, ad. 1. See also *ST* III, q. 66, a. 3, ad 5, and a. 10. It will also be fruitful to recall what Thomas says about the solemnity of the vow in the treatise on religion (*ST* II-II, q. 88, a. 7): "The manner in which a thing is solemnized depends on its nature: thus when a man takes up arms he solemnizes the fact in one way, namely, with a certain display of horses and arms and a concourse of soldiers, while a marriage is solemnized in another way, namely, the array of the bridegroom and bride and the gathering of their kindred. Now a vow is a promise made to God: wherefore, the solemnization of a vow consists in something spiritual pertaining to God; i.e. in some spiritual blessing or consecration which, in accordance with the institution of the apostles, is given when a man makes profession of observing a certain rule, in the second degree after the reception of Holy Orders."

liturgy, is based also on the history of the Eucharistic celebration, which clearly identifies the communal episcopal Mass as normative, the form from which every simplified—which is to say less *solemn*—form is derived.[16]

Entrusted to the Church, the sacramental signs should be celebrated in the most fitting manner possible. Entirely situated within the order of signs, analogy, and proportion, the liturgy must strive to manifest and measure up to the immense richness and profundity of the mystery. It does so by virtue of the dignity and authority of the Church, associated by Christ in the economy of her hierarchy to the instrumental causality of his sacred humanity. The Church in her liturgy has elevated a whole complex of words, gestures, things, and places to the order of grace in order to ensure that redeemed humanity has access to the interior plenitude of the sacramental treasure she has been charged to transmit. Her rites render apparent what is hidden and sensible what is abstract, that. Because they are located in the realm of sacramentality, which they surround and manifest, we can group this collection of secondary liturgical signs under the term *sacramentals*—as long as this term is disengaged from a reductive definition of a casuistic variety.

If Thomas did not dedicate a specific question in the *Summa* to sacramentals, the treatise on the sacraments in general, nevertheless, contains many allusions to them, and explicitly borrows the term *sacramentalia* from Peter Lombard's *Sentences*[17]—a term much more apt than the *sacramenta minora* earlier advanced by Hugh of Saint Victor.[18] In the mind of our Doctor, the sacramentals should not be reduced to certain minor isolated rites and devotionals. On the contrary, the hints contained in the aforementioned treatise of the

---

16. See Niels K. Rasmussen, "Célébration épiscopale et célébration presbytérale: Un essai de typologie," in *Segni e riti nella Chiesa altomedievale occidentale*, in *Settimane di studio del Centro italiano di studi sull'alto medioevo* 33 (Spoleto, Italy: Fondazione Centro Italiano Di Studi Sull'Alto Medioevo, 1987), 581–603.

17. See *ST* III, q. 65, a. 1, ad 8: "[Venial sin] is taken away by certain sacramentals, for instance, holy water and such like"; Peter Lombard, *Libri IV Sent.*, d. 6, no. 8.

18. Hugh of Saint Victor, *De sacramentis Christianae fidei*, bk. 2, part 9.

Summa permit us to define them by virtue of the similarity they bear to the sacraments under the aspect of sign. In fact, in imitation of the sacraments, the sacramentals are at the same time signs of grace and signs of cult, by virtue of a particular institution and in a particular mode that we must briefly outline here.

In contrast to the sacraments, the sacramentals, or liturgical signs, have not been the object of divine determination or institution. Rather, they have been determined or instituted by the authority of the Church. Charged by the Lord with using and dispensing the sacraments, the Church—whose horizon with respect to the effusion of grace remains instrumental and ministerial[19]—has received the fundamental trajectory to which she must relate everything, and on which depends the validity of the diverse secondary signs she has the power to establish. So, in instituting the sacramentals—religious signs that, without belonging to the essence of the sacraments, are more or less ordered to the sacraments—the Church claims the various exterior acts of religion as her own and orients them to the reception of grace and the supernatural signification proper to sacramental cult.

Therefore, like the sacraments, the sacramentals are signs. Most often, they have the same constitution as the sacraments, composed of sensible objects and words, but they are distinguished in a fundamental manner with respect to the efficacy of grace. Different from sacraments, which both signify and really cause sanctifying grace in virtue of a physical and perfective efficacy, the sacramentals for their part possess only a dispositive efficacy,[20] by which they prepare or

19. See *ST* III, q. 64, a. 5, 6, 8 & 9; q. 83, a. 3, ad 8 : "*Dispensatio sacramentorum pertinet ad ministros Ecclesiae, sed consecratio eorum est ab ipso Deo. Et ideo ministri Ecclesiae non habent aliquid statuere circa formam consecrationis: sed circa usum sacramenti et modum celebrandi.*" ["The dispensing of the sacraments belongs to the Church's ministers; but their consecration is from God Himself. Consequently, the Church's ministers can make no ordinances regarding the form of the consecration, but only the use and the manner of celebrating."]

20. *ST* III, q. 60, a. 2, ad 3: "Names are given to things considered in reference to their end and state of completeness. Now a disposition is not an end, whereas perfection

perfect the principal action of the sacraments.[21] Nevertheless, even if their efficacy is subject to the general laws that govern the efficacy of prayer, the sacramentals, as acts of the Spouse of Christ, transcend the moral dispositions of the subjects who practice or receive them. These sacramentals are distinct from the "sacred" realities of the cult of natural religion and the Old Law, in that they possess in themselves a certain objective value, the minister who performs them acting not in his own name but in the name of the Church, with whose prayers God is well pleased.

Further, like the sacraments, sacramentals are the signs of a sanctifying cult. Sensible signs instituted by the Church to manifest her cult and her faith, liturgical signs also predispose the soul for grace and serve as remedies against venial sin.[22] Nevertheless, by too often considering them under the aspect of efficacy, a certain sacramental theology has had the tendency, as Fr. Roguet noted, to "relegate sacramentals to the extreme circumference of the sacramental sphere,"[23] assigning them only a medicinal function.[24] If we hold, on the contrary, that the sacramentals are signs in their own right, signs of the Church that are ordered to the principal signs, which are the sacraments, we are on the way to understanding their real importance in the cultic organism of the New Law.

---

is. Consequently things that signify disposition to holiness are not called sacraments … ; only those are called sacraments which signify the perfection of holiness in man."

21. *ST* III, q. 65, a. 1, ad 6: "Holy water and other consecrated things are not called sacraments, because they do not produce the sacramental effect, which is the receiving of grace. They are, however, a kind of disposition to the sacraments: either by removing obstacles; thus holy water is ordained against the snares of the demons, and against venial sins, or by making things suitable for the conferring of a sacrament; thus the altar and vessels are consecrated through reverence for the Eucharist."

22. In addition to *ST* III, q. 65, a. 1, ad 6, see *ST* III, q. 87, a. 3 (in the treatise on the sacrament of penance).

23. Aimon-Marie Roguet, "Renseignements techniques: A. Notes doctrinales thomistes: IX. L'organisme sacramentel (Question 65)," in Thomas Aquinas, *Somme théologique: Les Sacrements*, 3^a, *Questions 60–65* (Paris: Éditions de la Revue des jeunes, 1945), 369–77, at 375.

24. According to Journet, "Questions détachées sur la sacramentalité," 147, this point of view is founded upon a hasty reading of *ST* III, q. 87, a. 3, and of *De malo*, q. 7, a. 12.

In fact, in the celebration and administration of the sacraments—*circa usum sacramenti et modum celebrandi*[25]—the Church, who "has a good intention both as to the validity of the sacrament and as to the use thereof,"[26] has established ritual ordinances that, the Angelic Doctor says, "are directed by the wisdom of Christ."[27] Under the direction of the Holy Spirit, she surrounds the sacraments—acts of the divine head—with prayers and rites that are ordered to them, that manifest the faith, and that express the intention of the Spouse. These prayers and these rites are thus endowed with a particular virtue in view of what they express and signify, which is the cult of Christ and the Church, a unique cult—having divine efficacy—in which they participate. In the celebration of the Eucharistic sacrifice, as we shall see, the gestures of offering, the Eucharistic prayer, and the diverse symbolic rites are there to manifest, according to Thomas, the representation of the sacrifice of Calvary, the faith of the Church in the mystery celebrated, and all the reverence due to the sacrament;[28] all this confirms the irreplaceable role of liturgical traditions in both approaching and understanding the sacrifice of the altar.[29]

For that matter, the rites of consecration and benediction of various places and objects, which are ordered in a more or less similar manner to the offering of sacrifice, can also enter into the category

25. *ST* III, q. 83, a. 3, ad 8.

26. *ST* III, q. 64, a. 10, ad 1.

27. *ST* III, q. 72, a. 12 : "On the contrary, it is the use of the Church, who is governed by the Holy Ghost. I answer that, Our Lord promised his faithful (Matthew 18:20) saying: 'Where there are two or three gathered together in My name, there am I in the midst of them.' And therefore we must hold firmly that the Church's ordinations are directed by the wisdom of Christ. And for this reason we must look upon it as certain that the rite observed by the Church, in this and the other sacraments, is appropriate."

28. See *ST* III, q. 83, a. 5. We analyze the body of the article at greater length *infra*.

29. See Roguet, "Renseignements techniques," 376 "[The sacrificial value of the Eucharist] is made precise and explicit by the rites, which are secondary but indispensable: words of the canon, use of the altar, signs of the cross, etc. etc. . . . which clarify that in pronouncing these words the priest is not engaging in a simple commemorative meditation, but truly performs a sacrifice. In the same way in the fore-Mass and the Divine Office attached to it, ought they not be considered as sacramentals of primary importance?"

of sacramentals. For these rites do more than separate places and objects from the profane realm, a sacralization that previous cultic regimes were capable of doing, but rather, and most properly, they designate them to signify a *spiritual* cult, acceptable and sanctifying, in which the divine power continuously operates.[30] After their fashion, the sacred realities ordered to the celebration of sacramental cult are at the same time both signs and instruments of spiritual virtue, in the sense that they possess a value of efficacy entirely relative to the interior cult of the supernaturalized soul in which they excite the acts of the infused virtue of religion. Thus Aquinas remarks, for example, that the material church and altar, being separated from the profane realm and consecrated by the priests and rites of the Church for the offering of the Eucharistic sacrifice, receive from the rite of consecration "special spiritual virtue from the consecration, whereby they are rendered fit for the divine worship, so that man derives devotion therefrom, making him more fitted for divine functions, unless this be hindered by want of reverence."[31]

As liturgical signs, sacramentals are a part of the Church, the contribution of her ministerial character to the celebration of the cult of the sacraments,[32] which she has received the mission to celebrate solemnly for the building of the Kingdom to the end of time. Also, as Hyacinthe-François Dondaine once wrote, the sacramentals

---

30. See *ST* III, q. 83, a. 3: "Hence we consecrate those things which we make use of in this sacrament; both that we may show our reverence for the sacrament, and in order to represent the holiness which is the effect of the Passion of Christ, according to Hebrews 13:12: 'Jesus, that He might sanctify the people by His own blood,' etc."

31. *ST* III, q. 83, a. 3, ad 3.

32. See Turrini, *L'Anthropologie sacramentelle*, 513: "Thomas knows full well that the Church has put something of her own into the sacraments such as he knew them in their liturgical expression. Despite the lack of historical and critical comfort regarding the formation and evolution of the Sacramentaries and Rituales, perhaps there was no difficulty for him in admitting that the sacramental actions bore elements of ecclesiastical institution. But that isn't the problem. Thomas traced a line of demarcation by which he was able to safeguard both the legitimacy of the Church's contribution to the sacramental organism and the relativity of this contribution. The power of the Church is for Thomas very circumscribed: it does not go beyond the world of man and has only an anthropological value."

and the solemnity proper to them "give the sacrament its full cultic dimensions."[33] We would add that, just as the sacraments are signs of the causality of Christ, who works through and in them, at the same time the sacramentals and liturgical rites are signs of the Church's agent causality. The Church, forming one body with her divine head, renders to the Father, in the unity of the Spirit, the cult that is pleasing to God, whence flows every grace, and at the center of which is the sacrifice of the Eucharist.[34] In order to understand the liturgy, to grasp its essence and its theology, it is thus necessary, as A.-M. Roguet insisted sixty years ago, to reunite "sacraments and sacramentals into one homogenous synthesis organized around the Eucharist."[35]

---

33. See Dondaine, "La définition des sacrements dans la *Somme théologique*," 226–27: "This definition [of sacrament as sign] reveals a fundamental and primary aspect of the sacramental institution; the way it is rooted in human nature and assumed into the divine economy of salvation through faith in Christ; its aspect as a sign of public profession of religious faith: *sacramenta fidei*. It also furnishes, right from the outset, a stable basis of intelligibility for the subject, useful to the research of the theologian, but also able to guide the conduct of the minister and the initiatives of the Church with respect to the *sacramentalia* and *solemnitas* that give the sacrament its full cultic dimensions. Useful, because it deals with an eminently human thing: signs." This is a much more comprehensive vision of sacramentals than that to which they have been too long confined, as explained by A.-M. Roguet: "For if the primary characteristic of sacramentals is the fact that they are instituted by the Church, aren't we compelled to classify those sacramentals by which the Church performs her sacerdotal action, the office of praise to her Spouse, as being of first rank, in preference to those isolated and voluntary rites by which individuals can obtain 'certain special spiritual effects,' such as medallions, Agnus Deis, and benedictions of the Blessed Sacrament?" (Roguet, "Renseignement techniques," 376).

34. Roguet, "Renseignements techniques," 377 : "It seems to us that our understanding of the sacramental organism that prolongs the action of the Incarnate Word among us would be greatly deepened and enriched if, instead of treating the several sacraments first and afterward the sacramentals, seen as a patchwork of isolated rites, we considered it in light of an organic image: it is a 'system'—as when we speak of a 'solar system.' Its sun is the Eucharist, the sacrament *par excellence*, from which all the other sacraments depend and to which all the other sacraments tend; they are like the planets that gravitate around this central star. And the sacramentals are like the asteroids, the fringes of this divine mantle of the continuing Incarnation."

35. Roguet, "Renseignements techniques," 377.

GENRE AND METHOD OF THE *EXPOSITIO MISSAE*

These considerations of a general nature constitute a sort of sketch of the liturgical theology of the Angelic Doctor. It was necessary to return to the foundations, to distinguish the framework on which the particular liturgical elements will be attached. We now approach the sanctuary and, under the guidance of our Doctor, we fix and exercise our regard on the ceremonies and the prayers of the Eucharistic sacrifice. But in the first place, what is Thomas's view of the Eucharistic celebration? In what manner, with what method, does he analyze the prayers and rites?

Genesis and Developments of the *Expositio Missae*

Forming a sort of insert into the *Summa*, articles 4 and 5 of question 83—the former on the words, the latter on the gestures of the Eucharistic sacrifice—belong to a genre of liturgical commentary that was very popular in the Middle Ages: the *expositio missae*.[36] In an article whose conclusions are still authoritative, Dom André Wilmart has shown that the Carolingian capitularies from the end of the eighth and the beginning of the ninth centuries, by dint of their marked insistence on the necessity of the clergy's comprehension of the prayers of the Mass, were in their primitive redactions a kind of liturgical gloss for the use of priests.[37] They were at first nothing but brief literal commentaries on the text of the Gregorian *ordo*, from the Preface to the *Ite missa est*. But very soon theological

---

36. The other articles of question 83, notably articles 2, 3, and 6, do not belong directly to the genre of *expositio missae*. Article 2 discusses the fittingness of a liturgical hour for the celebration, and article 3 that of place and consecrated objects. Article 6, where he details the accidents that might occur during the celebration in handling the Eucharistic species, corresponds to the chapter *De defectibus in celebratione missarum occurrentibus* of the Tridentine Missal.

37. André Wilmart, "Expositio missae," in *Dictionnaire d'archéologie chrétienne et de liturgie*, ed. Henri Leclercq, vol. 5, part 1 (Paris: Letouzey et Ané, 1922), 1014–27. The contents of this article were summarized and its biography brought up to date by Pierre-Marie Gy, "Expositiones missae," *Bulletin du Comité des études de la Compagnie de Saint-Sulpice* 22 (1958), 222–31.

reflections and allegorical elaborations were added. Word-by-word analyses of prayers gradually gave way to more structured expositions that gave more place to examination of the rites. They were intended for both the instruction of the faithful and for the understanding of the clergy and were often inserted inside general treatises on liturgy or even canonical and theological summas.[38]

From the Carolingian period, viz. shortly after the birth of the genre in the West, the *expositio missae* drew closer—and was perhaps influenced by—the Eastern method, particularly the "mystagogical catecheses" which, from the second half of the fourth century at Antioch and Jerusalem, later at Constantinople in the seventh and eighth centuries, had elaborated a symbolic understanding of the liturgy.[39] The ripest fruit of this evolution of the *expositio* was without contest the *De officio missae*, as seen in the third book of the *Liber officialis* of Amalarius of Metz,[40] a monumental liturgical treatise (after the fashion of Isidore of Seville) written around 827–832. Amalarius's

38. In fact, Wilmart distinguished two periods of the *expositio missae*, the first, that of the *expositio* properly speaking, executed through the insertion of spiritual and doctrinal commentaries. Thus he proposed an inventory of the "genuine *expositio missae*," so as not to confound them with the *ordines* and other treatises of the Amalarian tradition. However, we generally understand by the term *expositio missae* any explanation of the Mass in the medieval period, whether it constitutes a singular work or an insertion into a liturgical or even canonical or theological treatise. For study of the *expositiones* of the second period, Wilmart refers to the classic work of Adolph Franz (*Die Messe im deutschen Mittelalter* [Fribourg-en-Brisgau: Beiträge zur Geschichte der Liturgie und des religiösen Volkslebens, 1902]), but it is now useful to consult the studies of Mary Schaefer, "Latin Mass Commentaries from the Ninth through the Twelfth Centuries: Chronology and Theology," in *Fountain of Life*, ed. Gerard Austin (Washington DC: Pastoral Press, 1991), 35–49; and "Twelfth Century Latin Commentaries on the Mass: The Relationship of the Priest to Christ and to the People," *Studia liturgica* 15 (1983): 76–86. So also the work of Mazza, *The Celebration of the Eucharist*, 177–98.

39. See among others, Jean Daniélou, *The Bible and the Liturgy* (Notre Dame, Ind.: University of Notre Dame Press, 1956), 127–61; Gy, "*Expositiones missae*," 230–31; Paul Bradshaw, *The Search for the Origins of Christian Worship: Sources and Methods for the Study of Early Liturgy* (Oxford: Oxford University Press, 1993), 141–50; Robert F. Taft, *The Byzantine Rite: A Short History* (Collegeville, MN: Liturgical Press, 1992), 45–48; Enrico Mazza, *Mystagogy: A Theology of Liturgy in the Patristic Age* (New York: Pueblo, 1989); and Mazza, *The Celebration of the Eucharist*, 147–54.

40. Amalarius of Metz, *Liber officialis*, in *Amalarii episcopi opera liturgica omnia*, vol. 2, ed. J. M. Hanssens (Vatican City: Biblioteca Apostolica Vaticana, 1950).

expositio contained all at once ritual directions, didactic analysis, and doctrinal and mystical commentary. If the parallel between Scripture commentary and explication of the Mass did not receive systematic formulation here, still the method adopted was precisely the same as the method of Scripture commentary flourishing in the same period—that is to say, a research privileging the spiritual sense of the liturgy, above the *letter* of the prayer and the rite, in its triple allegorical, tropological, and anagogical dimension.[41] But Amalarius had a marked preference for the rememorative type of allegory. He set all his culture, his piety, and his imagination to its service. Besides the constant desire to attach figures of the Old Law to the rites of the altar, he finds especially in the development of the ceremonies of the Mass a veritable chronology of the work of redemption; from the Incarnation, represented by the liturgical rites of entry, right up to the Ascension, signified by the *Ite missa est* and the end of the celebration. As for the rites of the Canon, they trace precisely and represent perfectly the events of the Passion.[42]

Thus one is confronted in the liturgy with what M.-D. Chenu defined, a propos of scriptural allegorism, as "a continuous extrapolation of the literal content," even a "pulverization of the text."[43] This danger was not lost on those contemporaries of Amalarius who were anxious for an understanding of the Mass closer to the sense of the Fathers, such as that of the deacon Florus of Lyon, author, around 835–838, of an *Opusculum de actione missarum*.[44] In reaction to the

41. On the antiquity of this method in liturgical commentary, see Robert F. Taft, "The Liturgy of the Great Church, An Initial Synthesis of Structure and Interpretation on the Eve of Iconoclasm," *Dumbarton Oaks Papers* 34/35 (1980–1981): 45–75; *The Byzantine Rite*, 45–47.

42. Amalarius of Metz, *Liber officialis*, bk. 3, ch. 28 (ed. Hanssens, 355, no. 8): "Celebratio huius officii ita currit, ut ostendatur quid illo in tempore actum sit circa passionem Domini et sepulturam eius, et quomodo nos id ad memoriam reducere debeamus per obsequium nostrum, quod pro nobis factum est." See a summary of the celebration of the Mass according to Amalarius in Mazza, *The Celebration of the Eucharist*, 162–67.

43. Chenu, "Les deux âges de l'allégorisme scripturaire au Moyen Âge," 26.

44. Florus of Lyon, *De expositione missae*, PL 119, col. 15–72. See also Paul Duc, *Étude sur l'Expositio missae de Florus de Lyon, suivie d'une édition critique du texte* (Lyon: Belley, 1937).

imagination of the cleric of Metz, although without ever citing him by name, Florus chose to comment principally on the text of the *ordo*, resorting to citations of Scripture and the doctrine of the Fathers.[45] In contrast to Amalarius, he is almost entirely reticent with regard to rites.[46] But it was certainly this latter defect that would restrict the popularity of the Lyonnais deacon's austere and lofty opuscule; clergy and faithful preferred treatises that explained their roles as rapt actors and witnesses of the Franco-Roman rites.

Nevertheless, if allegorism was received by the greater part of commentators and liturgists of the Middle Ages, not everyone made the pious excesses of Amalarius their own. Some even preferred the method of Florus of Lyon, such as John of Fécamp († ca. 1078) in his *De corpore et sanguine Domini*,[47] Odo of Tournai († 1113) in his *Expositio in Canonem missae*,[48] and especially St. Albert the Great, who in his *De sacrificio missae*, without denying the legitimacy of the spiritual sense as such, vigorously attacks the so-called rememorative allegory.[49] Others, though tributaries of Amalarius, disputed a number

45. On the value of Florus's exposition, see André Wilmart, "*Expositio* missae," 1025–26; and Mazza, *The Celebration of the Eucharist*, 173–74.

46. See Mazza, *The Celebration of the Eucharist*, 173–74: "It may be said in summary that there is a radical difference in both object and method between the commentary of Florus and that of Amalarius. Florus comments on a text, that is, that which is *written* in the sacramentary, while Amalarius is not concerned with texts but comments on the rites that are performed and are *seen* by priests and faithful during the celebration. As far as method is concerned, Florus tries to be strictly literal, while Amalarius concentrates on the images, figures, and symbols to which allegory gives him access." See also Adolf Kolping, "Amalar von Metz und Florus von Lyon: Zeugen eines Wandels im liturgischen Mysterienverständnis in der Karolingerzeit," *Zeitschrift für katholische Theologie* 73, no. 4 (1951): 424–64.

47. John of Fécamp, *De corpore et sanguine Domini*, PL 101, col. 1085–1098.

48. Odo of Tournai, *Expositio in Canonem missae*, PL 160, col. 1053–1070.

49. Albert the Great, *De sacrificio missae*, in *Opera omnia*, vol. 38, ed. Auguste Borgnet (Paris: Apud Ludovicum Vivès, 1890), 1–189. See Jungmann, *The Mass of the Roman Rite*, 1:113–14: "First of all, [Albertus Magnus] presents an enlightened and theologically grounded explanation of the course of that Mass that is for the most part derived from the text of the Mass *ordo*. Besides he makes repeated thrusts at the allegorical exposition, especially at the rememorative. He says it is *mirabile* to refer the silence of the Mass proper to events in the story of our Lord's Passion—things in no way touched upon in the text of the Mass. In fact, in reference to the explanation that the kissing of the altar at the *Supplices* signified Judas' traitorous kiss, and the signs of the cross that follow signify the bonds

of his interpretations, such as Remigius of Auxerre († ca. 908) whose *Liber de divinis officiis* is however equally indebted to Florus;[50] Bernold of Constance († ca. 1100) in his *Micrologus de ecclesiasticis observationibus*;[51] and John Beleth, author, ca. 1160–1164, of a *Summa de ecclesiasticis officiis*;[52] among others. In the context of the Paschasian debates, several joined their theological interests to Amalarian allegorism: so Petrus Pictor in his *Liber de sacramentis* (ca. 1100);[53] Rupert of Deutz († ca. 1129), author of a treatise *De divinis officiis*;[54] Honorius Augustodunensis († 1156) in the commentary contained in his *Gemma Animae*;[55] Lothar of Segni, whose *De sacro altaris mysterio* was written around 1195–1197, before the author became Innocent III;[56] and others. Finally there were later disciples and continuators of Amalarius, including Ivo of Chartres († 1115) in his *Sermones de ecclesiasticis sacramentis*;[57] Praepositinus of Cremona († 1210) in his *Summa de officiis*;[58] Sicard of Cremona († ca. 1215), author of a volumi-

---

and ropes by which our Savior was led to Annas, he says scornfully: *omnino profanum est et omnibus fidelibus abominandum*. The different signification attached to the signs of the cross at the *Quam oblationem* he termed: *deliramenta et hominum illiteratorum.*"

50. Remigius of Auxerre, *Liber de divinis officiis*, ch. 60, PL 101, col. 1246–1271.

51. Bernold of Constance, *Micrologus de ecclesiasticis observationibus*, PL 151, col. 974–1022.

52. John Beleth, *Summa de ecclesiasticis officiis*, ed. H. Douteil, Corpus Christianorum Continuatio Mediaevalis (CCCM) 41A (Turnhout: Brepols, 1976).

53. Petrus Pictor, "Liber de sacramentis," in *Petri Pictoris Carmina : nec non Petri de Sancto Audemaro Librum de coloribus faciendis*, ed. L. van Acker, CCCM 25 (Turnhout: Brepols, 1972), 11–46.

54. Rupert of Deutz, *Liber de divinis officiis*, ed. H. Haacke, CCCM 7 (Turnhout: Brepols, 1967).

55. Honorius Augustodunensis, *Jewel of the Soul*, ed. and trans. Zachary Thomas and Gerhard Eger, 2 vols. (Cambridge, MA: Harvard University Press, 2023).

56. Innocent III, *De sacro altaris mysterio* (PL 217, col. 775–914). See the critical edition and French translation *Les mystères des messes: Présentation, édition critique et traduction française*, ed. and trans. Olivier Hanne, 2 vols. (Huningue: Presses universitaires Rhin & Danube, 2022). For a partial edition, see David Wright, "A Medieval Commentary on the Mass: *Particulae* 2–3 and 5–6 of the *De missarum mysteriis* (ca. 1195) of Cardinal Lothar of Segni (Pope Innocent III) (University of Notre Dame, PhD., 1977). For an English translation, see *The Mysteries of the Mass; The Four Images of Marriage*, trans. David M. Foley (Saint Marys, KS: Angelus Press, 2023).

57. Ivo of Chartres, *Sermones de ecclesiasticis sacramentis et officiis*, PL 162, col. 505–610.

58. Praepositinus of Cremona, *Praepositini Cremonensis Tractatus de Officiis*, ed. J. A. Corbett, Publications in Medieval Studies 21 (Notre Dame, IN: University of Notre Dame Press, 1969).

nous *Mitrale seu de officiis ecclesiasticis Summa*,[59] but overshadowed at the end of the century, around 1285–1295, by the *Rationale divinorum officiorum* of William Durandus, bishop of Mende (✝1296),[60] about whom Timothy M. Thibodeau has said that "it is incontestably the definitive work of a voluminous medieval literature of expositions on the liturgy."[61]

It is in the midst of this vast movement that we must now situate the Thomistic *expositio*.

59. *Sicardi Cremonensis episcopi Mitralis de officiis*, CCCM 228, ed. Gábor Sarbak and Lorenz Weinrich (Turnhout: Brepols, 2008). See Mazza, *The Celebration of the Eucharist*, 177–79, at 177: "One aspect of his work should be pointed out: for every rite on which he comments he provides the reader with a great many interpretations, one after another, without ever singling out one as better or more meaningful than the others. All the interpretations are logical and are strictly based on one or more passages of the Bible; all are traditional interpretations already developed by other authors, the Fathers or the Medieval commentators, and all are equally possible and acceptable. For Sicard, it is a matter of choosing a method, and this is something quite original; no less original is his realization that the method of the four senses, used in interpreting the Scriptures, can be applied also to the interpretation of the liturgy. He has thus grasped clearly, although perhaps unconsciously, a point that is characteristic of the patristic understanding of the liturgy, and he uses it skillfully and with freedom."

60. William Durandus, *Rationale divinorum officiorum*, bks. I–IV, ed. A. Davril and Timothy M. Thibodeau, CCCM 140 (Turnhout: Brepols, 1995).

61. Timothy M. Thibodeau, "Les sources du *Rationale* de Guillaume Durand," in *Guillaume Durand, évêque de Mende (v. 1230–1296), Canoniste, liturgiste et homme politique*, ed. Pierre Marie Gy, OP (Paris: Éditions du C.N.R.S., 1992), 143–53, at 143. See also Claude Barthe, "L'*esprit* et la *lettre*," introduction to *Le sens spirituel de la liturgie*, by William Durandus, trans. Dominique Millet-Gérard (Geneva: Ad Solem, 2003) 7–37, at 26: "A master teacher, [William Durandus] presents his liturgical subject as rigorously and systematically as he does his books of canon law (a law that, we must not forget, composed one body with dogmatic theology). He gathers everything that was said before him, classifies it, and augments it with distinctions if necessary. The reader must not be surprised by the fact that his very poetic material is classed like butterflies by an entomologist: according to whether the thurible has one, two, three, or four chains, it has different symbolic meanings, or more precisely degrees of meaning along the same line (i.e., the thurible basically represents Christ). But there is a grand cohesion underneath this rich veneer: the organization is not a simple catalogue of labels, but corresponds to theological-spiritual principles that are very clear and edifying to the soul. This arises from the systematic spirit of Durandus, but more profoundly from Christian tradition in general and Medieval tradition in particular, from its concern for orthodoxy and thus for unity and unification, which for the Medievals meant the collection and harmonization of authorities by means of interpretive clarifications that tried their best to master an inexhaustible material."

The Literal and Spiritual Senses of the Liturgy

In the wake of A. Wilmart[62] and liturgists such as J. A. Jungmann,[63] P.-M. Gy,[64] and more recently E. Mazza,[65] critiques have been mounted against the allegorical method of commentary, of which Amalarius, more than the inventor, was a sort of "high priest." They have highlighted the arbitrary constructions and the imaginative piety of these works. They have emphasized the decisive influence of the cleric of Metz on the greater part of the *expositiones missae* of the Middle Ages, from the *Liber de divinis officiis* of Remigius of Auxerre to the fourth book of the *Rationale divinorum officiorum* of Durandus of Mende, and thence on the ritual elaborations of the medieval period

---

62. See André Wilmart, *Expositio missae*, 1024: "From the Catholic doctrine that the Mass commemorates and reiterates the sacrifice of the cross, and from the authoritative examples of the Fathers and ancient liturgical writers, the 'high priest of symbolism,' as this friend of Louis the Pious was called, drew by his indiscreet zeal consequences one is obliged to qualify as absurd. Unfortunately, thanks to the success of his book and despite the soon-forgotten condemnation of the synod of Quiersy (838), he managed to infest nearly the entire liturgical literature of the Middle Ages with his fantasies. The Mass is, from beginning to end, nothing but a figure, or rather a drama, a sequence of scenes from the life of the Savior up to the Ascension, comprising the years of evangelical ministry and even, by consequence, the Old Testament; no improbability escapes this system, where everything is permitted under the pretext of piety. In this account, the ceremonies have no immediate sense, only what we give to them, something multiform, always admirable and admissible as long as it is symbolic. But the ceremonies in particular offer open season to the fantasy of the interpreter. The sturdy prayers of the Roman tradition cannot be treated so liberally and so, either they are simply omitted by the interpreter or else, if it is sometimes judged necessary to mention them, a brief mention is made of the literal meaning only, even at the risk of contradicting the wider exegesis of the texts of the Mass."

63. See Jungmann, *The Mass of the Roman Rite*, 1:87–91.

64. See Gy, "*Expositiones missae*," 230–31: "In the fourth century, the celebration of the stages of salvation history, till that time commemorated in the unity of the Paschal feast, were spread out across an annual liturgical cycle. Theodore of Mopsuestia and Amalarius wanted to do quite the same for the Mass: to discover in the sequences of ceremonies of the Mass the different stages of the history of salvation. But the procedure of Amalarius is artificial because he latches on to fictitious detail and superimposes his imaginative schema on the Eucharistic liturgy. Instead of helping us to understand the unfolding of the words and rites, instead of outlining the development of the text and the liturgical action, his symbolism actually hides them and obscures them."

65. See Mazza, *The Celebration of the Eucharist*, 162–72.

and the understanding of the Mass in general until the Reformation and beyond.

Setting aside the question of Amalarius's influence, real or overstated, claims like these have contributed to throw no little suspicion on the mystagogic approach to the liturgy and, in recent times, to discredit the value and the significance of medieval ritual developments that, grafted onto the ancient Gregorian *ordo* over the course of five centuries, have produced nothing but a "liturgy encumbered with secondary, not to say superfluous, signs."[66] Now, if we take this as our optic, our reading of the Thomistic *expositio* will show it be a carefully reasoned and commentated catalogue of obsolete ritual signs, or even a spiritual collection of *antiquitates liturgicae*. Then, the historical inquiry may be completed by identifying its sources and discovering its probable influences. Yet without downplaying the importance of historical inquiry, we believe that Thomas's text, precisely because it combines both the literal and the spiritual explanation of rites, invites the contemporary reader to reflect on the nature and role of rite itself, and thus perhaps to arrive at a more profound understanding of the spirit of the liturgy. The fact of liturgical allegorism, so rich in all of its consequences, thus merits to be better understood, even if only to better define its influence and mark its limits. The following remarks are meant as a contribution to this reflection.

For Amalarius and almost every one of the medieval commentators, there is a very direct line between the rite and the saving actions

---

66. Roguet, "Note explicative [52]" on 3^a, *Questions 79–83*, 317. See also, among others, Gy, "*Expositiones missae*," 231: "At the end of the Middle Ages, in the Latin West, the Amalarian method rediscovered the Eucharistic liturgy, and then it disappeared leaving only a few traces, thus: the multiplicity of signs of the cross in the Canon; see in the Germanic countries, the burial of Christ on Good Friday (the Eucharist was carried to the tomb) and the paraliturgy of the resurrection. A double evolution took place subsequently but in two directions that are not entirely homogenous: on one hand, the accent was placed on the Passion and its different phases, on the other there developed an epiphanic conception of the Mass regarded as the coming of the Lord among his people. The one and the other of these ways of understanding the Mass were imposed, preventing the faithful at that time from seeing the Mass as we see it."

of Christ. It is on this relation that the cleric of Metz desires to shed
light. In so doing, he continues in the Carolingian age the typological interpretation of the Eucharist found in the Fathers, that is to
say, he discovers the relation between the biblical figure and the sacramental reality. Now this reality, this mystery—the sacrament—is
composed of words and actions and is expressed in the order of liturgical signs. It is these signs, then, that we should explore, in the
light of spiritual science.[67] The procedure corresponds to that of
Theodore of Mopsuestia and classical Byzantine mystagogy.[68] Another fidelity to the thought of the Fathers and another point of contact with Eastern mystagogy; for Amalarius, the celebration of the
Mass constitutes a liturgical whole in which each particular rite has
its own importance relative to the global liturgical action. Consequently, various rites of the Mass, which is a global representation
of the redemptive Passion, are signs of various events of the Passion.
If Amalarius commits the error, however, of too much isolating the

67. See Maximus the Confessor, *Mystagogy*, in *Maximus the Confessor: Selected Writings*, trans. George C. Berthold (New York: Paulist Press, 1985), 183–225, at 189: "And
again, 'The invisible realities from the creation of the world have been perceived and are
recognized through the things he has made,' says the divine Apostle. And if we perceive
what does not appear by means of what does, as the Scripture has it, then much more
will visible things be understood by means of invisible by those who advance in spiritual
contemplation. Indeed, the symbolic contemplation of intelligent things by means of
visible realities is spiritual knowledge and understanding."

More than a century before Maximus, Pseudo-Dionysius the Areopagite, in his *Ecclesiastical Hierarchy*, gave a striking illustration of this principle: "And while the general
crowd is satisfied to look at the divine symbols, he, on the other hand, is continuously
uplifted by the divine Spirit toward the most holy source of the sacramental rite and he
does so in blessed and conceptual contemplations, in that purity which marks his life
as it conforms to God." *Pseudo-Dionysius: The Complete Works*, trans. Paul Rorem (New
York: Paulist Press, 1987), 211.

68. See Taft, *The Byzantine Rite*, 46: "Writing at the end of the fourth century—most
probably at Antioch in the decade before becoming bishop of Mopsuestia in 392, Theodore was the first to synthesize the two themes of the historical self-offering of Jesus and
the liturgy of the heavenly Christ in his *Catechetical Homilies* (15–16). Theodore offers
a synthesis of ritual representation in which the Jesus-anamnesis is conceived as a dramatic reenactment of the Paschal Mystery encompassing the whole eucharistic rite: the
earthly celebrant is seen as an image of the heavenly high priest, and the earthly liturgy as
an icon of his eternal heavenly oblation."

figures and rites and, under the influence of a juridical conception, constructs a symbolic edifice that is too complex, nevertheless, as E. Mazza writes, "the symbols expressing the relationship between the rite of the Mass and the Passion of Christ cannot be taken as purely allegorical, since they express a real relationship that has an ontological significance, although it is not based any longer on the philosophical conception that had been characteristic of the patristic period."[69]

Despite the presence of numerous dubious interpretations that a historical-liturgical study could permit us to assess, we must not hesitate to affirm—along with Amalarius and the medievals, thus with Thomas Aquinas but also with Theodore and the mystagogues of the Christian Orient—the intrinsic value of the rite, the link that it maintains with the spiritual reality that it signifies, without forgetting the essential role of the hierarch who exercises the sacramental function.[70] We pointed out above that it was a sort of indifference toward rite that certainly caused the "editorial" failure of Florus. Must we oppose a purely literal and intellectual approach to the mystical and luxuriant ritualism of Amalarius? Would that not risk minimizing the importance of rituality? Now, since in the regime of the religion of Christ the rite, as Geneviève Trainar said recently, "is the encounter of man—in his body and his soul—with the presence of the Spirit,"[71] it is truly important to take account of the liturgical signs

---

69. Mazza, *The Celebration of the Eucharist*, 169.

70. See Mazza, *The Celebration of the Eucharist*, 168–69: "That relation between the Mass and the work of redemption, that is, the passion of Christ, is a real one.... The origin and explication of this realism are posed in the person of the bishop who celebrates the Eucharist. The bishop is understood as the vicar of Christ, and this sacramental function is very justly linked to the imitation of Christ, expressed in the ritual practices of the celebration. Amalarius conserves the archaic language of typology, but he is not equipped to understand it as the Fathers understood it; the sacramental value of the rite as the imitation of Christ is lost, although not entirely. What saves it, at least in part, is the theology of the minister Amalarius makes use of. Because the bishop is a 'successor' and 'vicar' of Christ, the rites and actions of the Mass are a genuine imitation of the Passion."

71. Geneviève Trainar, *Transfigurer le temps: Nihilisme-symbolisme-liturgie* (Geneva: Ad Solem, 2003), 70.

and discover how to understand them. As for the superabundance of allegorical interpretations and the plurality of spiritual senses on a single theme, must we see it as a divergence from an original and unifying symbolism toward one that is arbitrary and extrinsicist? Could it not rather be, as D. Millet-Gérard suggests, the expression of a profound reverence for the plenitude of meaning and the splendor of the Mass, "the greatest monument of meaning that has ever existed"?[72]

In the Scholastic era, the canonists Sicard of Cremona and William Durandus composed two liturgical summas. Their strong, logical construction responded to a desire for systematization and was marked by a skillful weaving together of various symbolic meanings. Further, to justify their recourse to multiple explanations for a single rite, they both set their interpretation of the liturgy side by side with a scriptural exegesis in its four senses.[73] They did nothing more than to formulate a principle the medievals had known for centuries: just like Scripture, the liturgy, by virtue of the inspiration and assistance of the Holy Spirit, is the manifestation of the mystery and presence of Christ in his Church. There is a rite as it appears with its letter and its history, but above there is the plenitude of what it signifies, the work of the Holy Spirit, who has not only guided the Church's institution of the rite, but also gives it the ability to signify the infinite riches of the Kingdom.[74] It should therefore not be surprising if, to the original sense of the rite, whether it be practical, ceremonial, or *a fortiori* symbolic, other mystical, moral, and anagogical meanings may be added.

As in the case of Scripture, the problem thus arises of a reading

72. Dominique Millet-Gérard, "Manifestation et vérité: Le *Rational*, œuvre d'artiste et doctrine," preface to *Le Sens spirituel de la liturgie*, 38–61, at 59. See also Ansgar Santogrossi, "Symbolisme liturgique et spiritualité biblique," *Catholica* 81 (2003), 126–29.

73. See William Durandus, "Prohemium," in *Rationale divinorum officiorum*, CCCM 140, 6–8, no. 9–12.

74. See Santogrossi, "Symbolisme liturgique et spiritualité biblique," 128–29. With this author, but also with C. Barthe and D. Millet-Gérard, one sometimes gets the impression that the analytic monosemy of modern liturgists must be countered by a polysemy that is averse to synthesis.

that takes account of both the literal sense and the spiritual sense. For the allegorical sense is based on and develops from the literal sense. It is there to extend it, whether it explains what the institutor of the rite proposed to begin with, or whether, by dint of immemorial custom, or the commentaries of bishops and doctors, it assigns new meanings to it. Historical-liturgical investigation of the literal sense consequently proves to be fundamental. Historical inquiry is necessary to understand whether the symolism is original or the product of later developments. This seems to be the way to follow in order to avoid the extrapolations of a self-accommodating and imaginative exegesis of the liturgy. Nevertheless, what we have said about the nature of liturgical signs and the profound value of the spiritual sense of the liturgy should at the same time guard us from a rationalist and entirely *a priori* anti-allegorizing approach. We will see by what measure Aquinas—who always searches for the literal sense of Scripture before giving it a mystical significance, even in his analysis of the ceremonial precepts[75]—maintains equilibrium in his commentary between the two readings: literal and allegorical.

For there is a balance to maintain. As G. Trainar points out, our perception of rite implies, on one hand, that we do not deny the transcendent dimension of what is enacted there, but also, on the other, that we do not propose as transcendent what is often only personal, imaginary, convoluted, or even fantastical.[76]

Recently there has been a marked recovery of interest in the medieval liturgists and the spiritual exegesis of rites.[77] This renewed acquaintance with allegorical commentary on the liturgy is matched by a tendency to privilege research that is full of enthusiasm, to the detriment of intelligent, scientific research into the literal sense of

---

75. See *ST* I-II, q. 102, a. 2; Chenu, "La théologie de la loi ancienne selon saint Thomas," 485–97.

76. See Trainar, *Transfigurer le temps,* 58–59.

77. This interest bears principally upon the author who has been dubbed the "prince of liturgists," William Durandus, bishop of Mende (ca. 1286–1295), whose *Rationale divinorum officiorum* is rightly considered the culmination of the liturgical traditions of the Middle Ages, from the Carolingian period to the thirteenth century.

the sacred rites. But is this the proper response to modern reductive rationalism? Apart from the literary fervor that Huysmans and certain "symbolist" writers accorded it at the end of the nineteenth century, it is beginning from the second half of the seventeenth century that the allegorical method was abandoned, whether to counter Protestant objections with arguments based more upon the history and doctrine of the prayers and rites,[78] or because the nascent liturgical science—with the Benedictines Jean Mabillon (✝1707) and Edmond Martène (✝1739), the Theatine cardinal Joseph Tomasi (✝1713), and the Oratorian Pierre Lebrun (✝1729), among others— preferred studying sources and writing scholarly commentaries on liturgical documents over mystical explanations.

A complete study of rites must, therefore, allow us to define not only the limits but also the irreplaceable role of symbolism. This is what Pierre Lebrun does in his *Explication littérale, historique et dogmatique des prières et des cérémonies de la messe,* a work that to this day remains unsurpassed, and whose amplitude and complexity is expressed by the title.[79] In the preface, after remarking that allegorists like Lothar of Segni and William Durandus, "as able as they were, were not well-versed in antiquity, and ... had not the time to do the necessary research," Fr. Lebrun points out the manner in which it is fitting to use the numerous mystical explanations given by these authors:

> For a long time many learned and experienced men have desired that what is mysterious should not be confused with what is not. But however edifying the views presented in order to nourish the piety of the faithful, they must give way to the chief ideas proposed by the Church. Whether it was necessity, convenience, or seemliness that was the first cause of the ceremony in question, that we must say; and then rise as high as possible to discover the spiritual reasons the Church has, so to speak, superimposed

78. See, for example, Jacques-Benigne Bossuet, *Explication de quelques difficultés sur les prières de la messe à un nouveau catholique,* in *Œvres complètes,* vol. 42, ed. Gauthier Frères (Paris: Delusseux, 1828), 61–177.

79. Pierre Lebrun, *Explication littérale, historique et dogmatique des prières et des cérémonies de la messe,* 4 vols. (Paris: Séguin Aîné, 1716–1726). The first volume was republished several times.

upon the original reason of institution. The most recent ideas must come last in our consideration.[80]

One notices that P. Lebrun, far from denying the value of the "spiritual reasons," albeit superimposed, to the contrary invited the commentator to investigate their precise role.[81] He never ceased to oppose the liturgical rationalism of his era, in this case the absolute "literalism" of the Benedictine Claude de Vert.[82] In so doing—in the name of the literal sense itself—Lebrun defended and defined the legitimacy of recourse, in the explication of numerous rites, to the intentionally and fundamentally symbolic reasons that governed their institution: "The true literal and historical sense of a writing or a ceremony is that which the author or institutor had in mind, and it is often a figurative sense, of symbol and of mystery."[83]

For the reasons sketched above, our analysis of the *expositio missae* in Aquinas's *Summa* must pay careful attention to the literal sense of the prayers and rites, to those "chief ideas that have been held by the Church" in instituting them. Now these ideas most often relate

---

80. Lebrun, *Explication littérale*, 1:xv–xvi.

81. See Taft, *The Byzantine Rite*, 72: "When rites, once of practical import, outlive their original purpose, their continued survival demands reintegration into a new system. In the process, such relics often acquire new symbolic interpretations, unrelated to their genesis or original scope."

82. See Claude de Vert, *Explication simple, littérale et historique des cérémonies de l'Église*, 2 vols. (Paris: Florentin Delaulne, 1697–1698); Lebrun, *Explication littérale*, 1:xvi–xxxvii.

83. Lebrun, *Explication littérale*, 1:xxii. The author continues: "If we consider the scepter of kings and the crosier of bishops and abbots in a coarse and material fashion, we might say that it is given to them for support while walking, because this is the more ordinary use of staves, and because in fact in ancient times bishops and abbots availed themselves of staves in their travels. But since we are seeking the reason for the institution of the ceremony of the pastoral staff, we would distance ourselves from the true sense of the Church if we gave, as a reason of institution, the ordinary usage of support while walking; for the scepter and the crosier are given to both young and old to be used only in actions of magnificence and ceremony. The proper and historical significance of the scepter is to be the symbol of the power of the king in all his dominions, just as the pastoral staff is given by the Church to bishops and abbots to mark their authority in their diocese and in their monasteries, and because as pastors they have the crook to protect their flock and to chastise those who trouble its peace and good order. The Church herself teaches us these symbolic senses in her pontificals" (xxii–xxiii).

to the mystery. In the body of article 5, where he formulates the principles of his commentary, the Angelic Doctor establishes the role of mystagogical explication, a role that is fundamental because the Eucharistic action is situated in the order of sign. He first reminds us that the sacraments use both words and actions to signify, in order thus to be complete and "more perfect." In the case of the Eucharist, the sacrament of the Lord's Passion, "words are used to signify things pertaining to Christ's Passion, which is represented in this sacrament; or again, pertaining to Christ's mystical body, which is signified therein." It is the same for "certain actions," such as incensations, signs of the cross, and various movements of the priest at the altar, which "are not ridiculous gestures, [but] they are done so as to represent something else."[84] Thus Thomas firmly maintains the spiritual sense of the Eucharistic celebration—a fundamental mystagogy that bears principally on the Passion of which the Mass is not merely the *imago repraesentativa* and the *signum commemorativum*, but also on the *res tantum*, the Mystical Body of Christ, which celebrates the Eucharist and which the Eucharist constitutes in its unity.[85] Of course, mystagogical explication, discovery of the spiritual sense of the mystery celebrated, has been the object of pious excess and erroneous opinions, but it remains the royal road toward the fullness of the mystery. Our analysis must therefore not neglect it: for we are dealing with a mystical sense at the origin of the institution of a prayer or ceremony, even if it is one that a venerable tradition has superimposed, thereby conferring on the liturgical reality in question a richness to which it is disposed.

84. *ST* III, q. 83, a. 5, ad 5.
85. See de Lubac, *Corpus Mysticum*, 134: "Thus everything points to a study of the relation between the Church and the Eucharist, which we may describe as standing as cause each to other. Each has been entrusted to the other, so to speak, by Christ; the Church produces the Eucharist, but the Eucharist also produces the Church. In the first instance the Church is involved in her active aspect … in the exercise of her sanctifying power; in the second case she is involved in her passive aspect, as the Church of the sanctified. But in their last analysis it is the one Body which builds itself up through this mysterious interaction in and through the conditions of our present existence up to the day of its consummation."

If Thomas privileges the spiritual explanation, sometimes even in a very thoroughgoing manner, he is, nonetheless, aware that a number of prayers and ceremonies have no other reason than "devotion and respect toward the sacrament"[86]—and this seems to us to leave the door open for a history of Christian cultic forms. Where necessary, therefore, and in a manner proportionate to the genre of the article, we will draw on modern historical research. Though St. Thomas does not take a historical approach,[87] in many places he was careful to offer literal and sensible explanations, either hewing close to a prayer's plain sense or seeking for an original symbolism that could synthesize the various polysemic readings whose limits he must have perceived.[88] Further, his outline of the Mass is remarkable for its exactitude and for the accuracy of its divisions.

Parallel Passages and Sources of
the Thomistic *Expositio*

We find already in Thomas's *Commentary on the Sentences* a quite abundant exposition of the prayers and rites of the Mass,[89] one that is partially taken up again in the *Summa*. His *Commentary on the First Letter to Timothy* gives an outline of the Mass followed by a brief analysis, constructed according to the components of prayer given in 1 Tim 2:1 (*obsecrationes, orationes, postulationes, gratiarum actiones*). If the Pauline text is mentioned in the *Summa*, it is not apropos of the Mass but to illustrate the question of prayer in gener-

---

86. *ST* III, q. 83, a. 5. See also *ST* III, q. 83, a. 3: "There are two things to be considered regarding the equipment of this sacrament: one of these belongs to the representation of the events connected with our Lord's Passion; while the other is connected with the reverence due to the sacrament, in which Christ is contained verily, and not in figure only."

87. See Gy, "La documentation sacramentaire de Thomas d'Aquin," 425–31.

88. Also in *ST* II, q. 83, a. 5, ad 3, where after trying through force of details to make the various signs of the cross in the Canon correspond with the various events of the Passion, he briefly offers the spiritual explanation, which is the best and at the origin of the rite. We will return to this point.

89. See Thomas, *Commentary on the Sentences* IV, d. 8, expositio textus. See also Thomas, *Commentary on the Sentences* IV, d. 1, q. 1, a. 5, q^a 1, ad 2; d. 13, expositio textus; d. 15, q. 4, a. 3, q^a 1.

al.⁹⁰ We also point out that the Parma edition of the works of Thomas (t. 17) contains an *"Expositio missae quid significant illa quae fiunt ibi,"* an inauthentic work consisting of a compilation of extracts from the *Libellus de canone mystici libaminis* of Richard of Wedinghausen (from the end of the twelfth century).⁹¹

In the period when Thomas wrote the *expositio missae* of the *Summa*, or around 1272–1273, the best-known commentaries on the Mass were without any doubt those of Innocent III and Sicard of Cremona. Enjoying the authority of its author, the *De sacro altaris mysterio*, besides the addition of theological material, offered the "ecclesiological" advantage of commenting on the Pontifical Mass according to the usage of the papal chapel of the end of the twelfth century.⁹² We can, therefore, understand Aquinas's esteem for the *De sacro altaris mysterio*, to which he already referred in his treatise on the Eucharist.⁹³ However, as a work that lacks a systematic program of the Mass, Innocent's commentary could not have a decisive influence on Thomas's exposition. Though in the fifth article Thomas echoes the allegories contained in Lothar's work, he did not cite the future Innocent III as his source, likely due to the fact Lothar had only compiled the allegories he found in earlier explanations. From the fact that Thomas cites the opinions of certain commentators, without naming their authors, we may deduce that he was

90. See Thomas, *Commentary on 1 Timothy*, ch. 2, lect. 1; *ST* II-II, q. 83, a. 17 : "a gloss on 1 Timothy 2:1 says that 'in the Mass, the consecration is preceded by supplication,' in which certain sacred things are called to mind; that 'prayers are in the consecration itself,' in which especially the mind should be raised up to God; and that 'intercessions are in the petitions that follow, and thanksgivings at the end.'"

91. See De La Taille, *Mysterium fidei*, 267.

92. See Innocent III, *De sacro altaris mysterio*, prologue: "It is the customs [*consuetudinem*] of the Apostolic See, not the one we read about in ancient times but the one that is known to us today, that we have proposed to describe, for by the Lord's Providence she is the mother and head of all the other Churches (ed. Fioramonti, 34, no. 8); see also Pierre-Marie Gy, "La papauté et le droit liturgique au XIIᵉ et XIIIᵉ siècle," in *The Religious Roles of the Papacy: Ideals and Realities (1150–1300)*, ed. Christopher Ryan, Papers in Medieval Studies 8 (Toronto: Pontifical Institute of Mediaeval Studies, 1989), 229–45.

93. See *ST* III, q. 78, a. 2, ad 5; and q. 78, a. 3, sed contra.

familiar at least with certain *expositiones missae*.[94] Nothing would indicate, however, that he had the *Mitrale* of Sicard at hand.

We might be tempted to investigate the influences exercised on
the genre of *expositio missae* on the part of Dominican masters before
the Angelic Doctor. If the *Speculum ecclesiae* of Hugh of Saint-Cher
may have inspired the quadripartite plan of the Pauline commentary mentioned above, this would prove to be without consequence
in the articles that concern us.[95] For his part, Albert the Great seems
to have exercised some influence, not in his program of the Mass
(Thomas's is better structured and even more literal), nor especially in his anti-allegorist stance, which Aquinas must have known and
did not make his own. According to N. K. Rasmussen, the Angelic
Doctor's *expositio missae* could not have depended on liturgists pri-
or to the twelfth century, before whom one cannot find any rational
division of the Eucharistic action. Further, the Thomistic commentary could not be indebted to younger predecessors or contemporaries, but, "deeply rooted in the method of logical division peculiar
to his own time," his Mass program in both the *Commentary on the
Sentences* and the *Summa*, is "his own work, plain and simple."[96] Regarding his analysis of ritual details—still according to N. K. Rasmussen—Thomas is largely indebted to the *Opusculum super missam*
of William of Middleton, continuator (ca. 1255) of the *Summa* of Alexander of Hales.[97]

Finally, there are the canonical documents, decrees and decretals, which the Angelic Doctor invokes most often in articles 4 and 5
of question 83, for no other reason than to take the liturgical practice
of the Roman church into account. In question 83, article 4, ad 7, for

94. See *ST* III, q. 83, a. 5, ad 8 : "Quidam tamen dicunt …"
95. Hugh of Saint-Cher, *Tractatus super missam seu Speculum Ecclesiae*.
96. Rasmussen, *Saint Thomas et les rites de la messe*, 23–24.
97. The *Opusculum super missam* of William of Middleton is included in the *Summa
fratris Alexandri*, between art. 2 and 3 of q. 10, membrum V, *Tractatus de officio missae*: see
Stephen J. P. van Dijk, "De fontibus 'Opusculi super missam' Fr. Gulielmi de Melitona,"
Ephemerides liturgicae 53 (1939): 291–349.

example, the passage of *De corpore et sanguine Domini* of Paschasius Radbertus, which with Gratian he attributes to St. Augustine, was certainly read in the Decretals.

"ORDO AGENDORUM ET DICENDORUM"

"Incipit ordo agendorum et dicendorum a sacerdote, etc." was the title of the Mass ordinary compiled in 1243 by Haymon of Faversham, fourth Minister General of the Franciscans.[98] Better known as *Indutus planeta*, these two words being the first of the opening rubric, this *ordo*, principally destined for the celebration of private Mass, was widespread in the period when Aquinas wrote his *expositio missae*. Without being able to affirm the influence of Haymon on Thomas, we can observe that both see an "order of actions and words"[99] in the Mass. Thomas for his part examines what is said (art. 4) and what is done (art. 5). One might see here the application of a sacramental binary to the rites, though not a substantial one, with the word considered as giving the other sensible things their meaning. In any case, it is the relation between word and action, both constitutive of the liturgical rite, that establishes the link between the two articles.

We have elected to consider the rite of Mass according to the program laid out in the corpus of article 4. For each of its parts, defined by the order of the liturgical action and the articulations of its parts as distinguished by Thomas, we will examine what Aquinas says about both the words and the actions of the whole that is the rite. Numerous objections—nine in article 4 and twelve in article 5—bearing on precise points of the celebration, words or

98. See Stephen J. P. van Dijk, ed., *Sources of the Modern Roman Liturgy: The Ordinals by Haymo of Faversham and Related Documents* (1243–1307), vol. 2, *Texts*, Studia et documenta franciscana 2 (Leiden: Brill, 1963), 1–14.

99. See Rasmussen, *Saint Thomas et les rites de la messe*, 12: "It is permissible to see in these two texts [of Haymon and Thomas] the expression of the same consciousness of the existence of rational structures even inside the liturgy, a consciousness that is entirely faithful to the great intuitions of the thirteenth century."

actions that present peculiar difficulties, and the various responses, will be included here in the order of exposition.

As we have already said, historical-liturgical remarks will sometimes prove necessary. They will allow us to identify with precision the liturgical rite that is being commented upon in the *Summa*.

The Romano-Frankish Rite of the Thirteenth Century

The sacrament of Christ's immolation, the Eucharist, is the memorial of his work of redemption,[100] and for that reason embraces the entire mystery of salvation. That is why this sacrament "is ... performed with greater solemnity than the other sacraments." Thomas is referring to the cultic principle, that is, the binary *substantia-solemnitas*, simply formulated at the head of the corpus of article 4.[101]

To establish "the fittingness of all the words that accompany this sacrament," our Doctor refers in the *sed contra* to the authority of a decretal that attributes the order of the Eucharistic celebration to James, first bishop of Jerusalem, and to Basil of Caesarea. Aside from the problems concerning the attribution and date of composition of these liturgies, we may be surprised to see two pastors cited together who are separated by three centuries, and by the reference—from a writer who is about to comment on the Franco-Roman Mass—to the liturgies of Jerusalem-Antioch and Byzantium. What seems to us like a lack of historical sensitivity, or even an ignorance of the diversity of the liturgical families, perhaps testifies instead to a sense of the continuous and homogenous evolution of rites over the course of centuries, beginning with unwritten apostolic tradition.[102] Furthermore, would not Thomas see in the cultural richness of the various liturgical traditions a sign of the profound communion of the Mystical Body in the celebration of the sacrament? We find the same

---

100. See *ST* III, q. 83, a. 1, where Thomas cites the Secret prayer of the Ninth Sunday after Pentecost: "Whenever the commemoration of this sacrifice is celebrated, the work of our redemption is enacted."

101. See *ST* III, q. 83, a. 4; see also ad 1: "The consecration is accomplished by Christ's words only; but the other words must be added to dispose the people for receiving it."

102. See *ST* III, q. 64, a. 2, ad 1.

recourse to the *sensus Ecclesiae* in the *sed contra* of article 5, where it is a question of the rites to be performed. These receive their value and legitimacy from the custom or tradition of the Church (*Ecclesiae consuetudo*), which "cannot err, since she is taught by the Holy Ghost."

The Mass that Aquinas commentates in the *Summa* is the Mass *secundum consuetudinem romanae Ecclesiae*,[103] which is the rite of the Roman Curia as it established itself over the course of the thirteenth century as the result of both the growing identification between the *Ecclesia romana* and the *Curia romana*,[104] and the revisions by Franciscan liturgists.[105] In its own way, St. Thomas's choice shows the success of the process of unification of the Western liturgy around the usages of the papal chapel: this unification, desired by Innocent III and his successors—and powerfully assisted by the expansion of the Franciscan Order—soon extended beyond the Alps through the exile in Avignon. Since he was writing a universal summary of theology, Thomas seems to have desired to describe the Latin rite in its most "universal" form. For this reason, he does not describe the usages particular to the Dominican Order's rite of Mass, a rite determined in 1256 by the Master General Humbert of Romans[106]—he uses the names *introitus* and *graduale*, for example, which the Dominican books designated by the terms *officium* and *responsum*.

In so doing, the Dominican Doctor is aware that the difference between the two *ordines*, Franco-Roman and Dominican, is properly speaking only a matter of certain usages. For both had developed from one primitive Roman *ordo*, called the Gregorian. Of this "pure" Roman rite, we find an ample description in the *Ordo Romanus I*,[107]

---

103. See Stephen J. P. van Dijk, "Order of the Mass according to the use of the Roman Church (Court) before 1227," in *The Ordinal of the Papal Court*, 493–526.

104. See Gy, *La liturgie dans l'histoire*, ch. 4, "Typologie et ecclésiologie des livres liturgiques," 75–89 (particularly 81–82).

105. See Stephen J. P. van Dijk and J. Hazelden Walker, *The Origins of the Modern Roman Liturgy: The Liturgy of the Papal Court and the Franciscan Order in the Thirteenth Century* (Westminster, MD: Newman Press, 1960).

106. See Rousseau, *De ecclesiastico officio Fratrum Praedicatorum*; and González Fuente, *La vida litúrgica en la Orden de Predicadores*.

107. See Michel Andrieu, *Les Ordines Romani du haut Moyen Âge*, vol. 2, *Les textes*

a sort of liturgical directory of the papal Mass written on the end of the seventh century, as well as a short precis following the text of the Roman Canon in the Gregorian sacramentary called the *Hadrianum*,[108] from the name of Pope Hadrian I, who had it copied and sent to Charlemagne around 785. Transplanted into the Carolingian Empire, the ancient Roman *ordo*, although substituted for the Gallican Mass, borrowed indigenous ritual traditions and received over the course of the centuries numerous elaborations in the particular churches, monasteries, and collegiate chapters. The Franco-Roman sacramentaries and *ordines* in a former period, and later—beginning in the tenth and eleventh centuries—the missals and ordinaries,[109] are witnesses to numerous variations on the same theme: ceremonial adaptations and euchological elaborations of the ancient Gregorian *ordo* that principally affected three moments of the celebration: the entrance, the offertory, and the communion rites.[110] In the case of the entrance and offertory, it was a matter of "making speak" certain preexistent rites that until then had remained mute while the *schola cantorum* performed a chant. During the Introit, the celebrant's and ministers' prayers at the foot of the altar replaced the ancient prostration of the *Ordo Romanus I*; during the chanting of the Offertory antiphon, in a time when the adoption of unleavened bread had led to the suppression of the collective offering of the material of sacrifice, the so-called apology prayers henceforth

(*Ordines I–XIII*) , Spicilegium sacrum lovaniense 23 (Louvain: Université catholique, 1971), 1–108. The *Ordo Romanus I*, first in the general class and in the list of eucharistic *ordines* in particular, constitutes the first detailed description of the Roman Mass, and that at its highest typological level: the stational Mass of the Roman Pontiff. We know that the form described is the origin of other more or less amplified forms of celebration: the episcopal celebration, the solemn celebration of a simple priest, Low or Private Mass— all modes of celebration whose explanation must be based on the normative celebration of the Roman Pontiff.

108. See Jean Deshusses, vol. 1 of *Le Sacramentaire grégorien: Ses principales formes d'après les plus anciens manuscrits*, Spicilegium Friburgense 16 (Fribourg: Éditions universitaires de Fribourg, 1971), 85–92.

109. For a classification of the sources, see Vogel, *Medieval Liturgy*; and Palazzo, *Le Moyen Âge: Des origines au XIIIe siècle*.

110. See our study, "Ritual and Sacred Chant in the *Ordo Romanus Primus* (Seventh-Eighth Century)," *Antiphon: A Journal for Liturgical Renewal* 22, no. 2 (2018): 199–219.

accompanied the placing of the oblations on the altar. Further, the simplification of the fraction modified the arrangement of the communion rites. Finally, after the Postcommunion prayer, various conclusion formulas were introduced. Innumerable medieval missals offer the historian of cult infinite forms of the Franco-Roman apologies and witness to a wide variety of ceremonial uses, but for all that the various ordinaries of Mass, especially the Franco-Roman and Dominican ordinaries, never constituted independent liturgical families.

We should add that the history of the rite of Mass is also linked to the history of doctrine and spirituality, in particular to Paschasius Radbertus's reflection on the Lord's presence and to the great florescence of Eucharistic devotion that resulted from it. This spiritual movement—of which Thomas Aquinas, as author of the Office of Corpus Christi is certainly the most notable representative—attained its apogee in the Gothic period: it was the origin of what a number of modern liturgists have designated—not without disdain—the "dramatization of the Mass," as well as the development of acts of veneration toward the Eucharistic Body. The history of the Roman Mass, from the "pure Roman" Gregorian *ordo* to the *ordo missae* of the Roman Curia of the thirteenth century, far from a process of denaturation and "modernization"[111] of the original, is thus more of an organic and homogenous growth and a development, in the sense John Henry Newman intended, that unfolds according to the rhythm of the doctrinal and spiritual life of the Church.

As elaborated and variegated as the euchological and ritual adaptations were, they did nothing more than graft themselves onto the ancient *ordo*, whose structure remained always immutable. The normative form of celebration was still the solemn rite with its rigorous articulation of chants, prayers, and readings; at its heart was the

---

111. See Roguet, "Note explicative [52]" on 3^a, Q. 79–83, 317 : "The Middle Ages had rigorously 'modernized' the Mass by adding a quantity of secondary rites (signs of the cross, genuflections, elevations); they thought they were making the Mass more expressive of both the cross that it represents and the real presence that it effects. The exclusive and unhesitating practice of this liturgy encumbered with secondary, not to say superfluous, signs, considered as immutable and quasi-divine in all of its parts, could not help but favor allegorical interpretation."

Eucharistic celebration proper, the canon, running from the Preface to the *Pax Domini*,[112] just as Gregory the Great had redacted it in its impeccable stylistic and conceptual purity.[113] For a long time the later devotional prayers had been committed to memory and were said at the discretion of the celebrant. Their inclusion in the ordinary of the Mass did not become truly systematic until the thirteenth century. Certainly, the progressive normalization of the Low Mass played a decisive role in this process, bringing with it the gradual loss of liturgical moorings and a disregard for the basic structure of the Roman Eucharistic celebration.

Nevertheless, at the moment when Thomas Aquinas wrote his *expositio missae*, the movement did not yet seem irreversible. For if the Angelic Doctor, along with his whole epoch, may have lacked a historical consciousness of the liturgy, he still knows that the solemn rite of Mass is the norm whose structure must be elucidated, and that it is first and foremost the prayers of the canon that must be explained. His commentary follows the program of a Solemn Mass and, consequently, takes account of the fact that it is a public action involving the whole assembly. Thus, he offers an explanation of the Introit antiphon and not the private prayers of the ministers at the

---

112. See the study of Bernard Botte: "Histoire des prières de l'ordinaire de la messe," in *L'Ordinaire de la messe: Texte critique*, trans. and ed. Bernard Botte and Christine Mohrmann (Paris: Cerf, 1953), 5–27, at 15: "Until the thirteenth century there are no other fixed prayers in the Mass besides the Canon. The first part contained prayers, readings, and chants, but these are items that varied each day. The only prayers that were regularly repeated were the acclamations, the *Kyrie* and the *Gloria in excelsis*. There are no priestly prayers at the Offertory, and after the Communion there is nothing but the Post-communion, which varies each day. The true Ordinary is the canon, which runs from the Preface to the *Pax Domini sit semper vobiscum*. After all, *canon* means nothing other than a 'rule' for celebrating the Eucharist."

113. Botte, "Histoire des prières de l'ordinaire de la messe," in Botte and Mohrmann, *L'Ordinaire de la messe*, 27: "We should be grateful to the people of the Middle Ages for having preserved the canon in its purity, and not to have allowed their personal effusions or theological ideas to pass into it. One can imagine the complete sham we would have today if each generation had been permitted to remake the canon to the measure of their theological controversies or novel forms of piety. We can only hope that the good sense of these people will continue to be imitated, who had their own theological ideas, but who understood that the canon was not their playground. To their eyes it was the expression of a venerable tradition, and they felt that it could not be touched without opening the door to every sort of abuse."

foot of the altar. When he deals with "the praise of the people in the chant of the Offertory," and notes "the prayer of the priest, which asks that the people's oblation be acceptable to God," this is probably the prayer *super oblata* of the sacramentaries rather than the private apologies, about which he says nothing at all. Then he enters into the details of the text of the ancient prayer, the Canon, and explains the significance of the rites that confront and hold the attention of the participants.

Program of the Mass (q. 83, a. 4, corpus)

Thomas divides the celebration of the Mass into four parts: the first two, the preparation [1] and the instruction [2], precede the celebration of the mystery proper [3], which is itself divided into three moments: the oblation [3.1], the consecration [3.2], and the reception of the sacrament [3.3]; the celebration is concluded by the thanksgiving [4].

[1] The Preparation extends from the ascent of the altar to the Oration—the *oratio super populum* of the Roman sacramentaries, or *Collecta* in the Franco-Roman books. This part includes four moments: the Introit, the *Kyrie eleison*, the hymn *Gloria in excelsis Deo*, and finally the *Oratio* "which the priest makes for the people."

[2] The faithful people are now prepared to hear the instruction, the second part of the celebration of "the mystery of faith." The instruction is carried out in an ascending pattern. The Epistle comes first, drawn from the teaching of the prophets and apostles. The intercalary chants (Gradual, Alleluia, or Tract) are like an echo of this first teaching. The Gospel constitutes perfect instruction. Singing of the *Credo*, or symbol of faith, follows.

[3] The celebration of the mystery proper unfolds in three stages, for the mystery, says the Angelic Doctor, "is both *offered* as a sacrifice, and *consecrated* and *eaten* as a sacrament." Hence the distinction and the sequence: offertory (*oblatio*), consecration of the sacrament, reception of the consecrated gifts. Each of these three stages in turn is divided in a logical manner.

[3.1] In the offertory, the people express the joy of their offering by a chant, the *offertorium*, while at the altar the prayer of the priest (*oratio sacerdotis*) "asks for the people's oblation to be acceptable to God."

[3.2] The time of the consecration begins with the Preface and culminates in the Canon.

By the Preface, "the people are first of all excited to devotion." The Preface opens onto the *Sanctus*, the chant of the angels confided also to the faithful people.

During the *Sanctus*, the priest, "in a low voice (*secreto*)," begins the Canon. He recommends to God the offerers, namely the earthly Church in her hierarchical constitution: the pope, bishops, dignitaries, and faithful; in the prayer *Communicantes*, he commemorates the saints; finally he concludes these recommendations with the prayer *Hanc igitur*, a general expression of the needs of the offerers.[114] "Then he comes to the consecration itself." The Angelic Doctor understands the consecration to include here, in addition to the words of institution, which form their core, the prayer *Quam oblationem* that precedes them, as well as all the post-consecratory prayers, from *Unde et memores* up to the final doxology of the Canon.

[3.3] "Then follows the act of receiving the sacrament." This third time runs from the *Pater* up to the communion proper. Aquinas first distinguishes the preparation of the people that consists in the Lord's Prayer, followed by the prayer *Libera nos* and the peace. After the chanting of the *Agnus Dei*, the priest, and then the faithful, receive the sacraments.

[4] Finally comes the thanksgiving, by which, Thomas observes, the whole Mass celebration is finished—*tota missae celebratio in gratiarum actione terminatur*. In the Communion chant, "the people rejoicing for having received the mystery"; then, "the priest return[s] thanks by prayer."

No other concluding rite is mentioned.

---

114. See *ST* III, q. 83, a. 4, to note the summary of the prayer *Hanc igitur*: "Thirdly, he concludes the petition when he says: 'Wherefore that this oblation,' etc., in order that the oblation may be salutary to them for whom it is offered."

The Mass program of the *Summa* differs from that of the *Commentary on the Sentences*.[115] There, the Mass was divided into three parts: *principium, medium,* and *finis orationis*. The *principium orationis* corresponded to the preparation of the *Summa*, but with the difference that the Introit, the *Kyrie,* and the *Gloria* consisted in a disposition of the people toward the *ipsa oratio*, the Collect. Then the *medium orationis* extended from the Epistle to the reception of the Sacrament, a vast part divided into three times: the instruction of the people, the oblation of the matter to be consecrated, and the consumption of the sacrament, running from the Preface to the reception of communion. Only the third part, the *finis orationis,* including the thanksgiving, with the chanted Communion antiphon (already chanted after the Communion in Aquinas's day) and the Postcommunion prayer, has an exact counterpart in the *Summa*: the Thanksgiving, the fourth and last part of the program. Within each part distinguished in Thomas's *Commentary on the Sentences,* the various subdivisions are articulated most often in terms of allegorical schemas,[116] with some of them corresponding to distinctions in theological teaching.[117]

---

115. See Thomas, *Commentary on the Sentences* IV, d. 8, expositio textus.

116. See Thomas, *Commentary on the Sentences* IV, d. 8, expositio textus: "The instruction of the people is done through the word of God, which indeed reaches the people from God through his ministers; and so those things that pertain to the instruction of the people are not said by the priest, but by the ministers.

Now there are three kinds of ministry of the word of God. The first is from authority, which belongs to Christ who is called 'minister'.... The second is from the truth made plain which applies to the preachers of the New Testament.... The third is from prefiguration, which applies to the preachers of the Old Testament. And thus a deacon sets forth Christ's teaching; and because Christ is not only man, but God, the deacon says first, the Lord be with you, so that he might make men attentive to Christ as God. But the teaching of the preachers of the New Testament is announced by subdeacons. Nor is it inconsistent that sometimes in place of an epistle something is read by them from the Old Testament, since the preachers of the New Testament also preached the Old. But the teaching of the preachers of the Old Testament by lower ministers is not always read, but specifically on those days on which the configuration of the New and Old Testaments is indicated, as in the fasts of the four seasons, and when certain things are celebrated that were prefigured in the Old Law, like the Passion, the Nativity of Christ, his Baptism, and things like that" (trans. Mortensen, 7:377.)

117. Thomas, *Commentary on the Sentences* IV, d. 8, expositio textus: "Now the part that contains the sacrament's completion is divided in three, according to the

In relation to the Mass program of the *Commentary on the Sentences* and the one sketched in the *Commentary on the First Letter to Timothy*, the program of the *Summa* is distinguished by its greater simplicity and precision. Even in a time when allegorism was the most common method, and even after having applied that method in the two works previously cited, the Angelic Doctor has not resorted to the arbitrariness of a construction founded on allegorism, nor has he tried to make the divisions of the Eucharistic action correspond in an artificial manner to the logical divisions of sacramental theology. He has preferred to follow the text of the *ordo missae* and distinguish its parts with precision. It is remarkable that his analysis proved more "literal" and more historically based than that of Albert the Great and measures up to the accounts of historians of the Roman Mass. For example, contrary to Albert, who saw in the Collect the first stage of the Instruction, Thomas rightly understood that the first common oration formed the conclusion of the Preparation—which is clear from a reading of the normative *Ordo Romanus I*. Further, the fact that he attached the Preface to the consecratory action, so as not to isolate it or, again contrary to Albert, so as not to make it the conclusion of the Offertory, reveals a peculiar sensitivity to the genesis and coherence of the liturgical celebration. This matter of the placement of the Preface should be emphasized all the more because it coincides, as Michel Andrieu's critical edition has shown, with the primitive redaction of the *Ordo Romanus I*.[118] Only the fourth part, called "Thanksgiving," proves to be mistaken, since the Communion antiphon belongs to the reception of the sacrament, and the Postcommunion belongs to and concludes the Eucharistic rites proper.

---

three things that are integral to this sacrament: namely, what is the sacrament alone, what is the reality-and-sacrament, and what is the reality alone. In the first part, therefore, is contained the blessing of the matter offered, which is the sacrament alone; in the second part, the consecration of the body and blood of Christ, which is the reality-and-sacrament, at: 'bless and approve this our offering'; in the third, the request of the sacrament's effect, which is the reality alone, at: 'vouchsafe to look upon them with a gracious and tranquil countenance'" (trans. Mortensen, 7:379).

118. See M. Andrieu, *Les* Ordines Romani *du haut Moyen Âge*, 2:95–97, nos. 88 and 91.

The "Actors" of the Celebration: Priest, Ministers,
People, and *Schola Cantorum*

Since "things are mentioned in this sacrament which belong to the entire Church,"[119] the celebration of the Eucharist requires the participation of the entire Mystical Body. Consequently, not only the priest, the principal minister of the sacrament, but also others ministers of the priestly hierarchy, superior and inferior, and the whole people exercise a liturgical role.

The Priest   In the Mass the priest stands in the place of both Christ and the Church: "The priest, in reciting the prayers of the mass, speaks in the Church's stead (*in persona Ecclesiae*), in whose unity he remains; but in consecrating the sacrament he speaks as in the person of Christ (*in persona Christi*), whose place he holds by the power of his orders."[120]

If priestly action in God's name—*personam Dei gerit*[121]—pertains principally to the consecration, it is also manifested in other rites. For example, if the priest intones the angelic hymn and the symbol of faith, it is to signify that heavenly glory and faith "are things that have come to the people through divine revelation." In virtue of his participation in the priesthood of Christ, the priest at the altar transmits heavenly benefits to the people, but he also performs the ascending motion of the divine mediation: to bear the prayers of Christ's Church to the bosom of God. Thus, it is proper for the priest, according to the Letter to the Hebrews (5:1) cited by Thomas, "to offer up gifts and prayers for the people." Of these prayers, the Angelic Doctor observes, certain are said in a raised voice, such as the common prayers (Collect, Secret, Postcommunion) that "are common to priest and people alike." Others are uttered in a low voice, those "that belong to the

---

119. *ST* III, q. 83, a. 4, ad 6.
120. *ST* III, q. 82, a. 7, ad 3. See also *ST* III, q. 82, a. 5 and 6; q. 83, a. 1, ad 3.
121. *ST* III, q. 83, a. 4, ad 6.

priest alone, such as the Oblation [Offertory] and the Consecration [the Canon]."[122]

The Ministers   If he affirms the necessity of having several assistants in the solemn celebration of the Mass,[123] St. Thomas does not enter into detail about the functions of these ministers. Rigorously defined by their orders, major and minor, the functions of the ministers are definitely understood by Thomas to be among the number of those actions that "are done in order to represent ... the disposing of His mystical body."[124] We know that the deacon and the sub-deacon, both considered to be *in sacris* by the theology of the Dominican Order at that time, had access to the altar and performed there, in conformity with the orders they had received, a liturgical ministry in immediate service to the celebrant. The latter was charged with consecrating; the others were to instruct by performing readings of the Epistle and the Gospel. In so doing, they manifested "that this doctrine was announced to the peoples through ministers sent by God."[125]

The People   With regard to the presence and participation of the faithful people, the *expositio missae* offers frequent elaborations. Modern and contemporary liturgists have often the denounced liturgical neglect of the people of God ever since the High Middle Ages. Before taking up this question, it would evidently be useful to agree on the notion and modes of participation in the liturgy. Without entering into this debate now, we must take note of the fundamental importance, in the eyes of a theologian and commentator of the thirteenth century, of the presence of an assembly, a presence constitutive for the celebration, since it is for the faithful people that the Eucharistic sacrifice is offered.

An analysis of the celebration's development will permit us to

122. *ST* III, q. 83, a. 4, ad 6.
123. See *ST* III, q. 83, a. 5, ad 12.
124. *ST* III, q. 83, a. 5, sed contra.
125. *ST* III, q. 83, a. 4, ad 6.

highlight many more examples. Here we only point out that the priest, at the end of the preparation, pronounces the oration for the people "that they may be made worthy of such great mysteries."[126] It is for the faithful people that the rite proceeds next to the instruction, so that they may enter better disposed into the celebration of the mystery.[127] If the prayers of the Offertory and Canon pertain to the priest alone, if for this reason they are said in a low voice, Thomas emphasizes that the priest invites the people to unite themselves with him through the greeting, *Dominus vobiscum*, that he addresses to them, both at the beginning of the Offertory and at the beginning of the Preface-Canon. Though we may justly regret that the Angelic Doctor does not mention either the initial *Oremus* of the Offertory nor the entire Preface dialogue, he does note that in performing the Offertory and Canon the celebrant says *Per omnia saecula saeculorum* in order to request the assent of the assembly, which is expressed by their *Amen*.[128]

Now the question of *sine populo* celebration of the Eucharistic sacrifice arises. The idea of a solitary Mass, without even the assistance of a server, motivated by the devotion of the celebrant alone, is evidently not even imagined, so strange is it to the traditional conception of the Eucharistic celebration, of which Thomas is still the interpreter in the thirteenth century. It is not a matter of any hostility to the Low, or private, Mass. Widespread in the High Middle Ages, especially in the monastic context, this form of celebration concentrated the various functions of the solemn rite (chants, readings, actions) in the hands of the celebrant, but did not, for all that, constitute a personal and solitary Mass. On the authority of the Decretals, Aquinas is careful to recall the necessity of assistants during every celebration of the Mass. In private Masses, that is, non-public—in the sense that public goes hand in hand with solemn—"it suffices to have one server, who takes the place of the whole Catholic people,

---

126. *ST* III, q. 83, a. 4.
127. See *ST* III, q. 83, a. 4.
128. See *ST* III, q. 83, a. 4, ad 6.

on whose behalf he makes answer in the plural to the priest."[129] We should remark in passing this sort of "popular representation" with which the server is invested: it is in the name of the people that the server responds. We may note, however, that the history of the ministers and clerical hierarchies, as documented in particular by the *Ordines romani*, does not always hold the same opinion!

The Schola Cantorum   For St. Thomas, the people are represented also by the *chorus* of singers, the *schola cantorum* of the *Ordo Romanus I*: "some things which refer to the people are sung by the choir."[130] The prayers that the choir sings entirely, from beginning to end, without the intervention of the celebrant or the ministers at the altar, "[inspire] the entire people with them."[131] These chants, vehicles of the sentiments of the Christian people, are the Introit, the *Kyrie*, the intercalary chants of the Instruction, the Offertory antiphon, the *Sanctus*, the *Agnus Dei* and the Communion antiphon. In the case of the *Gloria* and the *Credo*, the people do not begin the chant, but continue the chant intoned by the celebrant, the representative of the One who alone dispenses glory and faith. But the Angelic Doctor's interpretation clashes with the history of the *schola cantorum*. From the start, the *schola* was not a choral substitute for a people who could not sing, either because they had fallen out of the habit or because the melodies had become too complicated, but as a clerical institution pure and simple, carried out first of all by the deacon.[132] The *schola cantorum* played a genuine liturgical role, forming a bridge between the altar and the assembly.[133]

---

129. *ST* III, q. 83, a. 5, ad 12.
130. *ST* III, q. 83, a. 4, ad 6.
131. *ST* III, q. 83, a. 4, ad 6.
132. For the history of ecclesiastical chant and of the *schola cantorum*, the seminal work of Philippe Bernard should be consulted: *Du chant romain au chant grégorien* (Paris: Cerf, 1996), 412–13.
133. We refer the reader once again to our study "Ritualité et chant sacré," 264–65.

The Actions at the Altar: Lavabo, Incensation,
Movements at the Altar, Signs of the Cross

Article 5 examines the rites performed by the priest during the Eucharistic sacrifice. Since they are repeated many times in the course of the liturgical action, it will be convenient to point out the general significance Thomas accords to them, so we can more easily include them afterward in our analysis of the *ordo missae*.

The idea of "representation" of the redemptive Passion constitutes Aquinas's principal argument in favor of the ritual movements of the celebrant, especially the gestures of the priest and the signs of the cross in the Canon. Respect for the sacrament, as well as the moral dispositions proper to the priest, also serve to establish the fittingness of certain rites. Besides desiring to prove that no gesture is ridiculous because of theirmystical or tropological significance,[134] St. Thomas takes care to clearly demarcate the Christian ritual from observance of the precepts of the Old Law. Thus, he justifies hand washings and incensation for their religious fittingness and symbolism, fundamental or allegorical, without recourse to a Mosaic typology of the Christian ritual. Contrary to a whole tradition of *expositiones missae*, Thomas does not search for figures and justifications of Christian liturgical usages in the ceremonies of the Temple, and moreover affirms that the Church does not observe the rites of the *lavabo* or the incensation "because it was prescribed under the Old Law, but because it is becoming in itself, and therefore instituted by the Church."[135] In both cases, he takes care to emphasize that the Church's observance of these two ceremonies differs from the Old Law. In the case of the *lavabo*, the Church asks the priest to wash only his hands at Mass, which is easier than washing the feet and sufficiently apt to symbolize perfect purity.[136]

---

134. See *ST* III, q. 83, a. 5, ad 5.

135. *ST* III, q. 83, a. 5, ad 1. See also ad 2.

136. See *ST* III, q. 83, a. 5, ad 1: "Hence it is not observed in the same way as it was then: because the washing of the feet is omitted, and the washing of the hands is observed; for this can be done more readily, and suffices for denoting perfect cleansing."

It will be noted that, in the economy of sensible rites, the Christian rite has a more *spiritual* dimension. Nevertheless, the Christian rite cannot be abstracted from this economy, because of the nature of religious man's condition and, at the same time, the cultic regime of the Divine Incarnation. In this sense, his later recourse to the authority of a gentile philosopher, Aristotle, supported by a verse taken from the Psalter, the Old Testament book that Christ's Church has made its office and its prayer,[137] seems to reveal a conception of Christian cult in which the universal religious man, the *katholicos*, is taken up, body and soul, into a religion of supernatural character, which by moving from an ancient and obsolete covenant toward the new eternal covenant is no longer linked to the history of Israel. It seems that in Thomas's view, nothing of the transitory religion of Israel abides as regards both the interior and exterior dimensions of the religious life, except that which accords with the general anthropological foundations of cult. Nothing in the cult of Israel that prefigured and announced the mystery of Christ has existence or the quality of figure any longer, after the consummation wrought in his blood by the divine Antitype.[138] On the contrary, after the Gospel has been proclaimed and known, the practice of the ceremonies of the Old Law, in addition to being null and void, become culpable and death-causing.[139] Hence the careful attention of Aquinas not to "Judaize," to use the Anselmian phrase,[140] the cult of Christ and

---

137. See *ST* III, q. 83, a. 5, ad 1: "For, since the hand is the 'organ of organs' (*De Anima* iii), all works are attributed to the hands: hence it is said in Psalm 25:6: 'I will wash my hands among the innocent.'"

138. See *ST* I-II, q. 103, a. 3, sed contra and ad 2; q. 103, a. 4, sed contra and ad 1. See also the *Commentary on the Letter to the Romans*, ch. 14, lect. 1.

139. See *ST* I-II, q. 103, a. 4 : "Consequently, just as it would be a mortal sin now for anyone, in making a profession of faith, to say that Christ is yet to be born, which the fathers of old said devoutly and truthfully; so too it would be a mortal sin now to observe those ceremonies which the fathers of old fulfilled with devotion and fidelity."; et ibid., ad 1: "But immediately after Christ's Passion they began to be not only dead, so as no longer to be either effectual or binding; but also deadly, so that whoever observed them was guilty of mortal sin."

140. See Anselm, *Epistola de sacrificio azymi et fermentati*, in *Anselmi Cantuariensis Archiepiscopi Opera Omnia*, vol. 2, sect. III, ed. F. Schmitt (Stuttgart-Bad Cannstatt:

the Church. Yet a number of his predecessors and contemporaries, even if they all possessed nearly the same "theology of Israel," proved to be less rigorous in the matter of cult, often providing high constructed parallels between the Mosaic cult and the ceremonies of the Church, so as to establish a ritual continuity in the history of salvation.[141] Innocent III did this, for example, apropos of the *lavabo*.[142]

The *Lavabo* and Incensations   Refusing to resort to Judaic precedents to explain the washing of hands and incensation of the altar, Thomas offers in each case first a literal explanation, then one of a more symbolic nature, both founded on the notion of the respect due to the sacrament. "Because we are not wont to handle precious objects except the hands be washed," the reverence due to the Eucharist does not permit "for anyone to approach so great a sacrament with hands that are, even literally, unclean."[143] Further, by spreading a pleasing fragrance about the sanctuary, we "remove any disagreeable smell that may be about the place."[144] In addition to literalism, in the manner of Claude de Vert, we see here a theme that is also dear to Byzantine liturgical theology: the super-elevation of the senses,[145] the notion of "supernatural senses."

F. Frommann Verlag, 1968), 226: "When they say we Judaize it is not true, because we do not sacrifice the azyme in order to observe the Old Law, but so that the sacrifice may be performed more carefully, and to imitate Our Lord who did not Judaize when he did this. For when we do what the Jews did, we do not Judaize if we do it not in so far as it is a Jewish custom but because of another cause."

141. See William Durandus, *Rationale divinorum officiorum*, bk. 4, ch. 1, CCCM 140 (243–44, nos. 13–16).

142. See Innocent III, *De sacro altaris mysterio*, bk. 2, ch. 55 (ed. Fioramonti, 186–89).

143. *ST* III, q. 83, a. 5, ad 1.

144. *ST* III, q. 83, a. 5, ad 2.

145. See Paul Evdokimov, *The Art of the Icon: A Theology of Beauty* (Redondo Beach, CA: Oakwood Publications, 1972), 23–30, at 27–28: "In this authoritative tradition are counted such witnesses as Macarius of Egypt, John Climacus, Maximus the Confessor, Symeon the New Theologian, Gregory Palamas and finally Seraphim of Sarov. Grace which is experienced, lived, and felt as sweetness, peace, joy, and light is a foretaste of the future age. St. Macarius spoke of 'divinity felt.' We are not dealing here with eliminating the senses which, due to the Fall, have lost all sense of direction nor with replacing them with a new organ of perception, but rather with the transfiguration of the senses we already have. We want to restore them to their normal condition, a condition lost in

As the hands are washed and the incense wafts, these gestures, already significant as acts of reverence for the sacrament, acquire a dimension more profoundly linked to the mystery being celebrated. Ablution, or purification of the extremities, signifies "cleansing from even the smallest sins.... Such cleansing is required of him who approaches this sacrament."[146] The smoke that rises about the altar represents "the effect of grace, wherewith Christ was filled as with a good odor." The Angelic Doctor does not mention the incensation of the altar, at the Introit, or of the book, before the chanting of the Gospel, but he does mention the incensation of the Offertory, considered the most important and indeed the one whose practice was most general. The incensation of the altar is when Christ, like grace, "spreads to the faithful by the work of His ministers"; and therefore "when the altar, which represents Christ, has been incensed on every side, then all are incensed in their proper order."[147] Here Thomas gives an explanation of incensation that privileges the descending aspect of the liturgical action: a sign of grace and benediction stemming from the honor due to the members of the Mystical Body. He omits the most popular symbolism, the ascending symbolism of the prayer emphasized in the words of Psalm 140, which accompanies the incensation of the altar in the rite of the Roman Curia.[148] Finally, we add that the reference to hierarchical order illustrates another dimension of ritual representation, which is the manifestation of the Church, the Mystical Body that God has constituted from sacramental elements.

---

the Fall but now being restored. In the economy of the Incarnation, the spiritual and the corporeal have been integrated together. In the liturgy, we hear sung chants, contemplate visible icons, smell incense, receive through the senses and eat matter in the sacraments: all this allows us to speak of liturgical sight, hearing, smell, and taste. Liturgy elevates matter to its real dignity and destiny, and we understand thereby that matter is not some autonomous substance but rather a function of the Spirit and a vehicle of the spiritual."

146. *ST* III, q. 83, a. 5, ad 1.

147. *ST* III, q. 83, a. 5, ad 2.

148. See Ps 140:2: "Dirigatur [Domine] oratio mea sicut incensum in conspectu tuo ..."

The Movements of the Priest at the Altar   Two objections in the same article 5, Lutheran *avant la lettre*, ridicule the "gesticulations" made by the priest at the altar: how he so often extends his arms and joins his hands, laces his fingers (*digitos complicat*) and bows (fifth objection), or turns himself so often toward the people to greet them (sixth objection). Whence the grave maxim: "nothing which appears ridiculous ought to be done in one of the Church's sacraments…. Consequently, such things ought not to be done in this sacrament."[149]

But Thomas responds that there is nothing to laugh at, for all these gestures, as we pointed out previously, "are done in order to represent Christ's Passion." Thus when the priest spreads out his arms after the consecration, following the custom widespread at that time and conserved in the Dominican *ordo missae* after its disappearance from the Roman, this "signifies the outstretching of Christ's arms upon the cross."[150] In the same way he raises his hands when he prays "to point out that his prayer is directed to God for the people, according to Lamentations 3:41: 'Let us lift up our hearts with our hands to the Lord in the heavens.'" When he joins his hands and bows, "praying earnestly and humbly, [he] denotes the humility and obedience of Christ, out of which He suffered." Finally, if the thumb and index finger of each hand remain joined after they have touched the body of the Lord at the consecration, it is out of respect for the sacrament "so that if any particle cling to the fingers, it may not be scattered."

One will have noticed that Aquinas puts the mystical explanation first. If this is obvious for the extension of the arms after the consecration, it is less convincing when it includes joining the hands and bowing, gestures of Franco-Roman piety signifying the dispositions of the religious soul. As for the ancient *orans* position, the splayed arms and the raised hands, Thomas considers it the great priestly gesture of common prayer. By the priest's *oratio*, we must

---

149. *ST* III, q. 83, a. 5, obj. 5.
150. *ST* III, q. 83, a. 5, ad 5.

understand the orations of the ancient sacramentaries and especially the Eucharistic anaphora pronounced for the whole Church, whereas the later prayers, pronounced with hands joined, express and excite the personal dispositions of the priest.

To account for the celebrant's greetings to the assembly, Thomas resorts to rememorative allegorism without offering a literal counterpart that would be able to chasten the undeniable artificiality of this sort of reading of the rites.[151]

The Signs of the Cross in the Canon   Two other objections involve the signs of the cross in the Canon,[152] one bearing on their multipli-

---

151. See *ST* III, q. 83, a. 5, ad 6: "Five times does the priest turn round towards the people, to denote that our Lord manifested Himself five times on the day of His Resurrection.... But the priest greets the people seven times, namely, five times, by turning round to the people, and twice without turning round ... and this is to denote the sevenfold grace of the Holy Ghost."

152. In the canon, the Roman *ordo missae* described by Thomas prescribes a certain number of signs of the cross to be performed over the offerings. We cannot say how many signs of the cross were performed originally; we only know that the priests of Gaul had a marked tendency to multiply them *sine intermissione*. In 751, Pope Zachary, in a response to St. Boniface, who had certainly asked him for advice in the matter, told the Apostle of Germany that he would send him, in the care of a priest, a roll of parchment containing the text of the Canon with the indications of the signs of the cross. The ancient Gelasian sacramentary (seventh to eighth centuries) indicates four signs of the cross in the *Te igitur*: "bene+dicas, haec + dona, haec + munera, haec + sancta sacrificia," and three others in the *Per quem haec omnia*: "sancti+ficas, vivi+ficas, bene+dicis." Slightly later (eighth to ninth centuries), in most manuscripts we find indication for signs of the cross at *Quam oblationem*, at the word *benedixit* before the consecration of the two species, and throughout the prayer *Unde et memores*. The signs of the cross over the offerings during the prayer *Supplices* seem to be slightly later, whereas the one performed by the celebrant over himself at the words *omni benedictione coelesti* do not appear in manuscripts until the twelfth century. The rites accompanying the doxology *Per ipsum* are the result of a transformation of the primitive rite. In the *Ordo Romanus I* the pontiff, while uttering the doxology, touched the chalice raised by the archdeacon with two consecrated pieces of bread (his personal offerings). In the *Ordo Romanus V* (ninth century), the bishop still touches the chalice *a latere* with the host, but he now does it tracing two signs of the cross on the outside of the chalice. These are linked to the two phrases *tibi Deo Patri + omnipotenti* and *in unitate Spiritus + Sancti*. When the Gallican use prevailed, already attested by Amalarius (*Liber Officialis*, Proem. 21), of placing the host and the chalice no longer side by side but the one behind the other above the corporal, the two signs of the cross were traced between the chalice and the celebrant. The sacramentaries from the end of the tenth century often mention three other signs of the cross, accompanying

cation, which is judged useless (third objection), the other on the unfittingness of their presence after the consecration (fourth objection). First the object of Protestant mockery, the signs of the cross repeated in the Canon encountered disfavor in the twentieth century with a number of experts and theologians writing for the most part in the wake of the "Liturgical Movement." The objections of this article indicate that this practice had already raised doubts in the time of St. Thomas.

We do not hesitate to admit that Thomas's long argumentation in their favor, which cleaves absolutely to mystical allegorism, does nothing to establish their sound foundation.[153] It is also certainly the most outmoded passage of the whole *expositio missae*, and the one that least demands our attention. We may ask ourselves whether the Angelic Doctor has not sacrificed something to the reigning fashion and whether he truly makes his own the laborious chronological and mystical constructions inherited from Amalarius via Innocent III, among others of the genre:

Now, Christ's Passion was accomplished in certain stages. First of all there was Christ's betrayal, which was the work of God, of Judas, and of the Jews; and this is signified by the triple sign of the cross at the words, 'These gifts, these presents, these holy unspotted sacrifices.' Secondly, there was the selling of Christ. Now he was sold to the Priests, to the Scribes, and to the Pharisees: and to signify this the threefold sign of the cross is repeated, at the words, 'blessed, enrolled, ratified.' Or again, to signify the price for which He was sold, viz. thirty pence. And a double cross is added at the words—'that it may become to us the Body and the Blood,' etc., to signify the person of Judas the seller, and of Christ Who was sold. Thirdly, etc.[154]

Whether or not he had read Albert's *De sacrificio missae*, Thomas would have known his master's inclinations against this genre of in-

---

each of the three other parts of the doxology: "Per + ipsum, cum + ipso et in + ipso." These signs of the cross are traced over the chalice, sometimes inside the cup, as a way of expressing the link between the two sensible species of the one mystery.

153. On this point we diverge from the opinion of David Berger in *Thomas Aquinas and the Liturgy*, 37–41.

154. ST III, q. 83, a. 5, ad 3.

terpretation, especially regarding the signs of the cross in the Canon. Without allying himself to Albert's condemnation, we clearly perceive in Aquinas, after he has consciously put forward just the sort of explanation denounced by Albert,[155] his desire to offer a briefer and more satisfying explanation: "In short, we may say that the consecration of this sacrament, and the acceptance of this sacrifice, and its fruits, proceed from the virtue of the cross of Christ, and therefore wherever mention is made of these, the priest makes use of the sign of the cross."[156]

Furthermore, his justification for the signs of the cross over the offerings after the consecration participates in the contemporary effort of theological-liturgical rationalization and at the same time assigns them value and legitimacy: "After the consecration, the priest makes the sign of the cross, not for the purpose of blessing and consecrating, but only for calling to mind the virtue of the cross, and the manner of Christ's suffering."[157]

Whether they be gestures of benediction or rememoration, the signs of the cross in the Canon are there to emphasize the identity of the Eucharistic sacrifice with the sacrifice of the cross that it represents. It was the notion of the representation of the redemptive Passion that induced Thomas to discover the tragic events of the Passion under the multiplicity of the signs of the cross. And as we will remark further on, it is in the Commingling, in which he contemplates a representation of the Resurrection, that he sees the culmination of the ordinances regarding the signs of the Canon.[158]

155. See Albert the Great, *De sacrificio missae*, tract. 3, ch. 13 (ed. Borgnet, vol. 38, 118), on, for example, the prayer *Quam oblationem*: "Some people give the most ridiculous explanations of this prayer, saying that because Christ was sold for thirty silver coins, which is three times ten, therefore three crosses are made in the first place; and because he was both sold and bought, therefore two crosses made in the second place.... In our opinion, this and other explanations like it are nothing but the fantastic concoctions of illiterate men who make a living passing off their insanities as true doctrine. Their efforts make theology detestable in the sight of everyone."

156. *ST* III, q. 85, a. 5, ad 3.

157. *ST* III, q. 85, a. 5, ad 4.

158. See *ST* III, q. 83, a. 5, ad 3: "Ninthly, the resurrection on the third day is represented by the three crosses made at the words—'May the peace of the Lord be ever with you.'"

N. K. Rasmussen saw in this a notable evolution in relation to the series of signs of the cross as presented in Thomas's *Commentary on the Sentences*,[159] toward an emphasis on the totality of the Paschal Mystery.[160]

In addition, the signs of the cross also serve to highlight certain sacred words, and thereby to designate the Holy Victim: "*hostiam* † *puram, hostiam* † *sanctam, hostiam* † *immaculatam, panem* † *sanctum vitae eternae, et calicem* † *salutis perpetuae*" (anamnasis prayer *Unde et memores*). This could very well be the reason for their multiple insertions into the anaphora.[161]

---

159. See Thomas, *Commentary on the Sentences* IV, d. 12, expositio textus.

160. See Rasmussen, *Saint Thomas et les rites de la messe*, 98.

161. In essence, we have put forth a hypothesis about the transformation of a primitive prayer posture, tied to the solemn prose of the canon, by which the celebrant would have designated the offerings with his hand, as is seen in certain oriental liturgies. Toward the eighth century, this gesture of designation would have been stylized in the form of a cross. It has also been considered an evolution of a gesture of imposition of hands over the offerings, a gesture that Hippolytus ordered to be practiced during the whole recitation of the anaphora: see Joseph A. Jungmann, *The Mass of the Roman Rite*, 2:142–47.

Appendix II

The *Expositio missae* of the *Summa theologiae* (IIIa, q. 83, a. 4–5), Part 2

In the previous appendix, we established that articles 4 and 5 of question 83 of the *Tertia pars* belong to the medieval genre of *expositio missae*. Further, we identified the liturgical rite Thomas commentates upon, presented the outline Thomas gives of it, and highlighted some general and preliminary liturgical principles. Here we come to his commentary on the prayers and rites according to the order of celebration of the Roman Mass.

ANALYSIS

The Preparation

And since it is written (Ecclesiastes 4:17): "Keep thy foot when thou goest into the house of God"; and (Sirach 18:23): "Before prayer prepare thy soul," therefore the celebration of this mystery is preceded by a certain preparation in order that we may perform worthily that which follows after.[1]

"Before prayer": this should be taken to mean before the celebration of the mystery properly speaking, or perhaps even before the act of consecration. As this latter is "accomplished by Christ's words only," it is necessary that "other words ... be added to dispose the

---

1. *ST* III, q. 83, a. 4.

people for receiving it."[2] Taken in this sense, "preparation" would have a wider sense that embraces all that relates to the "solemnity" of the sacrament.[3] The body of article 4, however, refers to a series of three chants concluded by a priestly oration.

The Introit

According to Thomas, the first of these chants, the Introit, expresses "the divine praise." Its text is usually drawn from the Psalms, which, for Pseudo-Dionysius (*Celestial Hierarchy*, 3.4) "embrace the whole content of Sacred Scripture in the mode of praise." To show the fittingness of a chant of praise at the opening of the celebration, the Angelic Doctor quotes Psalm 49:23: *"Sacrificium laudis honorificabit me, et illic iter quo ostendam illi salutare Dei."* The Psalm suggests that approaching the mystery of salvation or entering the path that leads there involves raising a sacrifice of praise.

One might justly desire, *a posteriori*, that this notion of sacrifice of praise should have denoted more than the opening chant, that a more correct understanding of the etymology of *eucharistia* would have permitted him to define the whole celebration in terms of it.[4] What's more, though Thomas refers to a path (*iter*) to be followed

---

2. *ST* III, q. 83, a. 4, ad 1.

3. We find this idea formulated a century later by Cabasilas—though the Byzantine commentator naturally does not restrict the "transformation of the gifts" only to the moment when the *verba Christi* are pronounced. See Nicolas Cabasilas, *A Commentary on the Divine Liturgy*, trans. J. M. Hussey and P. A. McNulty (London: SPCK, 1960), 25–26: "The essential act in the celebration of the holy mysteries is the transformation of the elements into the Divine Body and Blood; its aim is the sanctification of the faithful, who through these mysteries receive the remission of their sins and the inheritance of the kingdom of heaven. As a preparation for, and contribution to, this act and this purpose we have prayers, psalms, and readings from Holy Scripture; in short, all the sacred acts and forms which are said and done before and after the consecration of the elements.... Therefore, since in order to obtain the effects of the divine mysteries we must approach them in a state of grace and properly prepared, it was necessary that these preparations should find a place in the order of the sacred rite: and, in fact, they are found there. There, indeed, we see what the prayers and psalms, as well as the sacred actions and forms which the liturgy contains, can achieve in us. They purify us and make us able fittingly to receive and to preserve holiness, and to remain possessed of it."

4. See Gy, "La documentation sacramentaire de Thomas d'Aquin," 427–28.

toward the salvation that comes from God, nevertheless he does not offer the proper literal explanation, which is that the Introit antiphon is first of all a processional chant of approaching the altar—*ad introitum*—whose theme does not always involve praise and is generally adapted to the day or feast being celebrated. This defect is surprising, especially when one observes that, as Innocent III and William Durandus,[5] among others, bear witness, the chanting of the antiphon had not yet been restricted to the moment of the prayers at the foot of the altar, but still accompanied the entrance of the celebrant and his ministers.[6] Regarding the prayers at the foot of the altar, we find (in a. 5, ad 1) a mention of the *confession* at the foot of the altar included "in passing," as an example—along with the *lavabo*—of purification.

The Kyrie Eleison

Next comes the chanting of the *Kyrie eleison*, "a reference to our present misery" and an invocation of the divine mercy. The *Kyrie eleison* is sung thrice for the Person of the Father, then *Christe eleison* thrice for the Person of the Son, and again thrice *Kyrie eleison* for the Person of the Holy Spirit. Thomas adds that this triple invocation is said "against the threefold misery of ignorance, sin, and punishment; or else to express the circumincession of all the Divine Persons."[7]

Once the celebrant and his ministers have entered the sanctuary and put themselves in the presence of God, it is fitting that the

5. See Innocent III, *De sacro altaris mysterio*, bk. 2, ch. 18 (ed. S. Fioramonti, 126–29), and William Durandus, *Rationale divinorum officiorum*, bk. 4, ch. 5–6, 267–81.

6. See Rasmussen, *Saint Thomas et les rites de la messe*, 29: "One of the reasons for this absence is certainly St. Thomas's choice to comment on the texts first (*ea quae circa hoc sacramentum dicuntur*) and then the actions (*ea quae in celebratione huius sacramenti aguntur*). Thus it is very natural that the correlation between the entrance procession and the accompanying Introit chant escapes his notice.... For St. Thomas, its function becomes purely spiritual; it serves the general purpose of the preparation through divine praise. In this sense, we might call it functional, but only if we understand the aim of this function to be the edification of the Christians assembled in the church, and perhaps without an adequate appreciation of the liturgy's communal nature."

7. *ST* III, q. 83, a. 4.

entire assembly—priest, ministers, and faithful—implore the divine mercy. The *Kyrie* is certainly a vestige of a litany called the *Deprecatio Gelasii*, very similar to the synapties and ectenies that the Byzantine deacon still says on many occasions before the royal doors,[8] and each petitionary formula of which is coupled with the invocation *Kyrie eleison*. From the end of the sixth century it alternated with the invocation *Christe eleison*.[9] In the *Ordo Romanus I*, the litanic formulae have already disappeared, and all that remain are the invocations, repeated indefinitely until the celebrating pontiff signals the *schola cantorum* to cease.[10] The practice referenced here by Aquinas of chanting the invocations nine times is already attested in the *Ordo Romanus IV*, a Franco-Roman text from the second half of the eighth century.[11] Trinitarian symbolism is certainly at the origin of this practice. This explanation is found in the commentators of the ninth century, notably in Amalarius.[12] The allegorists all made reference to the nine choirs of angels. After mentioning this allegory in his *Commentary on the Sentences*,[13] Thomas no longer retains it in the *Summa*, preferring an artificial and unconvincing tropological meaning: "the threefold misery of ignorance, sin, and punishment."

The Gloria in Excelsis Deo

Following the plea for divine mercy, as a counterpart to the misery of man comes "the commemoration of the heavenly glory."

8. Synapte: a litany in the form of a series of invitations to pray for specific intentions. Ectene: literally "that which is lengthened, prolonged"; a series of invitations to pray for specific intentions. There is the Great Ectene said after the Gospel and two small ectenes, one after the transfer of the Holy Gifts, the other after the conclusion of the Anaphora.

9. See Mario Righetti, *Manuale di storia liturgica*, vol. 3, *La messa. Commento storico-liturgico alla luce del Concilio Vaticano II, con un excursus sulla Messa Ambrosiana di Pietro Borella* (Milan: Àncora, 1966), 213–18.

10. See Andrieu, *Les* Ordines Romani *du haut Moyen Âge*, vol. 2, 84, no. 52.

11. See Andrieu, "Ordo IV," in *Les* Ordines Romani *du haut Moyen Âge*, vol. 2, *Les textes (Ordines I-XIII)*, 159, no. 20.

12. See Amalarius of Metz, *Liber officialis*, bk 1, ch. 6 (ed. Hanssens, 282–84).

13. See Thomas, *Commentary on the Sentences* IV, dist. 8, expositio textus: "It is said nine times because of the nine choirs of angels, or because of faith in the Trinity" (Mortensen, 7:377).

Thomas notes the omission of the *Gloria* in offices of mourning, which "commemorate our unhappy state."[14]

No more than in the *Commentary on the Sentences*, Thomas does not choose to focus on the dimension of thanksgiving and praise that characterizes this ancient hymn often called the "great doxology." After dedicating the Introit to the expression of praise, here he prefers a brief explanation of an eschatological nature.

The Oration

Finally, at the end of the preparation, the oration takes place, "which the priest makes for the people, that they may be made worthy of such great mysteries."[15]

Since the oration is said for and in the name of the people, a salutation, the first of the celebration, is addressed to the people. Though mentioned in the *Commentary on the Sentences*,[16] this salutation is omitted here. Thomas chooses to underline the preparatory function of the oration, tying it more directly to the celebration and reception of the Eucharist. In the *Commentary on the Sentences*, however, the terms *oratio ad Deum pro populo fusa* signal the conclusive function of the *oratio*. Often designated in medieval missals under the term *collecta*, this oration *pro populo fusa* constitutes in fact a recapitulation, a collection—*collecta* comes from *colligere*—of the larger intentions of those who have assembled to implore the divine mercy and chant their praise and thanksgiving. The most ancient of these orations, those with provenance in the Roman sacramentaries, are characterized by the concision of their petitions and their more general character.[17]

14. *ST* III, q. 83, a. 4.

15. *ST* III, q. 83, a. 4.

16. See Thomas, *Commentary on the Sentences* IV, dist. 8, expositio textus: "Next comes the prayer poured out to God for the people, which the priest publicly pronounces after the Lord be with you; which is taken from Ruth 2:4. However, the high priest says: Peace be with you, bearing the type of Christ who addressed his disciples with these words after the Resurrection, in John 20:19 and 21" (trans. Mortensen, 7:377).

17. See Jungmann, *The Mass of the Roman Rite*, 1:372–90; and Christine Mohrmann, "Le latin liturgique," in Botte and Mohrmann, *L'Ordinaire de la messe*, 29–48, at 44–47.

The Instruction

"There precedes, in the second place, the instruction of the faithful, because this sacrament is 'a mystery of faith,' as stated above [*ST* III, q. 78, a. 3, ad 5]."[18] Here Thomas means *mysterium fidei* in the sense in which he explained the insertion of the formula in the consecration of the chalice: "The word 'mystery' is inserted, not in order to exclude reality, but to show that the reality is hidden, because Christ's blood is in this sacrament in a hidden manner, and His Passion was dimly foreshadowed in the Old Testament."[19]

The "mystery" that is hidden, the truth that is difficult to understand, shrouded in the veils of signs and language and rite, must be manifested, and for this one must resort to the instruction of Scripture.

For Thomas, instruction has a particular orientation toward the mystery of the presence of Christ in the Eucharist. It is the mystery of this presence that explains the obscure passages of the Old Testament, shadows that dissipate in the presence of the light of truth made manifest, and remembering such passages in turn serves to explain and glorify the divine Incarnation. In this perspective, the reading of Scripture is itself a disposition for the celebration of the mystery.[20] In the *Commentary on the Sentences*, the Mass program clearly indicates that the instruction—included under the *medium orationis*, that is, the celebration of the mystery proper—played a more important role. For the *Summa*, once the first movement of the liturgical assembly is achieved, the ministers of the Church dispense the Word of God to the people, granting a superior access to the "mystery of faith." In this sense the instruction is a catechesis on the mystery, the royal road of a progressive initiation into the mystery of the

18. *ST* III, q. 83, a. 4.
19. *ST* III, q. 78, a. 3, ad 5.
20. *ST* III, q. 83, a. 4: "Now this instruction is given 'dispositively' [through] the teachings of the prophets and apostles."

presence. One finds the same conception in Byzantium, in particular in the works of Nicholas Cabasilas.[21]

There is more to be said on the concept of the *mysterium fidei,* or simply the *mystery,* that we cannot get into here. We do not have to limit our understanding to the dimension of the real presence under the Eucharistic species, but can find in the *expositio missae* of the *Summa* more accents of that theology of mysteries, rooted in the doctrine of the Fathers and the liturgical traditions, of which Odo Casel has offered such a rich synthesis. The Caselian perspective, apart from certain necessary corrections, has shed great clarity on the question and permitted a renewed understanding of the essence of the liturgy: the presence of the entire mystery of redemption through the rite of the Church of Christ.[22] We would like to remark, nevertheless, how much this theology accords with the prayers and antiphons St. Thomas wrote for the office and Mass of Corpus Christi,[23] and with his reading (in *ST* III, q. 83, a. 1) of the ancient Roman oration containing these words: "*Quoties huius*

21. Nicholas Cabasilas, *A Commentary on the Divine Liturgy,* 26: "As for the lessons from the Holy Scripture, which proclaim the goodness of God, and his love for men, but also the severity of his justice and judgement, they instill in our souls the fear of the Lord, enkindle in us love for him, and thereby arouse in us great eagerness and zeal for the observance of his commandments. All these things, which make the souls of both priest and people better and more divine, make them fit for the reception and preservation of the holy mysteries, which is the aim of the liturgy."

22. See Odo Casel, "The Meaning of the Mystery," in *The Mystery of Christian Worship,* 104: "We act out the mysteries as the body of Christ; as his body we do all that the head does. In the rite we have an image of Christ's act in which we did not share while it was being fulfilled in time and place. The same thing is true of the last supper. Then Christ said, 'this act of sacrifice done once for all time on the cross is here being anticipated in image, and you are to imitate it afterwards in image.' The whole church does now what the Lord did at that moment. Yet certain men are chosen and consecrated to carry out this rite for the church."

23. See among others, the Oration: "*Deus qui nobis sub sacramento mirabili passionis tuae memoriam reliquisti ... ut redemptionis tuae fructum iugiter sentiamus*; the Secret: *Ecclesiae tuae, quaesumus, Domine unitatis et pacis propitius dona concede: quae sub oblatis muneribus mystice designantur*; and the Antiphon for the *Magnificat* at Second Vespers: *O sacrum convivium in quo Christus sumitur, recolitur memoria passionis eius, mens impletur gratia et futurae gloriae nobis pignus datur.*

hostiae commemoratio celebratur, opus nostrae redemptionis exercetur."[24] In this same vein, we cite once again the formula of article 4: "*In hoc sacramento totum mysterium nostrae salutis comprehenditur.*"

One will note that the instruction is meant for the "faithful people." Now, in the time of St. Thomas, and for a long time before, the readings were uttered in a language (Latin) that the majority of the faithful neither understood nor spoke, though it should not be forgotten that they were familiar with it from infancy. Nevertheless, since they could not understand the recitation, and since the greater part of them did not know how to read, how did this teaching reach them? On this point it is necessary to investigate the vernacular preaching and catechetical teaching of the Middle Ages. In the eyes of our Doctor, were these latter the privileged means of instructing the faithful? He does not say a word about preaching here. Yet in response to an objection bearing on "instruction in the faith," which in the context of the Mass refers specifically to the Epistle and the Gospel, he says that there exist two kinds of instruction: the one linked with Baptism (we might add post-baptismal catechesis) and so reserved to catechumens, and the other that happens in the celebration of the sacrament of the Eucharist, "for the faithful who take part in this sacrament."[25] He thus holds firmly for the truth and literalness of this instruction *intra missam*, independently of the problem of language, though it is evident that to his mind catechesis, and even preaching, help the faithful access an instruction which they cannot always understand in the moment.

Contrary to most commentators of his time, Thomas does not dodge the problem of the instruction's comprehensibility. Others before him had resorted to a mystical explanation of the moments and ceremonies of instruction, construing the subdeacon chanting the Epistle toward the altar as a figure of the prophets awaiting Christ, or as John the Baptist in the act of pointing out the Lamb of

24. *ST* III, q. 83, a. 1. This is the oration of the Ninth Sunday after Pentecost in the missal of the Roman Curia and, by consequence, of the missal of 1570.

25. *ST* III, q. 83, a. 4, ad 4.

God. By contrast, Aquinas is more cautious, bases his explanation on an obvious observation: lectors and subdeacons perform readings from the prophets and apostles, while by the deacons, "the higher ministers," "the people are instructed 'perfectly' by Christ's teaching contained in the Gospel."[26] In this way he identifies a progression in the instruction, from the teaching of the prophets and apostles to that of Christ.

Between these two instructions the choir performs several chants: the Gradual, Tract, or Alleluia, which "ought to result from the aforesaid teaching." A meditation and rumination on the Word of God, the intercalary chants pertain to the instruction and spiritual edification of the assembly. The mystical sense of the etymology of "gradual," according to Thomas, is that it is a sign of "progress in life (*profectum vitae*)," even though at its origin it is simply a *responsum* performed by a cantor on a step (*gradus*) of the ambo.[27] The Alleluia "denotes spiritual joy (*spiritualem exultationem*)." As for the Tract, chanted in place for the Alleluia at funeral offices and on Sundays and certain ferias of penitential seasons, has, for commentators since the seventh century, expressed "spiritual sighing (*spiritualem gemitum*)." This latter signification, however, is not original: its archaic melody was not reserved for penitential uses, and it owes its name simply to its mode of execution: an extended phrase (*tractim*) without antiphonic interruptions.[28]

Hearing the teaching of Christ contained in the Gospel elicits the assembly's profession of faith: "And because we believe Christ as the Divine Truth, according to John 8:46, 'If I tell you the truth, why do you not believe Me?' after the Gospel has been read, the 'Creed' is sung in which the people show that they assent by faith to Christ's doctrine."[29] Thomas justifies the Latin Church's practice of singing the *Credo* during the feasts of anyone mentioned in the

26. *ST* III, q. 83, a. 4.
27. See Righetti, *Manuale di storia liturgica*, 3:282.
28. See Righetti, *Manuale di storia liturgica*, 3:292–94.
29. *ST* III, q. 83, a. 4.

symbol—feasts of Christ, of the Blessed Virgin, and the Apostles, "who laid the foundations of this faith"—as well as on "other such days."

The homily is not mentioned here, just as it is not in the *Ordo Romanus I*. The modern reader may be surprised, since preaching is now considered an integral part of the liturgical action.[30] St. Thomas does not seem to share this view.[31]

The Celebration of the Mystery

So then, after the people have been prepared and instructed, the next step is to proceed to the celebration of the mystery, which is both offered as a sacrifice, and consecrated and received as a sacrament: since first we have the oblation; then the consecration of the matter offered; and thirdly, its reception. (q. 83, a. 4)

The treatise on the Eucharist in the *Summa theologiae* (III, q. 73–83) was not constructed around the distinction between *sacrifice* (cultic action) and *sacrament* (sanctifying reality). We know, on the contrary, how much Thomas has put forward the cultic dimension of sacramentality ever since the treatise on the sacraments in general. Likewise, in the first article of question 83, his treatment of the sacrificial value of the Eucharistic action sets the idea of sacramental immolation in the foreground. Thus, one is surprised to find the distinction, which seems to belong to the logical rather than conceptual order retained here, in the fourth article. Moreover, at first glance, this distinction seems to reduce the sacrificial act to oblation, here understood as the prayers and rites of the Offertory. But is not the consecration of the sacrament precisely that *aliquid sacrum,*

---

30. See Robert Cabié, *The Eucharist*, trans. Matthew J. O'Connell, vol. 2 of *The Church at Prayer*, ed. Aimé-Georges Martimort (Collegeville, MN: Liturgical Press, 1986), 106–7.

31. See Rasmussen, *Saint Thomas et les rites de la messe*, 40: "It is evident that this absence of the homily exercises an influence on the notion of the minister of the Word, especially as St. Thomas understands it in the *Sentences*, where he denies that this ministry pertains to priests." On the subject of the reticence of the Roman Church concerning the preaching of simple priests, see Righetti, *Manuale di storia liturgica*, 3:270–72.

performed over the offered matter, that constitutes the sacrificial act?[32] Then why does Aquinas seem to distance the Canon from the idea of sacrificial oblation? Has he not said elsewhere, earlier in the treatise, that "this sacrament has this in addition to the others, that it is a sacrifice"[33]? And when he comments later on the prayers of the Canon, does he not speak of sacrifice?[34]

When he evokes the consecration and reception of the sacrament, Thomas indeed maintains his conception of the sacrament as a sacrament of the Passion of Christ, a sacrament of that sacrifice whose virtue is eternal. Having established that the consecration brings together all the aspects of Eucharistic theology, and that the entire "celebration of the mystery," from the Offertory to the Communion, is nothing but the unfolding and making explicit of the substantial richness of the consecratory act, nothing prevents him from distinguishing certain parts that are ordained to this or that aspect of this sacrificial action that forms a unified whole. In so doing, at the precise moment when he articulates the program for the "celebration of the mystery," Thomas shows himself very faithful to what he said in the treatise on religion about the nature of sacrifice: in sacrifice there is offering and consecration.[35] It is thus that we have to consider, on the one hand, the offering of material (the bread and wine), and on the other, the consecratory act toward which this offering is oriented (the *sacrum facere* of which only Christ can be the author and in which he involves his Church).

32. *ST* II-II, q. 85, a. 3, ad 3: "A sacrifice, properly speaking, requires that something be done to the thing which is offered to God, for instance animals were slain and burnt, the bread is broken, eaten, blessed. The very word signifies this, since 'sacrifice' is so called because a man does something sacred [*facit sacrum*]."

33. *ST* III, q. 79, a. 7, ad 1.

34. In particular, St. Thomas will speak of sacrifice in article 4, in the *corpus* (in relation to the prayer *Supra quae propitio*), and also in ad 8.

35. *ST* II-II, q. 85, a. 3, ad 3: "An 'oblation' is properly the offering of something to God even if nothing be done thereto, thus we speak of offering money or bread at the altar, and yet nothing is done to them. Hence every sacrifice is an oblation, but not conversely."

The Offertory

Two actions accompany the oblation: the people's praise in the Offertory chant, which expresses the joy of those who are offering, and the prayer of the priest (*oratio sacerdotis*), which asks that the people's oblation be made acceptable to God.

Here we are faced with what we must call the sacrificial dimension of the Offertory: the people offer bread and wine, the matter of the sacrifice, and from that moment this matter is oriented and pointed toward the consecratory act. It is well known that modern liturgists have posed criticisms of the medieval Offertory prayers, seeing in their distinct oblative tenor a superfluous doubling of the Eucharistic prayer.[36]

This attitude was not part of the theological and liturgical thought of St. Thomas. N. K. Rasmussen asserts that, from a historical point of view, the Angelic Doctor shows himself "faithful to the conception of the Offertory as it had developed since Christian antiquity."[37] Thomas indeed sees the matter very correctly, at least with regard to history, when he speaks of the people's offering. At the end of the seventh century, the *Ordo Romanus I* paints the picture of a great collective act of offering, in which the whole assembly commits the sacrificial matter into the hands of the pontiff and his delegated hierarchs. This matter is then placed on the altar and reserved for the consecration.[38] Of course, at the time of Aquinas, as a result of the adoption of unleavened bread (the usual Western practice),

36. See notably Jungmann, *The Mass of the Roman Rite*, 2:97–100; Jean-Baptiste Molin, "Depuis quand le mot offertoire sert-il à désigner une partie de la messe?," *Ephemerides liturgicae* 77 (1963), 357–80; and more recently Cabié, *The Eucharist*, 180. On the influence of these critics in the reform of the Roman rite of Mass (*Novus Ordo Missae*, 1969), see Annibale Bugnini, *La Riforma liturgica, 1948–1975* (Roma: Edizioni liturgiche, 1997), 188, 337, 341, 375–76.

37. Rasmussen, *Saint Thomas et les rites de la messe*, 15.

38. See Andrieu, "Ordo I," in *Les* Ordines Romani *du haut Moyen Âge*, 2:91–95, nos. 69–85; Antoine Chavasse, *La liturgie de la ville de Rome du Ve au VIIIe siècle: Une liturgie conditionée par l'organisation de la vie* "in urbe" *et* "extra muros" (Rome: Pontificio Ateneo S. Anselmo, 1993), 37.

the offering of bread and wine by the assembly was no longer practiced. In spite of this fact, both the ancient and more modern prayers
were in agreement on the reality of an offering made by the entire
Church through the hands of the minister.

Originally, no prayer was connected to the action of the Offertory. Only a prayer, the *oratio super oblata*, also called the *secreta*, was
uttered at the end of the act of offering. If the *Ordo Romanus I* does
not mention the presence of this prayer,[39] nevertheless every Mass
formulary of the sacramentaries previous to and contemporary with
the *Ordo* furnishes a text, generally consisting of a brief formula of
oblation of the gifts.[40] Sometimes the prayer already asks for the consecration of the gifts and the graces connected to this consecration;
often, the theme of the oblation is adapted to the season or liturgical
feast being celebrated. Analysis of these orations proves that the origin of the oblative notions that would characterize the prayers of the
later epoch must be sought in these ancient texts.[41] This collection of
prayers, called *apologies*, began to accompany the placing of the offerings on the altar from the ninth century. The missal manuscripts
furnish an infinite variety,[42] of which the Romano-Franciscan, Car-
thusian, Dominican, and Lyonnaise, offer merely a few examples.
After having attempted in his *Commentary on the Sentences* a brief
systematization of the apologies of the Curial Missal, in the *Summa*
Thomas speaks of nothing but an *oratio sacerdotis*. Does this term refer to the ancient *super oblata*? Or is it a general term that applies to

39. See the hypothesis of Chavasse, *La Liturgia de la ville de Rome*, 35–39.

40. See, for example, the *Sacramentarium Veronense*, ed. Leo Cunibert Mohlberg,
Leo Eizenhöfer, and Peter Siffrin (Rome: Herder, 1956), 160: "Respice quaesumus, Domine, propitius ad munera quae sacramus, ut tibi grata sint."

41. On this point, we would like to indicate this passage from Jacques-Benigne
Bossuet in chapter 4 of *Explication de quelques difficultés sur les prières de la messe à un
nouveau catholique*, 72: "In order to understand what the Church does when she offers to
God the bread and the wine, we must consider the prayers that precede the consecration,
not only in the Canon of the Mass, but also in the orations called the secrets or *super
oblata*, for they are said over the oblations, i.e. over the bread and wine after they have
been placed on the altar."

42. See Paul Tirot, *Histoire des prières d'offertoire dans la liturgie romaine du VIIᵉ au
XVIᵉ siècle* (Rome: Edizioni liturgiche, 1985).

the whole of the apologies and the secret? Under the first hypothesis, Aquinas would show himself conscious of a true hierarchy in the prayers of the Mass, distinguishing between the prayers that accompany the actions, once performed without words, and the great Roman anaphora to which the more recent prayers lead up.

Whichever it may be, Thomas's interpretation of the Offertory is as well-founded as it is brief: a communal action of offering of a sacrificial nature. From the fact that it is the essence of sacrifice not to be a simple reality but a complex one unified by the unity of its end, the Offertory must be situated—as the history of its development also proves—amidst the whole larger context of the sacrificial offering: *offertur ut sacrificium*. In fact, the Offertory, in the words of Bernard Capelle, "is in no respect inchoate, the first stage of the oblation. It has the *full nature* of an oblation, though in its preparatory stage: *'tuo Nomini praeparatum.'* The Offertory is not a *partial* act on its way to becoming *absolute*; to the contrary it is a *total* if *relative* act, which is to say that in this moment the Christian makes his preparation for the consecration in a spiritual manner, by anticipation, his regard already fixed on the imminent sacramental oblation and in essential relation to it."[43]

In conclusion, to our mind, Thomas's commentary suggests two modest reservations. The first concerns his mystical interpretation of the Offertory antiphon, which he says is meant to express the joy of the offerers. N. K. Rasmussen has remarked: "This seems to be a sort of symbolization of the ancient Offertory, a procession accompanied by the chanting of an antiphon followed by several versets."[44] Second, as we have already pointed out, one might have expected some mention of the *Oremus* at the beginning of the Offertory, by which the pontiff invited the whole assembly to make a fervent act of offering with the purest possible spiritual dispositions.

---

43. Bernard Capelle, "Nos sacrifices et le sacrifice du Christ à la messe," in *La Messe et sa catéchèse*, ed. Emmanuel-Célestin Suhard (Paris: Cerf, 1947), 172.

44. Rasmussen, *Saint Thomas et les rites de la messe*, 43.

The Consecration

By *consecration* Thomas means to designate not only the act of uttering the words of the Savior over the bread and wine, an act "performed by supernatural power,"[45] and which he will call later the *ipsa consecratio*, but the whole of the Canon with its prayers and rites, from the Preface to the final doxology and the "assembly's Amen." Despite the exclusive efficacy he attributes to the words pronounced in the name of Christ by the priest, the Angelic Doctor, according to N. K. Rasmussen, "has implicitly recognized the coherence of all the parts of the great Eucharistic prayer, and this without resorting to the scholastic notion of *solemnitas*."[46] This agrees with our observation above, following B. Botte, about the respect the medievals had for the Roman Canon, which they generally believed to be of apostolic origin and from which they never dared to subtract under any circumstances, and even less to modify its order.

The Preface and the Sanctus

Originally a part of the Canon, the Preface's purpose is "to excite the people to devotion." For this reason, Thomas continues, "they are admonished 'to lift up their hearts to the Lord,'"[47] in such a way that, according to the words of Cyprian of Carthage, "they may be admonished that they should ponder on nothing but the Lord."[48]

P.-M. Gy has demonstrated that the medievals, Thomas among them, were hampered in their ability to conceive the anaphora as a prayer of thanksgiving by their ignorance concerning the full significance of the Greek word *eucharistia*.[49] Even so, the solemn procla-

---

45. *ST* III, q. 83, a. 4.

46. Rasmussen, *Saint Thomas et les rites de la messe*, 44.

47. *ST* III, q. 83, a. 4.

48. *ST* III, q. 83, a. 4, ad. 5. The citation from Cyprian is taken from the *De Dominica Oratione*, ch. 31, in *Saint Cyprian: Treatises*, ed. and trans. Roy J. Deferrari (New York: Fathers of the Church, 1958), 154.

49. Gy, "La documentation sacramentaire de Thomas d'Aquin," 427–29: "The whole Middle Ages employed [the word *eucharistia*] to signify the sacrament par excellence, something very holy, but it was thought that *eucharistia* signified *bona gratia* and it was

mation of thanksgiving made at the opening of the Canon in the celebrant's chant furnished grounds for such an understanding. One is
thus surprised that the Angelic Doctor, even if he could not identify
the expression *nos tibi semper et ubique gratias agere* with the Greek
term *eucharistia*, was not struck at this point by the importance of
the theme of thanksgiving, when Innocent III himself had noted it.[50]
It is all the more surprising in our time, when there is a strong tendency among some authors to separate or even to oppose thanksgiving and sacrifice, when the two are, on the contrary, so linked that
there exists no better term, we think, for designating and defining
the entire celebration than "Eucharistic sacrifice."

At the Preface the heart turns and raises itself toward God, putting aside all earthly thoughts so better to enter into the Holy of Holies. Then, having arrived at the sanctuary steps, it lifts up a noble
prayer of thanksgiving. Lebrun says: "We render him thanks principally for the benefit of the Incarnation, which allows us to offer the
body of Jesus Christ in sacrifice for the redemption of our sins."[51]
This thanksgiving for the immensity of the divine benefits, and especially for the gift of the redemptive Passion about to be represented sacramentally, leads directly to adoration. The liturgical act tran-
scends time; the cult rendered upon the earth rises up to heaven,
enters into contact and represents the heavenly liturgy (composed of
adoration and praise[52]) celebrated by the angelic choirs. The Church
on earth, at the moment she is to accomplish this spiritual sacrifice, surrounds the Eucharistic action with a celestial melody and

---

not known that the corresponding Greek word meant 'giving thanks.' During the passage
from Greek to Latin, *eucharistia* in the sense of an action was translated by *gratiarum
actio* and the word *eucharistia* was only transposed into Latin to designate the holy thing,
the eucharistic bread and wine, consecrated by the *eucharist*-prayer. If the medievals
had known the description of the Mass by St. Justin, who was rediscovered in the sixteenth century, they would have found this very illuminating connection between the
Eucharist-as-action and the Eucharist-as-holy-thing."

50. See Innocent III, *De sacro altaris mysterio*, bk. 2, ch. 62 (ed. Fioramonti, 200–203).

51. Pierre Lebrun, *Explication littérale, historique et dogmatique des prières et des cérémonies de la messe*, 1:308.

52. *ST* I-II, q. 103, a. 3.

borrows, or, more precisely, makes her own the angelic *Trisagion*. According to Byzantine liturgical theology, as P. Evdokimov has remarked, the "Eucharistic" adorer becomes the object of a veritable transfiguration.[53]

On this point the Thomistic commentary falls short of this plenitude of meaning, for it is too much preoccupied with Eucharistic realism. When they say *Sanctus, sanctus, sanctus*, the people are united to the angels and praise the divinity of Christ with devoted hearts. Then, by the words *Benedictus qui venit ...*, which the West joined to the angelic acclamation very late,[54] the same people unites itself to the children of Jerusalem to praise the humanity of Christ.[55]

The Structure of the Canon

Certain words have been imposed over the original structure of the Roman Canon—even if the history of its origins and formation remains a question open to investigation.[56]

The primitive redaction of the Canon, possibly derived from a Greek original, probably dates from the middle of the fourth century and certainly included nothing more than the central part extending from the prayer *Quam oblationem* to the prayer *Supplices te rogamus*.

---

53. Evdokimov, *The Art of the Icon*, 15: "What the pre-eternal Council of God has decided about the destiny of man is summed up in Revelations and expressed in the eternal praise of God: 'And all the angels, the elders, and the four animals, prostrated themselves before the throne, and worshiped God seated there on his throne, and they cried, 'Amen, Alleluia.' Then a voice came from the throne; it said, 'Praise our God, you servants of his' (Rv. 7:11; 19:4). A saint is not a superman but someone who lives his truth as a liturgical being. The fathers have found the most exact definition of man in the expression 'Eucharistic adoration.' A human being is a person of the *Sanctus* who joining the angelic choirs 'in an eternal unchanging movement around God sings and blesses the triple face of the unique God with triple blessings' [Maximus the Confessor, *Mystagogy*, I, 21] The *Sanctus* hymn during the liturgy is a *theologia*, that is, a hymn produced by the Holy Spirit."

54. See Righetti, *Manuale di storia liturgica*, 3:364–65.

55. See *ST* III, q. 83, a. 4.

56. See Mazza, *The Celebration of the Eucharist*, 62–66. Besides Jungmann, *The Mass of the Roman Rite*, 2:101–9; and Righetti, *Manuale di storia liturgica*, 3:342–56, we are indebted here to the ever-valuable analysis of Botte: "Histoire des prières de l'ordinaire de la messe," in Botte and Mohrmann, *L'Ordinaire de la messe*, 15–27. On the stylistic and literary qualities of the Canon, see Christine Mohrmann, "Le latin liturgique," in Botte and Mohrmann, *L'Ordinaire de la messe*, 37–40.

This central body contains the consecratory act and certain prayers united around the theme of anamnesis. It is this text that Ambrose recorded ca. 390 in his *De sacramentis* and which passed, not without certain variations, into the Roman sacramentaries of the seventh to the eighth centuries. From the fifth century, the original prayer is preceded, just after the *Sanctus*, by a *commendatio oblationum* (*Te igitur ... haec sancta sacrificia illibata*) to which another recommendation or commemoration for the offerers is logically joined: the memento of the living. To this prayer for the offerers was also associated, on the model of the Alexandrian liturgy, the commemoration of a series of personages in communion with the Church whom she has judged opportune to specially recall before God and the community, either by reason of their sanctity (the Blessed Virgin, apostles and martyrs in the *Communicantes* prayer) or their functions (pope, emperor, bishop, and priests in the latter part of the *Te igitur*). At first the celebrant merely introduced the various *commendationes* by means of a general formula, while the deacon read in a loud and intelligible voice the various names inscribed on two hinged tablets (the diptychs). After the reading of the diptychs, the celebrant concluded with a brief prayer. The deacon read the diptychs of the faithful departed only during Masses *pro dormitione*. As for the prayer *Nobis quoque peccatoribus*, which is clearly meant to encompass the intentions of the offering clergy, it seems to have been an appendix to the *commendationes*.

The revision and final redaction of the Canon was accomplished near the end of the fifth century, probably under the pontificate of Gelasius (492–496), and perhaps even by the pope's own hand. The redactors set the place of the diptychs in the Eucharistic prayer. The insertion of various *commendationes* in the ancient formulary is identifiable from the presence of the formula *Per Christum Dominum nostrum* which concludes each distinct section of the Canon: after the prayers *Communicantes, Hanc igitur, Supplices te rogamus*, the memento of the dead, and the prayer *Nobis quoque peccatoribus*. The Canon concludes with two doxologies, *per quem haec omnia* and *Per ipsum.* We owe the insertion *diesque nostros in tua pace...* in the *Hanc igitur* to St. Gregory. The several *Amens*, apart from the one that concludes the whole Canon, were added between the tenth and thirteenth centuries.

Te igitur, *Memento of the living*, Communicantes, Hanc igitur

The preceding observations on the structure of the Canon and, more precisely, on the notions of recommending the offerings and memorializing the offerers, permit us at this point to appreciate the correctness and concision of the Thomistic commentary.

As he begins the Canon,

The priest makes a "commemoration" [in a low voice], first of those for whom this sacrifice is offered, namely, for the whole Church, and "for those set in high places" (1 Timothy 2:2), and, in a special manner, of them "who offer, or for whom the mass is offered." Secondly, he commemorates the saints, invoking their patronage for those mentioned above, when he says: "Communicating with, and honoring the memory," etc.[57]

Because "the Eucharist is the sacrament of the unity of the whole Church," in the course of offering the sacrifice the priest mentions all those who compose the Church, who have some interest in its celebration and "all that belongs to the salvation of the entire Church"[58]: clerics and faithful of the Church militant, the heavenly choir, and the souls of the faithful departed. The prayer of the Canon that concerns the whole Church is thus not reserved exclusively to the priest. A little later (a. 4, ad 6), however, Thomas justifies the silence of the consecration in virtue of sacerdotal exclusivity. The silence of the Canon, which he does no more than mention (*sacerdos secreto ...*), would thus require a better-supported argument in its favor.[59] Also

---

57. *ST* III, q. 83, a. 4.
58. *ST* III, q. 83, a. 4, ad 3.
59. The practice of silence during the Canon certainly depends on the idea of the sacred preserve and special reverence due to the consecratory act. After the solemnity of the Preface chant, there comes a period of even more elevated solemnity, in which only silence can lead one to grasp the mystery. For the history of the silent Canon in the Roman

noteworthy is the absence of reference, contrary to the *Commentary on the Sentences*, to the honor rendered to the saints by the celebration of the Eucharistic sacrifice.[60] The prayer *Hanc igitur* closes the series of prayers recommending the offerings and offerers. It expresses in its conclusion the principal and general intention, which Thomas summarizes by means of a brief formula that includes the prayer's key words: "that the oblation may be salutary to them for whom it is offered (*ut fiat oblatio pro quibus offertur salutaris*)."[61]

Ad ipsam consecrationem

"Then [the priest] comes to the consecration itself."[62] The Angelic Doctor includes, in addition to the mere words of institution, also the petition for the consecration (*Quam oblationem*) that precedes them as well as all the prayers of the Canon that follow them. This remarkable fact testifies, it seems, to a more valorizing approach to the Church's liturgical action, and moreover, one better founded on tradition when compared to the hypothesis posited earlier in the

---

liturgy, we note that the *OR I* tells us nothing about the manner in which the pontiff pronounced the canon nor the liturgical actions that he performed. Following the mode of the *Preface*, did he say the prayer while modulating the text with vocal inflexions, using a musical scheme more or less similar to the ferial tone of the Preface? Did he read it in a loud voice *recto tono*, in a recitative manner? Or did he already say it in a low voice? In the context of the Roman basilica and its usually ample dimensions, it is difficult to imagine a simple reading of the Canon in a loud voice and without chant, which would have been intelligible only to those assistants standing nearest to him—unless of course it was understood that only the clergy should hear it: see volume 3 of Andrieu, *Les "Ordines Romani" du haut Moyen Âge*, 102, no. 39. The development toward a silent Canon attested in the later *ordines* (see Andrieu, "Ordo V," in *Les* Ordines Romani *du haut Moyen Âge*, vol. 2, *Les textes* (*Ordines I-XIII*), 221, no. 58) would thus be nothing more than an inevitable consequence. In addition, there is no trace of a change in vocal tonality for the *Per ipsum*.

60. Thomas, *Commentary on the Sentences* IV, dist. 8, expositio textus: "He commemorates those in whose reverence it is offered, at: [*Communicantes*], and there is included the Virgin who offered Christ in the temple, the Apostles who handed down this rite of offering to us, and the martyrs who offered themselves to God, but not confessors, because in ancient times the Church did not invoke them in solemnizing, or because they did not suffer like Christ, whose Passion this sacrament is the memorial of" (trans. Mortensen, 7:379).

61. *ST* III, q. 83, a. 4.

62. *ST* III, q. 83, a. 4.

treatise, according to which, isolated from the solemn liturgical context normally required, the words and rites of consecration are able to suffice for the production of the sacrament.[63]

In the *Quam oblationem* prayer the priest, Thomas notes, "asks … for the effect of the consecration." The last prayer pronounced *in persona Ecclesiae* before the *verba Christi* are uttered, the *Quam oblationem* forcefully expresses the intention of the Church.[64] One may join J. A. Jungmann in seeing at this moment "the consecratory epiclesis of the Roman Mass," when the Church, intending the transubstantiation of the oblations, earnestly invokes the Divine power.[65] Nevertheless, one should not attribute the intention of transubstantiation through the Holy Spirit to the Roman formula in the same way that Byzantine theology credits the Eastern epiclesis.[66] Not only

---

63. See *ST* III, q. 78, a. 1, ad 4: "If the priest were to pronounce only the aforesaid words with the intention of consecrating this sacrament, this sacrament would be valid because the intention would cause these words to be understood as spoken in the person of Christ, even though the words were pronounced without those that precede. The priest, however, would sin gravely in consecrating the sacrament thus, as he would not be observing the rite of the Church."

64. See Lebrun, *Explication littérale, historique et dogmatique des prières*, 358: "The ancient authors are always careful to join the prayers of the Church to the words of Jesus Christ, *as having great power in the consecration*, to use an expression of St. Basil. Why is this so? Because the intention of the Church must be expressed in the sacraments. Now the prayers that accompany the words of Jesus Christ indicate the intention, the desires, and the mind the Church has in pronouncing these words, which without the former might be regarded as a mere narration of history. It is the Church who, by the authority of Jesus Christ, consecrates priests to whom she indicates that which they must do in the great action of sacrifice. The priest is the minister of Jesus Christ and the Church. He must speak in the person of Jesus Christ and as the deputed representative of the Church. In the name of the Church he begins to invoke God's omnipotence over the bread and wine, so that they might become the body and the blood of Jesus Christ. From then on, he speaks no more in his own name, as the Fathers say. He pronounces the words of Jesus Christ, and therefore it is the word of Jesus Christ that consecrates. That is to say, the word of the one by whom all things were made. Thus it is Jesus Christ who consecrates … ; but he does it through the mouth of priests, and in response to their prayers.… He does it through priests who pray and bless with signs of the cross, according to the ecclesiastical authors and the councils."

65. See Jungmann, *The Mass of the Roman Rite*, 2:187–94.

66. On this subject see Sévérien Salaville, "L'Épiclèse: Examen de la question, Note complémentaire 3" in Nicolas Cabasilas, *Explication de la divine liturgie*, SC 4 bis (Paris: Cerf, 1967), 313–18.

does Aquinas not employ the term "epiclesis," it does not seem that he had any knowledge of the Eastern prayer.

On the contrary, one objection alleges the uselessness of a prayer that demands the completion (*perfectionem*) of a sacrament when one knows with certainty that only divine power can effect it. Hence the response: "the priest does not seem to pray there for the consecration to be fulfilled, but that it may be fruitful in our regard,"[67] a fact confirmed by the words "[*acceptabilemque facere digneris*] *ut nobis corpus et sanguis fiat.*"[68] This occasion allows the Angelic Doctor to offer a spiritual commentary on the many solemn epithets, of such juridical precision, by means of which the Church mounts an earnest cry to the divine power: *Benedictam, adscriptam, ratam, rationabilem, acceptabilemque facere digneris.* This spiritual commentary, in the wake of its predecessor in the *Commentary on the Sentences*,[69] rather than cleaving closely to the text and following the movement of the objective sacrificial offering, comments on the spiritual benefits flowing from the acceptance of the offering: those who offer it with a right intention will be "blessed," "enrolled in heaven," "counted among Christ's members," reasonable or spiritual[70]—which is to say, "torn from all beastly sensuality"— and finally "acceptable" to the Father.[71] If we also take into account his explanations concerning the signs of the cross that accompany each of the epithets in

---

67. *ST* III, q. 83, a. 4, ad 7.

68. For a complete examination of the significance of the prayer *Quam oblationem*, one may refer to the primitive version of the prayer, recorded in the *De sacramentis* of Ambrose, which does not contain the words cited by Aquinas, but rather the following formula—which seems to me to bolster the epicletic tenor of the prayer: "*Fac nobis hanc oblationem adscriptam, ratam, rationabilem, acceptabilem, quod figura est corporis et sanguinis Domini nostri Jesu Christi.*"

69. See Thomas, *Commentary on the Sentences* IV, dist. 8, expositio textus: "In a third way, it can be referred to the effect, hence he says, blessed, by which we are blessed; approved, by which we may be enrolled in heaven; ratified, by which we may be counted among Christ's members; reasonable, by which we may be torn from all beastly sensuality; acceptable, by which we may be accepted by God" (trans. Mortensen, 7:380).

70. On the meaning of *rationabilis*, see Bernard Botte, "Rationabilis," in Botte and Mohrmann, *L'Ordinaire de la messe*, 117–22.

71. *ST* III, q. 83, a. 4, ad 7.

question,[72] we will have a striking example of the plurality of spiritual, tropological, and allegorical senses in the present case.

The priest completes the consecration *per verba Salvatoris*.[73] Thomas merely cites the first words of the institution (*Qui pridie*) and passes on. He does not enter into detail, since he has already treated the form of the sacrament at length in question 78. According to N. K. Rasmussen, Thomas assigns only a relative and secondary value to the solemn rite that surrounds the act of consecration, the only necessary part: "at this point it would almost be inappropriate in his eyes to address this central point."[74] Though this claim deserves more nuance, we agree that, to the mind of a theologian composing a *Summa*, the question of the form of the Eucharist requires a treatment that is beyond the scope of a succinct *expositio missae*. For their part, the redactors of more ample liturgical commentaries often analyzed the words and rites of the consecration, and certain of them, including Innocent III, offer enough material to merit the name of veritable theological treatises.

Only one difficulty detains our Doctor here (a. 4, obj. 2): why is it that in the consecration of the sacrament in the Roman Canon we use words that are not found in the Gospel?

For we do not read in the Gospel, of Christ lifting up His eyes to heaven while consecrating this sacrament: and similarly it is said in the Gospel: "Take ye and eat" [*comedite*] without the addition of the word "all," whereas in celebrating this sacrament we say: "Lifting up His eyes to heaven," and again, "Take ye and eat [*manducate*] of this." Therefore such words as these are out of place when spoken in the celebration of this sacrament.

Thomas responds with an argument from tradition: as we read in the Gospel of John (21:25), the Lord said and did many things that were not written down. The Angelic Doctor places among these things the fact that at the Last Supper Jesus raised his eyes to heaven, and concludes that the Church has received this practice from

---

72. See *ST* III, q. 83, a. 5, ad 3.
73. *ST* III, q. 83, a. 4.
74. Rasmussen, *Saint Thomas et les rites de la messe*, 51.

apostolic tradition.[75] According to J. A. Jungmann, where the liturgical texts of the institution narrative do not reproduce the scriptural texts exactly, it is because they "go back to a pre-Biblical tradition." Thus the divergences of the biblical texts in this case may be explained by the diversity of the primitive liturgical texts, and the institution narrative of the Roman Canon may be the result of an evolution from a primitive text.[76] Furthermore, Thomas argues that it would seem logical (*rationabile*) that Christ raised his eyes toward the Father at this solemn instant: had he not done so on other occasions, for example before raising Lazarus (Jn 11:41) and before praying for his disciples (Jn 17:1)?[77] As for the word *manducate* (in place of the Vulgate's *comedite*) and the addition of *omnes*, besides the fact that "those words are not part of the [sacramental] form, as stated above (III, q. 78, a. 1, ad 2,4)," they in no way contradict the sense of the Gospel words.

The following prayers, *Unde et memores*, *Supra quae propitio*, and *Supplices te rogamus*—these latter two are one in the primitive version of *De sacramentis*—constitute the "anamnesis-offering" section of the Roman anaphora. This section, which E. Mazza has shown to originate in the Antiochian anaphora, or even the Alexandrine paleo-anaphora,[78] specifies the value of the sacrificial oblation of the consecratory action about to take place.

"Anamnesis" refers to the part of the Eucharistic prayer that immediately follows the commandment of the Lord at the end of the institution narrative: *Haec quotiescumque feceritis, in mei memoriam facietis* (Roman Canon). The Church commemorates the Paschal Mystery, the mystery of the death and triumph of the Lord,

---

75. *ST* III, q. 83, a. 4, ad 2.

76. See Jungmann, *The Mass of the Roman Rite*, 2:194–96; also Rasmussen, *Saint Thomas et les rites de la messe*, 69–70.

77. See *ST* III, q. 83, a. 4, ad 2. Thomas might have added the multiplication of the loaves as another significant occasion (Mt 14:19). On this gesture in the liturgy, see Bernard Botte, "'*Et elevatis oculis in coelum*': Étude sur les récits liturgiques de la dernière Cène," in *Gestes et paroles dans les diverses familles liturgiques*, ed. Constantin Andronikof (Rome: Centro liturgico Vincenziano, 1978), 77–79ff.

78. Mazza, *The Celebration of the Eucharist*, 49ff.

by offering the sacrifice in the sacramental order of the Eucharistic oblations, hence the prayer *Unde et memores*. Unfortunately, Aquinas does not develop his thoughts on the subject of the anamnesis. While in the *Commentary on the Sentences* the prayer is a *rei consecratae commemoratio*, in the *Summa* it is only a kind of apology: after performing the consecration, the priest "makes excuse for his presumption in obeying Christ's command, saying: 'Wherefore, calling to mind,' etc."[79] As we have seen, the only thing that detains his attention is the position of the arms in the form of a cross,[80] as well as the signs of the cross charged with rememorative allegory.[81] On this point Aquinas proves inferior to Innocent III and William Durandus.

But the prayer *Supra quae propitio* does garner his attention. Here the priest "asks that the sacrifice accomplished may find favor with God."[82] It is thus a development of the anamnesis's theme of sacrificial offering. The sacerdotal and thus ecclesial presumption that for Thomas is excused in virtue of the divine commandment, is here seen in a new light. What we dare to offer to God, despite our unworthiness, is the sacrifice of his Son: that he might deign to turn a propitious and serene countenance upon us—*propitio ac sereno vultu*. According to the words of Bossuet, "in this sacrifice there is Jesus Christ who is offered, and there is the man who offers him; the sacrifice is always agreeable from the point of view of Jesus Christ who offers it; it may not be so from the point of view of the man who offers him, for he can offer him worthily only if he himself is pure enough to be offered with him."[83] For this reason, Thomas remarks that in this prayer "the priest asks that this sacrifice may be accepted by God through the devotion of the offerers."[84] This sacrifice, because it is the sacrifice of Christ, is agreeable in itself. Therefore it is

79. *ST* III, q. 83, a. 4.
80. See *ST* III, q. 83, a. 5, ad 5.
81. See *ST* III, q. 83, ad 3.
82. *ST* III, q. 83, a. 4.
83. Bossuet, *Explication de quelques difficultés*, 140.
84. *ST* III, q. 83, a. 4, ad 8.

the interior dispositions of the offerers, the spiritual act of those who are admitted to participate in the sacrifice of Christ, that we ask God to look upon with favor; in fact, quoting Bossuet again, "the perfection of this sacrifice is not only that we offer and receive holy things, but rather that we who offer them and participate in them may become holy."[85]

We pray that God will consider our sacrifice acceptable, just as the ancient sacrifices were acceptable to him "through the devotion of the offerers"[86]: the *spiritual* sacrifices of Abel, Isaac, Melchisedech, and all the just "who have raised innocent hands to God, and offered him gifts with a pure conscience."[87] In order to arrive at a more profound understanding of this question, which encompasses the whole cultic economy of the history of salvation, one must go back to what Thomas said about sacrifice (in the treatise on the moral virtue of religion)[88] and more precisely about the Old Testament sacrifices—figures, types, and shadows of the unique sacrifice to come and, therefore, of the Eucharist (treatise on the Old Law).[89] Here is E. Mazza's summary: "The Eucharist is related to the ancient sacrifices as 'antitype' to 'type,' or 'truth' to 'figure'; the 'antitype' is the basis for defining the 'type,' and the 'truth' for defining the 'figure,' and not the other way around. Redemption, then, has a properly cultic component which the tradition has described in the word 'sacrifice.'"[90]

The sacrificial oblation is expressed in a third way by the prayer *Supplices te rogamus*. J. A. Jungmann has emphasized that "a gift is fully accepted not when it has drawn to itself a friendly glance, but when it is actually taken into the recipient's possession."[91] This is undoubtedly the primary and most precise meaning of this beautiful prayer, *"sublime"* in the sense that the acceptability of the sacrifice

85. Bossuet, *Explication de quelques difficultés*, 142.
86. *ST* III, q. 83, a. 4, ad 8.
87. Bossuet, *Explication de quelques difficultés*, 142.
88. *ST* II-II, q. 85.
89. *ST* I-II, q. 101; q. 102, a. 3; q. 103, a. 2 and 3.
90. Mazza, *The Celebration of the Eucharist*, 292.
91. Jungmann, *The Mass of the Roman Rite*, 2:231.

is regarded here from the point of view of the divine majesty, before the throne of God and the heavenly altar. Indeed, what is begged is that God will command these Eucharistic offerings to be transported by the hands of a holy angel—*per manus sancti angeli tui*—to the altar on high, in the sight of his divine majesty.

What is this angel? The response involves several difficulties, depending on whether the singular or plural, miniscule or majuscule is being used. The primitive version of the Canon, that of the *De sacramentis*, does not suggest the ministry of a particular mysterious Angel but of the angels in general: *per manus angelorum tuorum*. One might suppose therefore that, in the wake of the Preface and Sanctus, what is referred to here is a ministry of the angels that consists in presenting the prayers of the Church to the Most High. This explanation was given by Innocent III, among others, yet without citation of the primitive version.[92] For his part, Thomas holds rigorously to the singular of the so-called Gregorian version of the Canon; the angel is one who "standing by at the Divine mysteries [presents] to God the prayers of both priest and people, according to Apocalypse 8:4: 'And the smoke of the incense of the prayers of the saints ascended up before God, from the hand of the angel.'"[93] But also, he continues, "by the angel we are to understand Christ Himself, Who is the 'Angel of great counsel' (Isaiah 9:6 LXX), who unites His mystical body with God the Father and the Church triumphant." This solution places a new mystical sense side by side with a primary "literal" sense that does not exclude the angelic ministry mentioned in the prayer. Therefore, it is more correct to speak of an overlapping of senses rather than a plurality of senses; both senses are certainly intended, the one by the first redactor, the other by the reviser, who in "correcting" the primitive version did not deny the previous

92. See Innocent III, *De sacro altaris mysterio*, bk. 5, ch. 5 (ed. Fioramonti, 352–55). On the history of the text of *Supplices*, see Bernard Botte, "L'ange du sacrifice et l'épiclèse romaine au Moyen Âge," *Recherches de théologie ancienne et médiévale* 1, no. 3 (1929), 285–308.

93. *ST* III, q. 83, a. 4, ad 9.

tradition, but in a certain sense made it more profound. And so the two senses have become complimentary, each one clarifying the other, and St. Thomas seems to suggest that they both prove necessary for analyzing the liturgical text.

If the two senses were not mutually clarifying, the mystical extrapolation would be of no consequence at this point. For example, the angel, as a spirit by definition, might be perceived very simply as the Spirit who is sent from heaven, the Paraclete, whom Thomas elsewhere identifies (following Paschasius Radbertus) as the one who works, along with the Word of the Creator, in the consecration of the body and blood of Christ.[94] Byzantine theologians, especially Nicholas Cabasilas, see the prayer *Supplices* as the Roman consecratory epiclesis. If Cabasilas offers no comment on the person of the Angel, he very clearly asserts that the Latin prayer effects the consecration.[95] In the Greek tradition the latter is attributed to the invisible power of the Holy Spirit acting through the ministry of the priest. The modern editor of Nicholas Cabasilas, S. Salaville, has remarked further that "under a different literary form," the Roman prayer's petition for the oblation's ascension "corresponds in meaning to the petition for the Holy Spirit's transubstantiatory intervention" in the Eastern epiclesis.[96] Therefore, Aquinas's opting instead to exploit the theme of the Angel means that he offers no support for a consecratory epiclesis. It even seems that he was entirely unaware

94. See *ST* III, q. 82, a. 5: "On the contrary, Augustine (Paschasius) says (*De Corp. Dom.* xii): 'Within the Catholic Church, in the mystery of the Lord's body and blood, nothing greater is done by a good priest, nothing less by an evil priest, because it is not by the merits of the consecrator that the sacrament is accomplished, but by the Creator's word, and by the power of the Holy Spirit.'"

95. See Nicholas Cabasilas, *Commentary on the Divine Liturgy*, ch. 30, trans. Hussey and McNulty, 76–79, especially page 78: "The priest then prays that the offerings may be carried up to the heavenly altar—in other words, that they may be consecrated and transformed into the heavenly Body of the Lord. There is no question of a change of place, a passage from earth to heaven, since we see that the offerings remain among us, and that even after the prayer their appearances remain." See also the "Note complémentaire 4" by the editor, Sévérien Salaville: "L'Épiclèse: examen de la question," 313–18.

96. Sévérien Salaville, "L'Épiclèse orientale et l'oraison romaine « Supplices te rogamus… jube haec perferri. »: in Salaville , Explication de la divine liturgie, 320.

of the particular esteem of Byzantine theologians and liturgists for the *Supplices* prayer.

In addition, this exegetical choice in favor of the Angel allowed the Angelic Doctor to introduce the etymological question of the word *missa*. We do no more than point out the Thomistic contribution to a difficult question that the linguists still have not been able to resolve.[97] In Thomas's solution the mystical *sending* does not even leave room for the more prosaic *dismissal*: "And from this the Mass derives its name [*missa*]; because the priest sends [*mittit*] his prayers up to God through the angel, as the people do through the priest. Or else because Christ is the victim sent [*missa*] to us: accordingly the deacon on festival days 'dismisses' the people at the end of the mass, by saying: 'Ite, missa est,' that is, the victim has been sent [*missa est*] to God through the angel, so that it may be accepted by God."[98] The ascending dimension of the prayer, which, following the sense of the Latin expressions (*perferri; in sublime altare tuum; in conspectu divinae majestatis tuae*), raises the spiritual offering of the Church up to heaven, does not in fact mean to signify the transportation of the oblations to heaven, but of the mystical body who offers them: the priest utters the prayer of ascension "for Christ's mystical body, which is signified in this sacrament."[99] Through the Eucharistic celebration, the Church on earth is fully constituted in society and communion with the Divine. The *Supplices* prayer thus intends union with God as "the effect of this sacrifice and sacrament," as Thomas noted briefly in the corpus of the article. Union with God is the effect of the acceptance of the sacrifice; the prayer invokes the Eucharistic communion in which it will be consummated.[100] To the

97. See Claudio Balzaretti, *"Missa": Storia di una secolare ricerca etimologica ancora aperta* (Rome: Edizioni liturgiche, 2000).

98. *ST* III, q. 83, a. 4, ad 9.

99. *ST* III, q. 83, a. 4, ad 9.

100. See Jungmann, *The Mass of the Roman Rite*, 2:234–35: "The second half of the *Supplices* takes a new turn; bringing our sacrifice up to the heavenly altar should give rise to a *fruitful reception* of the holy gift by the assembled congregation—such is the prayer we take up. Our view thus turns away to the concluding act in the celebration of

ascending movement of sacrifice there corresponds a further de-
scendent movement from the divine Throne-Altar, the gift of every
grace and heavenly blessing: *Ex hac altaris participatione sacrosanctum Filii tui Corpus et Sanguinem sumpserimus, omni benedictione coelesti et gratia repleamur.*

The memento of the dead and the *Nobis quoque peccatoribus*
prayer also regard, according to St. Thomas, the effect of the acceptance of the sacrament.

After having asked for graces and blessings for the offerers on
earth, the priest requests the effect of the Church's sacrifice "for the
dead, who can no longer receive it, saying: 'Be mindful also, O Lord,'
etc."[101] For the Eucharist is the sacrifice of the whole Church, "the
sacrament of the unity of the whole Church."[102] Not only does the
Eucharistic sacrifice fill with grace those who unite themselves to its
offering here below, but also, in virtue of its propitiatory mediation,
it procures great relief—Cabasilas says a genuine sanctification[103]—
for the souls of the faithful departed for whom the Church offers.

Thomas proposes a brief interpretation of the subsequent prayer,
Nobis quoque peccatoribus, which has in fact proven to be the most
common among historians and commentators on the Roman Canon. An appendix to the *commendatio* of the oblations, it is a particular intercession "for the priests themselves who offer [the sac-
rifice]."[104] The plural certain hearkens back to the great sacerdotal
action, at once hierarchical and common, of the *Ordo Romanus I*.
Nevertheless, J. A. Jungmann has suggested enlarging the perspective

---

the Eucharist, the Communion.... The Communion is the second great event which the
celebration of the Eucharist comprises, the second intervention of God in the activity of
the Church. The Christian sacrifice is so constituted that, from the very beginning, the
congregation making the oblation is invited to the sacrificial meal. As soon, then, as the
oblation is completed, the expectant gaze is turned without further ado to the sacrificial
repast, and it is quite seemly that this expectation should become a humble prayer."

101. *ST* III, q. 83, a. 4.

102. *ST* III, q. 83, a. 4, ad 3.

103. See Nicholas Cabasilas, ch. 42 (trans. Hussey and McNulty, 96–98) and ch. 45
(101–2).

104. *ST* III, q. 83, a. 4.

and integrating an eschatological dimension that includes all the offerers, clergy and people.[105]

The conclusion of the Canon, alas, receives no commentary. The two doxologies, the one descending (*Per quem haec omnia*), which was formerly linked to the benediction of the fruits of the earth and later to that of the holy oils on Holy Thursday,[106] and the other ascending (*Per ipsum*), a final expression of the oblation of Christ and the Church, receive no mention. In the *Commentary on the Sentences*, only the first *Per quem haec omnia* is noted, as part of an articulated commentary on the Christic origin and identity of the consecrated gifts.[107]

The Communion

After the Eucharistic prayer is finished, all that is left is to complete the Dominical action: to distribute and consume the Eucharistic gifts. The necessity of the fraction of the consecrated bread and the desire to excite certain spiritual dispositions in the souls of the communicants are the basis for a complex of prayers and rites that have undergone various evolutions over the course of the centuries.

The *Pater Noster* and Its Embolism   The displacement of the *Pater noster* chant from the moment immediately preceding the reception of the sacrament to its current place, where it introduces the ensemble of prayers and rites connected to the distribution, has been attributed to St. Gregory the Great. In a letter to the bishop John of Syracuse, Gregory argued for the fittingness and apostolic origin of the recitation of the Lord's Prayer just after the performance of the

---

105. See Jungmann, *The Mass of the Roman Rite*, 2:257: "After the *Memento* of the dead the concept is raised a degree and the plea is for a final participation in the blessedness of the elect. Being about to eat the bread of life everlasting, we have prayed for the dead that God might be mindful of them and vouchsafe them entry into the place of light and peace. And it is this place of light and peace, viewed as the home of the saints, that we beg also for ourselves, *nobis quoque peccatoribus famulis tuis.*"

106. See Righetti, *Manuale di storia liturgica*, 3:419–22.

107. See Thomas, *Commentary on the Sentences* IV, dist. 8, expositio textus [(trans. Mortensen, 7:380).

Savior's action in the Eucharistic prayer.[108] He goes on to justify the Roman practice, which he points out is different from that of the Greeks, of reserving the chanting of the *Pater noster* to the celebrant alone,[109] with those assisting replying by the final petition. It does not appear that Thomas knew of this letter. If he had had the text in his hands, would he have said of the *Pater noster* that it is "the common prayer of the congregation ... in which we ask for our daily bread to be given us"?[110] Or did he see in the appropriation of the *Pater noster* by the priest, an immemorial Roman custom he witnessed every day, a sort of sacerdotal presentation of the common prayer,[111] just as he saw (wrongly) in the chant of the *schola cantorum* a substitution for the chant of the people?

The final petition of the Lord's Prayer, the one chanted by the people, in which P. Lebrun saw a recapitulation of the whole prayer,[112] has received a kind of epilogue for the very reason of its peculiar liturgical modality: the prayer *Libera nos*, called an "embo-

108. See Gregory the Great, "Letter to John of Syracuse," in *Gregory the Great, Ephraim Syrus, Aphrahat*, ed. Philip Schaff and Henry Wace, trans. James Barmby, Nicene and Post-Nicene Fathers: Second series 13 (Buffalo, NY: Christian Literature Publishing, 1898), 9: "But the Lord's prayer (*orationem Dominicam*) we say immediately after the prayer (*mox post precem*) for this reason, that it was the custom of the apostles to consecrate the host of oblation to (*ad*) that same prayer only. And it seemed to me very unsuitable that we should say over the oblation a prayer which a scholastic had composed, and should not say the very prayer which our Redeemer composed over His body and blood."

109. See Gregory the Great, "Letter to John of Syracuse," 9: "Among the Greeks, the Lord's prayer is said by the whole people, but among us by the priest alone."

110. *ST* III, q. 83, a. 4.

111. See Lebrun, *Explication littérale, historique, et dogmatique des prières*, 443–44: "In the Greek Church, and formerly before Charlemagne in the Churches of Gaul, the priest and people said the Lord's Prayer together.... The Roman Church had deemed it appropriate that the priest recite the *Pater* alone in a loud voice, of the opinion, it seems, that everyone would hear it more distinctly; and thereafter, so that the people could also take part, they were given to recite the final petition."

112. See Lebrun, *Explication littérale, historique, et dogmatique des prières*, 444: "[The people] must say [the final petition] as a sort of recapitulation of the Lord's prayer: for it is as if they said, deliver us from evil, Lord, so that you may be forever glorified in us, so that you alone may reign in us; that we may do your will, that out of your goodness we may obtain spiritual and temporal goods, that we may merit the forgiveness of our sins by sincere love for our brothers, and that our weakness may not be exposed to temptations."

lism" (Ἐμβολίσμος, from ἐμβολή: insertion, addition). Insofar as it is a development of the petition for all those assisting, this prayer was first recited in a loud voice. Around the year 1000, whether due to an already ancient rite of transferring the paten that first punctuated then divided this recitation, or whether in virtue of a mystical reading of the prayer and rites that accompany it,[113] or perhaps for both these reasons together, the embolism of the *Pater* was thenceforth pronounced in a low voice—though not without exception: the Ambrosian and Lyonnaise rites, the Roman Mass of the Presanctified on Good Friday, and a few others. It is thus no surprise that the Angelic Doctor sees in the *Libera nos* prayer a "private prayer, which the priest puts up specially for the people."[114]

The Fraction, Commingling, Peace and *Agnus Dei*

"Secondly, the people are prepared by the '*Pax*' which is given with the words, 'Lamb of God,' because this is the sacrament of unity and peace." The relation between the rite of peace and the *Agnus Dei* chant, and the analyses of article 5 (ad 7, ad 8, and ad 9) on the rite of fraction, with their reference to the symbolic doctrine of "threefold *corpus*" inherited from Amalarius, make it necessary to refer back to the articulation of the rites in the "normative Mass" of the *Ordo Romanus I*. Though in the present case Thomas remains far removed from any historical perspective, nevertheless such a perspective may be the best way to clarify Thomas's reading of a rite whose evolution is often characterized by simplification and interpolation of the rites and prayers of the original pontifical rite.

In the *Ordo Romanus I*, following the embolism *Libera nos* and the return of the paten to the altar, the pontiff says: *Pax Domini sit*

---

113. See Jungmann, *The Mass of the Roman Rite*, 2:289–90: "But about the year 1000 the Roman Mass changed to a quiet recitation of the embolism, except for Good Friday. It seems that the factor that led to this change was the consideration that the embolism was still within that portion of the Mass which represented the Passion of Christ. The termination of the Passion was the Resurrection, which since the sixth century was increasingly considered as symbolized in the ceremony of commingling."

114. *ST* III, q. 83, a. 4.

semper vobiscum while placing in the chalice a portion of the oblations consecrated during the previous pontifical Mass—the first
commingling, or commingling of the *fermentum* (*OR I*, nᵒˢ 94–
95).[115] The pontiff then proceeds to the fraction of a Eucharistic
bread from his own offering (first fraction), leaves the part he has
detached on the altar and places the rest of his oblation on the paten
(nᵒ 97). Then he leaves the altar for the throne (nᵒ 98). Meanwhile,
after the pope says *Pax Domini*, the archdeacon transmits the *pax* in
hierarchical order: first to the bishops, then the other members of
the clergy, and finally to the people (nᵒ 96). After the rite of peace,
the general fraction of the Eucharistic bread takes place. The oblations are first transported from the altar to the pope, bishops, and
priests (nᵒ 100–104). Then at the precise moment when the fraction
is about to begin, the archdeacon makes the sign to the *schola cantorum* to commence the *Agnus Dei* (nᵒ 105), a chant of Eastern origin addressed to the Holy Victim, Bread of life given and broken.
Repeated uninterrupted throughout the whole time of the fraction,
the invocation always ends with *miserere nobis*. However, the concomitance of the kiss of peace suggested, in later times, an interpolation containing an allusion to the peace—*dona nobis pacem*—which
prevailed almost everywhere. The fraction of the oblations completed, the pope communicates at the throne (nᵒ 106). While doing so, the pontiff detaches a piece from the consecrated bread that
he will consume. He places this part in the chalice held by the archdeacon (second commingling), saying: *Fiat commixtio et consecratio corporis et sanguinis domini nostri Jesu Christi accipientibus nobis
in vitam aeternam. Amen.* He addresses the archdeacon: *Pax tecum.*
The archdeacon responds: *Et cum spiritu tuo.* The pope then takes

---

115. We will use the numeration of Andrieu's edition: *Les* Ordines Romani *du haut
Moyen Âge*, vol. 2, *Les textes* (*Ordines I-XIII*), "Ordo romanus primus," 67–108. The reason for this first Commingling is to be found in the ancient use of the *fermentum*, but
here with the difference that the *fermentum* joins two successive Masses celebrated by
the pope, and not the Mass celebrated by the priest of a *titulus* with the stational Mass
of the Roman Pontiff. See the commentary of Michel Andrieu, *Les* Ordines Romani *du
haut Moyen Âge*, 2:61–64.

the Precious Blood in the chalice, which is held by the archdeacon (nᵒ 107). Then comes the communion of the whole assembly, clergy and people, administered in hierarchical order (nᵒˢ 109–18).

One thus observes a very direct progression and overlapping of the elements of the commingling, fraction, peace, and the communion proper. The key to reading this complex ritual resides evidently in the conception of the Eucharist as a sign of the unity of the Church. In imitation of Christ's action, the bread is broken. The fraction rite is surrounded with a great solemnity: the pope performs it at the throne; all the bishops and priests also take part in it —and this for a very practical reason. Recalling that the expression *fractio panis* served—following the Acts of the Apostles (2:42)—to designate the Eucharistic action itself, one might ask whether the solemn fraction, and with it the *ad thronum* communion of the *Ordo Romanus I*, is not meant to emphasize, in the exemplary context of the supreme pastor's Eucharistic celebration, the unity of the entire Church. The fraction is always followed by the act of commingling in the chalice a particle of the broken oblation: the commingling of the *fermentum* requires a particle broken during the preceding stational Mass. The second commingling, performed by the pope at the moment of his own communion, consists in placing in the chalice a particle of the oblations just consecrated. In both cases, it is a question of peace. We are to understand that the liturgical transmission of peace, which takes place immediately after the first commingling and precedes the fraction, is the sign of the union of the apostles around the Lord during the Last Supper. Everything thus hearkens back to the theme of ecclesial unity achieved through the Eucharist,[116] here seen in the tripartite division of the Eucharistic body: a part dropped into the chalice, another destined for consumption, and a third reserved on the altar both for the communion of the dying and in order to assure this Eucharistic continuity of which the *fermentum* rite is the expression.

116. See *ST* III, q. 83, a. 4.

The Roman ritual attached to the Eucharistic communion, a ritual also observed by St. Thomas, thus evinces a great richness and a no less great complexity. In the eyes of those who want to render an account of it, the literal and mystical reasons are nearly always overlapping, so that it is often impossible to circumscribe them exactly, and even less to oppose them. Since it is not possible to proceed with such an inventory, we will content ourselves with observing the commentaries of Aquinas, which all resort to the spiritual sense in this case.

The importance of the fraction rite is highlighted in the ad 7 of article 5 by the attribution of a triple signification: "the rending of Christ's body, which took place in the Passion;[117] ... the distinction of His mystical body according to its various states; ... the distribution of the graces which flow from Christ's Passion, as Dionysius observes (Eccl. Hier. iii)."[118] If the fraction and commingling are directly connected, as they should be, the primary signification, that is, the fraction as sign of the Passion of Christ, recalls the Paschal symbolism Thomas gave earlier to the three signs of the cross punctuating the commingling rite with the words *Pax Domini sit semper vobiscum*.[119] In fact, with the separate consecration of the bread and wine representing the death of the Lord on the cross and signifying the separation of his body and blood, the reunion in the chalice of the body and blood of Christ is consequently the sign of the glorious "reunion" of the Resurrection.

117. See *ST* III, q. 77, a. 7: "And as the sacramental species are the sacrament of Christ's true body, so is the breaking of these species the sacrament of our Lord's Passion, which was in Christ's true body."

118. According to Niels K. Rasmussen, "from a historical point of view, it must be said that the three explanations given do not get at the origin of the fraction rite. One might rightly wonder why St. Thomas does not mention the Gospel action in the institution of the Eucharist 'benedixit, fregit, deditque' and that he does not notice that the fraction is undertaken in view of the distribution. It is true that this thought is present in the quotation from St. Denys, but at the point at which this quotation is placed, next to two others that are purely symbolic, the idea easily loses any substance it did have and becomes a pure symbol of the graces of the Passion" (*Saint Thomas et les rites de la messe*, 111).

119. See *ST* III, q. 83, a. 5, ad 3: "The resurrection on the third day is represented by the three crosses made at the words—'May the peace of the Lord be ever with you.'"

The second signification given to the fraction, and thus to the commingling, regards the Church: "The breaking of the consecrated host, and the putting of only one part into the chalice, regards the mystical body."[120] Here Thomas makes his own the most ancient and most universally received of the allegorical commentaries, originating in Amalarius and generally known as the doctrine of the *corpus triforme*.[121] As E. Mazza has justly observed, Amalarius's idea is more an allegorical interpretation of the rite than a genuine doctrine,[122] even if it offers valuable material to the historian of theology about the Church-Eucharist relationship.[123] In the ad 8 of article 5, Thomas follows Gratian in attributing this commentary to the authority of Sergius I (687–701). He adds a brief commentary on the citations of Amalarius's text:

As Pope Sergius says, and it is to be found in the Decretals (De Consecr., dist. ii), "the Lord's body is threefold; the part offered and put into the chalice signifies Christ's risen body," namely, Christ Himself, and the Blessed Virgin, and the other saints, if there be any, who are already in glory with their bodies. "The part consumed denotes those still walking upon earth," because while living upon earth they are united together by this sacrament; and are bruised by the passions, just as the bread eaten is bruised by the teeth. "The part reserved on the altar till the close of the

---

120. *ST* III, q. 83, a. 6, ad 6.

121. See Amalarius, *Liber officialis*, bk. 1, ch. 35 (ed. Hanssens, 367–68).

122. See Mazza, *The Celebration of the Eucharist*, 170–71: "The idea of the *corpus triforme* is not strictly speaking a doctrine but simply an interpretation of the liturgical rite of the fraction, but an interpretation in the customary allegorical mode of Amalarius.... The idea of the *corpus triforme* needs to be appraised in terms of the author's method of explanation, that is as an interpretation of a rite. On the other hand, the Mozarabic Rite, also known as the Visigothic, already had something similar, inasmuch as the host is there broken into nine parts which are arranged on the paten in the form of a cross and interpreted as signifying nine mysteries of the life of Christ, from the incarnation to the coming of the Kingdom. In the system established in Amalarius' commentary, the question of the *corpus triforme* is not very important; as I have indicated, the idea is set forth in a few lines and in passing, without the author formally committing himself to it. It was Florus, deacon of Lyons and a fierce opponent of Amalarius, who turns the latter's comment on the rite of the fraction into a true and proper doctrine, while imputing this to Amalarius along with the accusation of having destroyed the unity of the body of Christ."

123. See Henri de Lubac, "Amalarius's 'Threefold Body' and What Became of It," in *Corpus Mysticum*, part II, 265–301.

mass, is His body hidden in the sepulcher, because the bodies of the saints will be in their graves until the end of the world": though their souls are either in purgatory, or in heaven.

Of this latter rite, in which a part of the host was reserved on the altar until the end of the Mass and beyond (*OR I*, nº 97), Thomas recognizes its disappearance. He is not equipped to identify its origins in the papal liturgy nor to observe, by consequence, that it is a simplification and adaptation of a complex ritual; he simply thinks that the rite "is no longer observed, on account of the danger." But, he says, the symbolism remains valuable, and it has been expressed nicely in a metrical composition.[124] Some advance another explanation: "The part put into the chalice denotes those still living in this world. while the part kept outside the chalice denotes those fully blessed both in soul and body; while the part consumed means the others."

Yet this last interpretation does not seem to impress Thomas. When he wants to explain the symbolism of the chalice in which the Eucharistic body and blood of the Lord will be reunited, the Dominican Doctor relies on classic Amalarian distinctions that permit him to distinguish a double representation of the cross and of glory: "Two things can be signified by the chalice: first, the Passion itself, which is represented in this sacrament, and according to this, by the part put into the chalice are denoted those who are still sharers of Christ's sufferings; secondly, the enjoyment of the Blessed can be signified, which is likewise foreshadowed in this sacrament; and therefore those whose bodies are already in full beatitude, are denoted by the part put into the chalice."[125]

124. See *ST* III, q. 83, a. 5, ad 8: "Hostia dividitur in partes, tincta beatos plene, sicca notat vivos, servata sepultos." [The host is divided into parts. The dipped one denotes the blessed, the dry one the living, and the reserved one the dead.] The author of the quatrain remains anonymous.

125. *ST* III, q. 83, a. 5, ad 9. See Rasmussen, *Saint Thomas et les rites de la messe*, 119: "From the point of view of content ... St. Thomas's conception of the chalice seems particularly correct. It takes account at the same time of the eschatological character of the heavenly banquet and of the profound Biblical roots of the chalice and of blood." He immediately follows this profound interpretation, however, with a more modest remark

Reception of the Sacrament   Once the commingling is complete, it is time for the Communion proper. Unlike in the *Commentary on the Sentences*, Thomas does not mention in the *Summa* any of the prayers of a private character that entered the *ordo missae* in previous centuries, by which the celebrant prepares himself for the reception of the sacrament.[126] He is content to observe that "the priest [receives] first [the sacrament], and afterwards [gives] it to others."[127] He finds a justification of this order in one of his favored works, the *Ecclesiastical Hierarchy* of Pseudo-Dionysius: "he who gives Divine things to others, ought first to partake thereof himself."

Is it possible to administer Communion to the people with hosts consecrated during a previous Mass? This question was raised by the eleventh objection of article 5: since the Paschal Lamb of the Old Law, the figure of the Eucharistic reality, must be entirely consumed, "it is improper therefore for consecrated hosts to be reserved, and not consumed at once." Aquinas's response is an affirmation of the most traditional practice, attested by the *Ordo Romanus I*, based on the direct connection between the act of offering the material of sacrifice and its reception in the course of the same celebration. Of course, the disappearance of the collective rite of offering of bread and wine on the part of the whole assembly, a disappearance that followed the progressive and universal adoption in the West of unleavened bread between the ninth and twelfth centuries, would have made the structure of the Eucharistic action much less discernible. Nevertheless, we do observe a recollection of the *ideal* from Aquinas's thirteenth century perspective, upheld by the authority of a

---

that, if understood *largo sensu*, leads one to suppose that he misunderstood the Greek manner of communicating: "And it is to be observed that the part put into the chalice ought not to be given to the people to supplement the communion, because Christ gave dipped bread only to Judas the betrayer" (*ST* III, q. 83, a. 5, ad 9).

126. See Thomas, *Commentary on the Sentences* IV, dist. 8, expositio textus: "However, the special preparation of the priest before consuming happens through the prayers he says privately, Lord, Jesus Christ, and whatever others there are" (trans. Mortensen, 7:381).

127. *ST* III, q. 83, a. 4.

decretal from Pseudo-Clement but tempered by the exigencies of pastoral life:

> The truth ought to be conformable with the figure, in some respect: namely, because a part of the host consecrated, of which the priest and ministers or even the people communicate, ought not to be reserved until the day following. Hence, as is laid down (De Consecr., dist. ii), Pope Clement I ordered that "as many hosts are to be offered on the altar as shall suffice for the people; should any be left over, they are not to be reserved until the morrow, but let the clergy carefully consume them with fear and trembling." Nevertheless, since this sacrament is to be received daily, whereas the Paschal Lamb was not, it is therefore necessary for other hosts to be reserved for the sick. Hence, we read in the same distinction: "Let the priest always have the Eucharist ready, so that, when anyone fall sick, he may take Communion to him at once, lest he die without it."[128]

We should note that in Thomas's day the only thing that imposes the necessity of Eucharistic reservation is the viaticum, since Eucharistic adoration outside of Mass was not yet much developed.

Is it fitting that the priest, after drinking the Precious Blood, should pour unconsecrated wine into the chalice? What does this ritual practice signify? Thomas points out that this rite "belongs to reverence for the sacrament."[129] He does not say that a quantity of wine should be poured into the chalice sufficient to cover and "purify" the part of the cup in which the Precious Blood was contained. Instead he gives the explanation that is an ablution or purification of the mouth (*ablutio oris*), which history informs us was also for a long time the case for lay communicants.[130] As a liquid, wine is capable of washing (*ablutivum*). Therefore, "[the priest receives it] in order to rinse the mouth after receiving this sacrament, lest any particles remain" of Eucharistic bread or wine. Citing the authority of a decretal, Aquinas adds that "it is for the same reason that wine is poured over the fingers with which he had touched the body of Christ."[131]

---

128. *ST* III, q. 83, a. 5, ad 11.
129. *ST* III, q. 83, a. 5, ad 10.
130. See Righetti, *Manuale di storia liturgica*, 3:525–26.
131. See *ST* III, q. 83, a. 5, ad 10: "Consequently it is received in order to rinse the

The Thanksgiving

The fourth and final part of the Mass according to the program proposed in the *Summa* will detain us only for a brief moment. We have already noted that it corresponds to the *finis orationis* in the program of the *Commentary on the Sentences*. Very briefly, Thomas sees in it the simple conclusion of the Mass in an act of thanksgiving: "the people [rejoice] for having received the mystery (and this is the meaning of the singing after the Communion);" then, just as Christ "said a hymn" (Mt 26:30) at the close of the supper with His disciples, "the priest returns thanks by [the Postcommunion] prayer."[132] There is no other element included in this part, despite the fact that the greater part of thirteenth century *ordines missae* contain conclusion rites.[133] Only if Thomas had mentioned these rites would he have been justified in positing a fourth part, however brief it would have been, because from a historical perspective it seems evident that both the Communion antiphon and the Postcommunion oration belong to the rite of the Communion: the Communion antiphon accompanies the communion, as the Introit and Offertory accompanied the going up to the altar and the offering; the Postcommunion concludes the complex of prayers and rites linked to the reception of the sacrament.

We join P. Gy in affirming that it is undoubtedly because he does not identify the term *eucharistia* with the prayer of thanksgiving that Thomas wanted to give a special place to this spiritual disposition

---

mouth after receiving this sacrament, lest any particles remain: and this belongs to reverence for the sacrament. Hence (Extra, *De Celebratione missae*, ch. Ex parte), it is said: 'The priest should always cleanse his mouth with wine after receiving the entire sacrament of Eucharist: except when he has to celebrate another mass on the same day, lest from taking the ablution-wine he be prevented from celebrating again'; and it is for the same reason that wine is poured over the fingers with which he had touched the body of Christ."

132. *ST* III, q. 83, a. 4.

133. See Stephen J. P. van Dijk,, "Order of the Mass according to the use of the Roman Church (Court) before 1227," in *The Ordinal of the Papal Court from Innocent III to Boniface VIII and related documents*, 493–526, at 523–25 and 531.

of "thanksgiving," making it the crowning moment of the entire celebration of the Eucharistic sacrifice. The regrettable practice of chanting the Communion antiphon, no longer during, but after the distribution of the sacrament, which seems to have been the most widespread practice in the thirteenth century, must have contributed to this relegating of the chant—and thus the oration that follows—to the position of a euchological appendix. The sentiments of the ancient Gregorian orations *ad complendum* are *Eucharistic* sentiments in the full sense of the term, and for Aquinas they thus serve to define the last part of the Mass.

CONCLUSION: REDISCOVERING RITE

Even limited as it is to two articles at the end of a long theological treatise, the *expositio missae* of St. Thomas Aquinas has provided us quite a complex reading of the ritual action, sometimes literal, often allegorical, without ever losing the perspective of a theologian. If one endeavors to situate the Thomistic commentary within the history of medieval *expositiones*, it must be observed that it responds to the desire for systematized knowledge that characterized thirteenth-century Scholasticism. In that period, attention was increasingly focused on organizing the Eucharistic celebration into logical parts that surround and converge upon the consecratory act. Despite the importance it retains for a form of allegory that, over and above the letter, plumbs the depths of intentions hidden under the veil of signs, there is, nevertheless, a clear tendency to analyze the concrete realities of the liturgy. The two approaches, literal and spiritual, cohabit, and rare are the doctors who follow Albert by placing them in opposition. The history of Christian cult teaches us, to the contrary, that an equilibrium between these two methods is the key to reading the vast complex of medieval liturgical signs.

And yet, if the theological tendency to define the Mass almost uniquely in terms of the act of consecration (instead of considering it as a whole) was a boon for dogmatic reflection, it unfortunately led to downgrading the status of the other prayers and rites considered thenceforth to be little more than an expression of cultic *solemnity*. In this development we may discern the rise of a new conception of the liturgy—denounced vigorously by Louis Bouyer—according to which the liturgy is nothing but the official and canonical form of the exterior cult of the Church.[134] This exteriorization of cult, making it a sort of "etiquette" around the valid and efficacious act that renders the Lord present, had a corresponding effect on the spiritual writers, whose interiorized religious devotion lacked a direct connection or true comprehension of the liturgical rites—at least when the scaffolding of allegorical mysticism did not rear its head once again. Therefore, it would seem to be a mistake to overemphasize Aquinas's distinction between the *substance* and *solemnity* of the sacramental rite. Any study of Thomas's sacramental doctrine requires a correct understanding of the theology of cult, developed in particular in the earlier treatises on the Old Law and on religion. In this sense, the two articles of the *expositio missae* that we have analyzed are one more proof of the interest that Thomas has in the external acts of cult.

In their affirmation of the importance of rituality, medieval commentaries present a liturgical theology that is profitable for contemporary reflection. Faced with the general anti-ritualism of modernity and with a certain liturgical minimalism that continues to look upon rite and symbol with suspicion, it is urgent to propose a rediscovery of the liturgy in all the riches of its anthropological, historical, theological, and spiritual dimensions. In the context of a renewed global reflection on the essence and spirit of the liturgy, to which Cardinal Ratzinger—now the happily reigning Benedict XVI—has again recently invited us,[135] in order to rediscover the sense of what Aquinas

---

134. See Louis Bouyer, *Liturgical Piety* (Notre Dame, IN: University of Notre Dame Press, 1965), 1–9.

135. See Ratzinger, *The Spirit of the Liturgy*, 168–69. "[The liturgy] is God's descent upon our world, the source of real liberation. He alone can open the door to freedom. The more priests and faithful humbly surrender themselves to this descent of God, the more 'new' the liturgy will constantly be, and the more true and personal it becomes.

calls the "Rites of the Christian Religion,"[136] to go toward this cult "in spirit and in truth"—at once the sign of the redemptive cult and the figure of the liturgy of the Kingdom, a liturgy of memorial and a liturgy of promise—means first of all, we repeat, rediscovering the meaning of rite itself. To aid us in this *rapprochement* with rite and to renew our celebration and participation in the Eucharistic sacrifice: that is perhaps the principal interest that the *Summa theologiae*'s expositio holds for us today.

Yes, the liturgy becomes personal, true, and new, not through tomfoolery and banal experiments with the words, but through a courageous entry into the great reality that through the rite is always ahead of us and can never quite be overtaken."

136. *ST* III, q. 62, a. 5: "Likewise by His Passion He inaugurated the Rites of the Christian Religion by offering 'Himself—an oblation and a sacrifice to God' (Ephesians 5:2)."

Bibliography

PRIMARY SOURCE BIBLIOGRAPHY

PL [Patrologia Latina] indicates volumes in the series Patrologiae cursus comple-
tus, series latina, ed. J.-P. Migne (Paris: J.-P. Migne, 1844–; facsimile reprint,
Turnhout: Brepols, 1956–).

CCCM indicates volumes in the series Corpus Christianorum Continuatio Mediaevalis, publishing manager, Luc Jocqué (Turnhout: Brepols, 1967–).

CCSL indicates volumes in the series Corpus Christianorum Series Latina, publishing managers Tim Denecker, Bart Janssens, Julian Yolles (Turnhout: Brepols, 1953–).

CCSG indicates volumes in the series Corpus Christianorum Series Graeca, ed.
Bart Janssens (Turnhout: Brepols, 1977–).

DS indicates the *Enchiridion symbolorum definitionum et declarationum de rebus
fidei et morum.* Edited by Henricus Denzinger and Adolfus Schönmetzer.
Rome: Herder, 1967.

Albert the Great. *Commentarii in IV Sententiarum.* 2 vols. Edited by Augustus Borgnet. Vols. 25–26 in *B. Alberti Magni Opera omnia.* Paris: Ludovicum Vivès,
1894.

———. *De sacrificio missae.* In *Opera omnia,* vol. 38. Edited by Auguste Borgnet,
1–189. Paris: Apud Ludovicum Vivès, 1890.

Alexander of Hales. *Glossa in IV libros Sententiarum Petri Lombardi.* 4 vols. Bibliotheca Franciscana Scholastica Medii Aevi 12–15. Rome: Quaracchi, 1951–1957.

Amalarius of Metz. *Liber officialis.* In *Amalarii episcopi opera liturgica omnia,* vol. 2,
edited by J. M. Hanssens. Vatican City: Biblioteca Apostolica Vaticana, 1950.

Anselm. *Epistola de sacrificio azymi et fermentati.* In *Anselmi Cantuariensis Archiepiscopi Opera Omnia,* vol. 2, edited by F. S. Schmitt, 223–32. Stuttgart-Bad
Cannstatt: F. Frommann Verlag, 1946.

Augustine. *De civitate Dei.* Edited by Bernhard Dombart and Alphonsus Kalb.
CCSL 47–48. Turnhout: Brepols, 1955.

Beleth, John. *Summa de ecclesiasticis officiis*. Edited by H. Douteil. CCCM 41A. Turnhout: Brepols, 1976.

Bernold of Constance. *Micrologus de ecclesiasticis observationibus*. PL 151, col. 974–1022.

Bonaventure. *Liber IV Sententiarum*. Bonaventurae Opera Theologica Selecta 4. Rome: Quaracchi, 1949.

Cajetan, Tommaso de Vio. *Summa totius theologiae S. Thomae de Aquino*. Edited by Serafino Capponi. Hildesheim: Georg Olms Verlag, 2000–2003.

———. *Instructio nuntii circa errores libelli de cena Domini, sive de erroribus contingentibus in eucharistiae sacramento*. Edited by Franz A. von Gunten. Rome: Angelicum, 1962.

Catholic Church. *Catechism of the Catholic Church*. 2nd ed. Vatican: Libreria Editrice Vaticana, 2012.

Cyprian. *De Dominica Oratione*. In *Saint Cyprian: Treatises*. Edited and translated by Roy J. Deferrari, 125–159. New York: Fathers of the Church, 1958. Original language in CCSL 3A. Edited by C. Moreschini, 90–113. Turnhout: Brepols, 1976.

Durandus. *See* William [Guillaume] Durandus.

Florus of Lyon. *De expositione missae*. PL 119, col. 15–72

Gratian. *Decretum Magistri Gratiani*. Edited by Emil Friedberg. In *Corpus Iuris Canonici*, vol. 1. Leipzig: Bernhard Tauchnitz, 1879; reprint, Graz: Akademische Drucku, Verlagsanstalt, 1959.

Gregory the Great. "Letter to John of Syracuse." In *Gregory the Great, Ephraim Syrus, Aphrahat*, edited by Philip Schaff and Henry Wace, translated by James Barmby, 8–9. Nicene and Post-Nicene Fathers: Second series 13. Buffalo, NY: Christian Literature Publishing, 1898. In Latin: *Registrum epistularum 9.26*. CCSL 140A. Edited by Dag Norberg, 586–587. Turnhout: Brepols, 1982.

Honorius Augustodunensis. *Jewel of the Soul*. 2 vols. Edited and translated by Zachary Thomas and Gerhard Eger. Dumbarton Oaks Medieval Library 79–80. Cambridge, MA: Harvard University Press, 2023.

Hugh of Saint Victor, *De sacramentis Christianae fidei*. Ed. by Rainer Berndt. Corpus Victorinum 1. Münster: Aschendorff, 2008.

Hugh of Saint-Cher. *Tractatus super missam seu Speculum Ecclesiae* (or *Expositio missae*). In *Opuscula et textus historiam ecclesiae eiusque vitam atque doctrinam illustrantia*, edited by Gisbertus Sölch, Series liturgica 9. Münster: Aschendorff, 1940.

Innocent III. *De sacro altaris mysterio*. PL 217, col. 775–914.

———. *Les mystères des messes: Présentation, édition critique et traduction française*. Edited and translated by Olivier Hanne. 2 vols. Huningue: Presses universitaires Rhin & Danube, 2022.

———. *The Mysteries of the Mass; The Four Images of Marriage*. Translated by David M. Foley. Saint Marys, KS: Angelus Press, 2023.

Isidore. *Etymologiarum sive originum libri XX*. 2 vols. Edited by W. M. Lindsay. Oxford: Clarendon, 1911.

Ivo of Chartres. *Sermones de ecclesiasticis sacramentis et officiis*. PL 162, col. 505–610.

John of Fécamp. *De corpore et sanguine Domini*. PL 101, col. 1085–1098.

Peter Lombard. *Magistri Petri Lombardi Parisiensis episcopi Sententiae in IV libris distinctae*. Grottaferrata: Editiones Collegii S. Bonaventurae ad Claras Aquas, 1971.

Maximus the Confessor. *Maximi Confessoris Mystagogia: Una cum latina interpretatione Anastasii Bibliothecarii*. CCSG 69. Edited by Christian Boudignon. Turnhout: Brepols, 2011. English translation: *Mystagogy*, in *Maximus the Confessor: Selected Writings*, translated by George C. Berthold, 183–225 (New York: Paulist Press, 1985).

Nicolas Cabasilas. *A Commentary on the Divine Liturgy*. Translated by J. M. Hussey and P. A. McNulty. London: SPCK, 1960. Original language in *Explication de la divine liturgie*, edited by Sévérien Salaville, René Bornert, Jean Gouillard, and Pierre Périchon, Sources Chrétiennes 4 bis (Paris: Cerf, 1967).

Odo of Tournai. *Expositio in Canonem missae*. PL 160, col. 1053–1070.

Petrus Pictor. *Liber de sacramentis*. Edited by L. van Acker. In *Carmina*, CCCM 25, 11–46. Turnhout: Brepols, 1972.

Praepositinus of Cremona. *Praepositini Cremonensis Tractatus de officiis*. Edited by J. A. Corbett. Publications in Medieval Studies 21. Notre Dame, IN: University of Notre Dame Press, 1969.

Pseudo-Dionysius. *Corpus Dionysiacum*. 4 vols. Edited by Beate Regina Suchla, Günter Heil, and Adolf M. Ritter. Berlin: De Gruyter, 1990. English translation: *Pseudo-Dionysius: The Complete Works*, translated by Paul Rorem (New York: Paulist Press, 1987).

Remigius of Auxerre ("Pseudo-Alcuin"). *Liber de divinis officiis*. PL 101, col. 1246–1271.

Rupert of Deutz. *Liber de divinis officiis*. Edited by H. Haacke. CCCM 7. Turnhout: Brepols, 1967.

Sacramentarium Veronense. Edited by Leo Cunibert Mohlberg, Leo Eizenhöfer, and Peter Siffrin. Rome: Herder, 1956.

Sicard of Cremona. *Sicardi Cremonensis episcopi Mitralis de officiis*. CCCM 228. Edited by Gábor Sarbak and Lorenz Weinrich. Turnhout: Brepols, 2008.

Thomas Aquinas. [*Commentary on Boethius's "De Trinitate"*] *Super Boetium de Trinitate*. Leonine edition, *Opera omnia*, vol. 50. Edited by P.-M. Gils. Vatican City: Ex Typographia Polyglotta S.C. de Propaganda Fide, 1992.

———. [*Commentary on the Letter to the Galatians*] *Super Epistolam ad Galatas Lectura*. In *Super Epistolas S. Pauli Lectura*, vol. 1, edited by R. Cari. Turin: Marietti, 1953. 563–49.

———. [*Commentary on the Gospel according to St. John*] *Super Evangelium S. Ioannis Lectura*. Edited by R. Cai. Turin: Marietti, 1952.

———. [*Commentary on the Letter to the Hebrews*] *Super Epistolam ad Hebraeos lectura*. In *Super Epistolas S. Pauli lectura*, vol. 2, edited by R. Cari. 335–506. Turin: Marietti, 1953.

———. [*Commentary on the Letter to the Romans*]. Original language in *Super*

Epistolam ad Romanos lectura. In *Super Epistolas S. Pauli lectura*, vol. 1, edited by R. Cari. Turin: Marietti, 1953. Translated by Fabian Larcher. Steubenville, OH: Aquinas Institute, 2020.

———. [*Commentary on the Psalms*] *In Psalmos Davidis Expositio.* In *Opera omnia*, vol. 14. Parma: Typis Petri Fiaccadori, 1863.

———. *Commentary on the Sentences Book IV. Scriptum super libros Sententiarum.* Ed. P. Mandonnet and M. Moss. Paris: P. Lethielleux, 1929–47, 3 vols. Translated by Beth Mortensen. Green Bay, WI: Aquinas Institute, 2018.

———. [*Compendium of Theology*] *Compendium theologiae*, in Opuscula 1 : Treatises, Opera omnia vo. 55. Steubenville, OH: Aquinas Institute ; Emmaus Academic, 2018.

———. [*Disputed Questions on Truth*] *Quaestiones disputatae de veritate.* 3 vols. Edited by A. Dondaine. Rome: Editori di San Tommaso, 1970–1976. Translated by Robert W. Schmidt, S.J. as *Truth: Questions 21–29*, vol. 3. Chicago: Henry Regnery Company, 1954.

———. [*On the Ten Commandments.*] *Opusculum in duo praecepta caritatis et in decem praecepta legis.* In *Opuscula Theologica*, ed. R. Spiazzi, vol. 2. Turin: Marietti, 1954.

———. [*Quodlibetal Questions*] *Thomas Aquinas's Quodlibetal Questions*, trans. Turner Nevitt and Brian Davies (Oxford: Oxford University Press, 2020), Original language: *Quaestiones de quolibet.* Leonine edition. Edited by R.-A. Gauthier. 2 vols. Paris: Cerf, 1996.

———. *Summa contra Gentiles.* Leonine edition. 3 vols. Rome: Typis Riccardi Garroni, 1918–1930. Translated into English by Anton C. Pegis, James F. Anderson, Vernon J. Bourke, and Charles J. O'Neil, 4 vols. (Notre Dame, IN: University of Notre Dame Press, 1975).

———. *Summa theologiae.* Leonine edition. 9 vols. Rome: Typographia polyglotta S. C. de Propaganda Fide, 1888–1906.

Vatican Council II. Constitution *Sacrosanctum Concilium.* December 4, 1963.

William Durandus. *Pontificale.* In *Le pontifical de Guillaume Durand*, vol. 3 of *Le pontifical romain au Moyen Âge*, edited by Michel Andrieu. Studi e Testi 88. Rome: Vatican Library, 1940.

———. *Rationale divinorum officiorum.* Edited by A. Davril and Timothy M. Thibodeau. CCCM 140, 140 A, 140 B (Turnhout: Brepols, 1995).

William of Melitona. *Opusculum super missam.* Included as part of Alexander of Hales's unedited *Tractatus de officio missae.* In *Summa theologiae* IV, q. 10, m. 5, a. 2.

SECONDARY SOURCE BIBLIOGRAPHY

Andrieu, Michel. *Les* Ordines Romani *du haut Moyen Âge.* Vol. 2, *Les textes* (*Ordines I–XIII*). Spicilegium sacrum Lovaniense 23. Louvain: Université Catholique, 1971.

Augier, Barnabé. "Le Sacrifice rédempteur." *Revue thomiste* 37 (1932): 394–430.

Balzaretti, Claudio. *"Missa": Storia di una secolare ricerca etimologica ancora aperta.* Rome: Edizioni liturgiche, 2000.

Barrois, Augustin. "Le sacrifice du Christ au Calvaire." *Revue des sciences philosophiques et théologiques* 14, no. 2 (1925): 145–66.

Barthe, Claude. *A Forest of Symbols: The Traditional Mass and Its Meaning.* New York: Angelico, 2023.

———. "L'*esprit* et la *lettre*." Introduction to *Le sens spirituel de la liturgie*, by William Durandus, 7–37. Translated by Dominique Millet-Gérard. Geneva: Ad Solem, 2003.

Bastide, Roger. "Anthropologie religieuse." In *Encyclopedia Universalis*, vol. 2, 271–275. Paris: Encyclopedia Universalis, 1990.

Berger, David. *Thomas Aquinas and the Liturgy.* Naples, Fla.: Sapientia Press, 2005.

Bernard, Philippe. *Du chant romain au chant grégorien.* Paris: Cerf, 1996.

Blázquez, Pelegrín. "El carácter como disposición a la gracia sacramental según Santo Tomás." *Studium* 13 (Madrid): 321–35.

Bonino, Serge-Thomas. "Le sacerdoce comme institution naturelle selon saint Thomas d'Aquin." *Revue thomiste* 99, no. 1 (1999): 33–57.

Bossuet, Jacques-Bénigne. *Explication de quelques difficultés sur les prières de la messe à un nouveau catholique.* In *Œvres complètes*, vol. 42, edited by Gauthier Frères, 61–177. Paris: Delusseux, 1828.

Botte, Bernard. "L'ange du sacrifice et l'épiclèse romaine au Moyen Âge." *Recherches de théologie ancienne et médiévale* 1, no. 3 (1929): 285–308.

———. "'*Et elevatis oculis in coelum*': Étude sur les récits liturgiques de la dernière Cène." In *Gestes et paroles dans les diverses familles liturgiques*, edited by Constantin Andronikof, 77–86. Rome: Centro liturgico Vincenziano, 1978.

Botte, Bernard, and Christine Mohrmann. *L'Ordinaire de la messe: Texte critique, traduction et études par Bernard Botte et Christine Mohrmann.* Paris: Cerf, 1953.

Bouyer, Louis. *Liturgical Piety.* Notre Dame, IN: University of Notre Dame Press, 1965.

Bradshaw, Paul. *The Search for the Origins of Christian Worship: Sources and Methods for the Study of Early Liturgy.* Oxford: Oxford University Press, 1993.

Bugnini, Annibale. *La riforma liturgica, 1948–1975.* Rome: Edizioni liturgiche, 1997.

Cabié, Robert. *The Eucharist.* Translated by Matthew J. O'Connell. Vol. 2 of *The Church at Prayer*, edited by Aimé-Georges Martimort. Collegeville, MN: Liturgical Press, 1986.

Caillois, Roger. *Man and the Sacred.* Champaign: University of Illinois Press, 2001.

Capelle, Bernard. "Nos sacrifices et le sacrifice du Christ à la messe." In *La messe et sa catéchèse*, edited by Emmanuel-Célestin Suhard, 154–173. Paris: Cerf, 1947.

Casel, Odo. *The Mystery of Christian Worship, and Other Writings.* Edited by Burkhard Neunheuser. Translated by I. T. Hale. Westminster, MD: The Newman Press, 1962.

Chardonnens, Denis. "Eternité du sacerdoce du Christ et effet eschatologique de l'Eucharistie." *Revue thomiste* 99, no. 1 (1999): 159–80.

Chavasse, Antoine. *La liturgie de la ville de Rome du Ve au VIIIe siècle: Une liturgie conditionnée par l'organisation de la vie "in urbe" et "extra muros."* Rome: Pontificio Ateneo S. Anselmo, 1993.

Chenu, Marie-Dominique. "Les deux âges de l'allégorisme scripturaire au Moyen Âge." *Recherches de théologie ancienne et médiévale* 18 (1951): 19–28.

———. *Introduction à l'étude de saint Thomas d'Aquin.* Montreal: Institut d'études médiévales, 1954.

———. "La théologie de la loi ancienne selon saint Thomas." *Revue thomiste* 61 (1961): 485–97

———. "Pour une anthropologie sacramentelle." *La Maison-Dieu* 119 (1974): 85–100.

Congar, Yves-Marie. "Le sens de l'économie salutaire dans la théologie de saint Thomas d'Aquin." In *Festgabe J. Lortz,* vol. 2, edited by E. Iserloh and P. Manns, 73–122, Baden-Baden: B. Grimm, 1958.

Daniélou, Jean. *The Bible and the Liturgy.* Notre Dame, IN: University of Notre Dame Press, 1956.

d'Argenlieu, Jean-Benoît. "Note sur deux définitions médiévales du caractère sacramentel." *Revue thomiste* 33 (1928): 271–75.

Dehau, Pierre-Thomas, *La structure liturgique de la messe d'après saint Thomas d'Aquin.* La Clarté-Dieu 7. Lyon: Éditions de l'Abeille, 1943.

Deshusses, Jean. *Le Sacramentaire grégorien: Ses principales formes d'après les plus anciens manuscrits.* Vol. 1. Spicilegium Friburgense 16. Fribourg: Éditions universitaires de Fribourg, 1971.

Dondaine, Hyacinthe-François. "La définition des sacrements dans la *Somme théologique.*" *Revue des sciences philosophiques et théologiques* 31 (1947): 214–28.

Duc, Paul. *Étude sur l'Expositio missae de Florus de Lyon, suivie d'une édition critique du texte.* Lyon: Belley, 1937.

Durkheim, Emile. *The Elementary Forms of Religious Life.* London: George, Allen, & Unwin, 1915.

Dykmans, Marc. *Le cérémonial papal de la fin du Moyen Âge à la Renaissance.* Vol. 25, *De Rome en Avignon, ou le Cérémonial de Jacques Stefaneschi,* and vol. 26, *Les textes avignonnais jusqu'à la fin du Grand Schisme d'Occident.* Rome: Bibliothèque de l'Institut historique belge de Rome, 1981–1983.

Eliade, Mircea. *History of Religious Ideas.* 3 vols. Chicago: University of Chicago Press, 1981.

———. *The Sacred and The Profane: The Nature of Religion.* New York: Harcourt, 1987.

———. *Images and Symbols.* Princeton, NJ: Princeton University Press, 1991.

Ellebracht, Marie Pierre. *Remarks on the Vocabulary of the Ancient Orations in the Missale Romanum.* Nijmegen: Dekker & Van de Vegt, 1963.

Evdokimov, Paul. *The Art of the Icon: A Theology of Beauty*. Redondo Beach, CA: Oakwood Publications, 1972.

Fernández Rodríguez, Pedro. "Hombre y sacramento en Santo Tomás." *Studi tomistici* 44 (1991): 245–52.

Fiedrowicz, Michael. *The Traditional Mass: History, Form, and Theology of the Classical Roman Rite*. New York: Angelico, 2020.

Franz, Adolph. *Die Messe im deutschen Mittelalter*. Freiburg im Breisgau: Beiträge zur Geschichte der Liturgie und des religiösen Volkslebens, 1902.

———. "La teologia nella liturgia e la liturgia nella teologia in san Tommaso d'Aquino." *Angelicum* 74 (1997): 359–417 and 551–601.

Gamber, Klaus. *The Reform of the Roman Liturgy: Its Problems and Background*. San Juan Capistrano, CA: Una Voce Press, 1993.

González Fuente, Antolín. *La vida litúrgica en la Orden de Predicadores: Estudio en su legislación: 1216–1980*. Dissertationes historicae 20. Rome: Institutum Historicum FF. Praedicatorum, 1981.

Gribomont, Jean. "Le lien des deux testaments selon la théologie de saint Thomas." *Ephemerides theologicae Lovanienses* 22 (1946): 70–89.

Gy, Pierre-Marie. "Expositiones missae." *Bulletin du Comité des Études de la Compagnie de Saint-Sulpice* 22 (1958): 222–31.

———. "Le texte original de la *Tertia pars* de la *Somme théologique* de saint Thomas d'Aquin dans l'apparat critique de l'édition léonine: le cas de l'eucharistie." *Revue des sciences philosophiques et théologiques* 65 (1981): 608–16.

———. "La papauté et le droit liturgique au XIIe et XIIIe siècle." In *The Religious Roles of the Papacy: Ideals and Realities (1150–1300)*, edited by Christopher Ryan, 229–45. Papers in Medieval Studies 8. Toronto: Pontifical Institute of Mediaeval Studies, 1989.

———. *La liturgie dans l'histoire*. Paris: Cerf, 1991.

———. "Avancées du traité de l'Eucharistie de saint Thomas dans la *Somme* par rapport aux *Sentences*." *Revue des sciences philosophiques et théologiques* 77, no. 2 (1993): 219–28.

———. "Divergences de théologie sacramentaire autour de saint Thomas." In Pinto de Oliveira, *Ordo sapientiae et amoris*, 425–33.

———. "La documentation sacramentaire de Thomas d'Aquin." *Revue des sciences philosophiques et théologiques* 80 (1996): 425–31.

———. "Bulletin de liturgie." *Revue des sciences philosophiques et théologiques* 81, no. 3 (1997): 491–92.

———. "*L'esprit de la liturgie* du Cardinal Ratzinger est-il fidèle au Concile, ou en réaction contre?" *La Maison-Dieu*, no. 229 (2002): 171–78.

Hameline, Jean-Yves. "Éléments d'anthropologie, de sociologie historique et de musicologie du culte chrétien," *Recherches de sciences religieuses* 78, no. 3 (1990): 397–424.

Hering, Hyacinthe-Marie. "De loco theologico liturgiae apud S. Thomam." *Pastor Bonus* 5 (1941): 456–64.

Hubert, Henri, and Marcel Mauss. "*Essais sur la nature et la fonction du sacrifice.*" *Année sociologique*, no. 2 (1889): 29–138.

Humbrecht, Thierry-Dominique. "L'eucharistie, 'représentation' du sacrifice du Christ, selon saint Thomas." *Revue thomiste* 98, no. 3 (1998): 355–86.

Journet, Charles. "Questions détachées sur la sacramentalité." *Vie spirituelle-supplément* 19 (1928): 121–50.

———. *The Church of the Word Incarnate*. Translated by A. H. C. Downes. Vol. 1. New York: Sheed & Ward, 1955.

———. *La Messe, présence du sacrifice de la croix*. Bruges: Desclée De Brouwer, 1957.

Jungmann, Joseph. *The Mass of the Roman Rite: Its Origins and Development* (*Missarum Sollemnia*). 2 vols. Translated Francis A. Brunner. Notre Dame, IN: Ave Maria Press, 2012.

Kolping, Adolf. "Amalar von Metz und Florus von Lyon: Zeugen eines Wandels im liturgischen Mysterienverständnis in der Karolingerzeit." *Zeitschrift für katholische Theologie* 73, no. 4 (1951): 424–64.

Labourdette, Michel. *Cours de théologie morale: Vertus rattachées à la justice*. Toulouse: Parole et Silence, 1961.

Lameri, Angelo. *La* Traditio instrumentorum *e delle insegne nei riti di ordinazione*. Bibliotheca ephemerides liturgicae subsidia 96. Rome: Edizioni liturgiche, 1998.

Lang, Uwe Michael. *The Roman Mass: From Early Christian Origins to Tridentine Reform*. Cambridge: Cambridge University Press, 2022.

———. *Signs of the Holy One: Liturgy, Ritual, and Expression of the Sacred*. San Francisco: Ignatius, 2015.

Lebrun, Pierre. *Explication littérale, historique et dogmatique des prières et des cérémonies de la messe*. 4 vols. Paris: Séguin Aîné, 1716–1726.

Leroy, Marie-Vincent. Review of *Saint Thomas d'Aquin: Les clés d'une théologie*. Albert Patfoort. *Revue thomiste* 84 (1984): 298–303.

———. "Un traité de Cajetan sur la messe." In Pinto de Oliveira, *Ordo sapientiae et amoris*, 469–86.

Levering, Matthew. *Christ's Fulfillment of Torah and Temple: Salvation according to Thomas Aquinas*. Notre Dame, IN: University of Notre Dame Press, 2002.

Lubac, Henri de. *Exégèse médiévale: Les quatre sens de l'Écriture*. 4 vols. Paris: Aubier, 1959–1964.

———. *The Splendor of the Church*. Translated by Michael Mason. San Francisco: Ignatius, 1986.

———. *Medieval Exegesis*. 3 volumes. Translated by Mark Sebanc. Grand Rapids, MI: Eerdmans, 1998.

———. *Corpus Mysticum: The Eucharist and the Church in the Middle Ages*. Translated by Gemma Simmonds, Richard Price, and Christopher Stephens. Notre Dame, IN: University of Notre Dame Press, 2006.

Łuczyński, Irénée Georges. "Le caractère sacramentel comme pouvoir instrumental selon saint Thomas d'Aquin." *Divus Thomas* 68, no. 1 (1965): 3–14.

Maccarrone, Michele. *Studi su Innocenzo III*. Padova: Editrice Antenore, 1972.

Mailhiot, Marie-Dominique. "La pensée de saint Thomas sur le sens spirituel." *Revue thomiste* 59 (1959): 613–63.

Matthijs, M. "'Mysteriengegenwart' secundum St. Thomam." *Angelicum* 34, no. 4 (1957): 393–99.

Mazza, Enrico. *Mystagogy: A Theology of Liturgy in the Patristic Age*. New York: Pueblo, 1989.

———. *The Celebration of the Eucharist: The Origin of the Rite and the Development of Its Interpretation*. Collegeville, MN: Liturgical Press, 1999.

Mennessier, A.-I. "Les réalités sacrées dans le culte chrétien." *Revue des sciences philosophiques et théologiques* 20, no. 2 (1931): 276–86.

———. *Saint Thomas d'Aquin: L'homme chrétien*. Paris: Cerf, 1965.

Millet-Gérard, Dominique. "Manifestation et vérité: Le Rational, œuvre d'artiste et doctrine." Preface to *Le sens spirituel de la liturgie: Rational des divins offices - Livre IV de la messe*. Ed. Claude Barthe, 38–61.

Molin, Jean-Baptiste. "Depuis quand le mot offertoire sert-il à désigner une partie de la messe?" *Ephemerides liturgicae* 77 (1963): 357–80.

Morard, Martin. "L'eucharistie, clé de voûte de l'organisme sacramentel chez saint Thomas d'Aquin." *Revue thomiste* 95 (1995): 217–50.

———. "Sacerdoce du Christ et sacerdoce des chrétiens dans le *Commentaire des psaumes* de saint Thomas d'Aquin." *Revue thomiste* 99, no. 1 (1999): 119–42.

Nichols, Aidan. *Looking at the Liturgy: A Critical View of Its Contemporary Form*. San Francisco: Ignatius, 1996.

Otto, Rudolf. *The Idea of the Holy*. Oxford: Oxford University Press, 1958.

Palazzo, Eric. *Le Moyen Âge: Des origines au XIIIe siècle*. Paris: Beauchesne, 1993.

———. *Liturgie et société au Moyen Âge*. Paris: Beauchesne, 2000.

Patfoort, Albert. *Saint Thomas d'Aquin: Les clés d'une théologie*. Paris: FAC, 1983.

———. *La Somme de saint Thomas et la logique du dessein de Dieu*. Saint-Maur: Parole et Silence, 1998.

Péguy, Charles. *The Mystery of the Holy Innocents*. Translated by Pansy Pakenham. *The mystery of the holy innocents and other poems* (Eugene, Or.: Wipf and Stock, 2018). Original language in *Charles Péguy: Œuvres poétiques complètes*. Paris: Éditions Gallimard, 1957, 671–823.

Perrin, Bertrand-Marie. "Le caractère de la Confirmation chez saint Thomas." *Revue thomiste* 98, no. 2 (1998): 225–65.

Pickstock, Catherine. *After Writing: On the Liturgical Consummation of Philosophy*. Oxford: Blackwell, 1998.

———. "Thomas Aquinas and the Quest for the Eucharist." *Modern Theology* 15, no. 2 (April 1999): 158–80.

Pinto de Oliveira, Carlos-Josaphat, ed. *Ordo sapientiae et amoris: Image et message de saint Thomas d'Aquin à travers les récentes études historiques, herméneutiques et doctrinales; hommage au Professeur Jean-Pierre Torrell à l'occasion de son 65e anniversaire.* Fribourg: Éditions universitaires, 1993.

Piolanti, Antonio. *Il mistero eucaristico.* Vatican City: Libreria Editrice Vaticana, 1983.

Pius XII. Encyclical Letter *Mediator Dei.* November 20, 1947.

———. Apostolic Constitution *Sacramentum Ordinis.* November 30, 1947. In *Acta Apostolica Sedis* 40 (1948): 5–7.

Quoëx, Franck. "Ritual and Sacred Chant in the *Ordo Romanus Primus* (Seventh-Eighth Century)." *Antiphon: A Journal for Liturgical Renewal* 22, no. 2 (2018): 199–219.

Rasmussen, Niels K. "Saint Thomas et les rites de la messe: Étude historique sur la *Somme théologique* IIIa Pars, q. 83, aa. 4 et 5." PhD diss., Saulchoir, 1963.

———. "Célébration épiscopale et célébration presbytérale: Un essai de typologie." In *Segni e riti nella Chiesa altomedievale occidentale,* 581–603. Settimane di studio del Centro italiano di studi sull'alto medioevo 33. Spoleto, Italy: Fondazione Centro italiano di studi sull'alto medioevo, 1987.

Ratzinger, Joseph. *The Spirit of the Liturgy.* Translated by John Saward. San Francisco: Ignatius Press, 2000.

———. "*L'esprit de la liturgie* ou la fidélité au Concile, Réponse au Père Gy." *La Maison-Dieu,* no. 230 (2002): 114–20.

Remy, Gerard. "Sacerdoce et médiation chez saint Thomas." *Revue thomiste* 99, no. 1 (1999): 101–18.

Ries, Julien. *Trattato di antropologia del sacro.* Vol. 1, *Le origini e il problema dell'Homo religiosus.* Milan: Jaca Book, 1989.

Righetti, Mario. *Manuale di storia liturgica.* Vol. 3, *La messa: Commento storico-liturgico alla luce del Concilio Vaticano II, con un excursus sulla Messa Ambrosiana di Pietro Borella.* Milan: Àncora, 1966.

Roguet, Aimon-Marie. "Renseignements techniques: A. Notes doctrinales thomistes: IX. L'organisme sacramentel (Question 65)." In *Somme théologique: Les Sacrements, 3ª, Questions 60–65,* by Thomas Aquinas, ed. A.-M. Roguet, 369–77. Paris: Éditions de la Revue des jeunes, 1945.

———. trans. and ed. *Somme théologique.* By Thomas Aquinas. Vol. 2, *L'Eucharistie.* Paris: Desclée, 1967.

Rousseau, Louis. *De ecclesiastico officio Fratrum Praedicatorum secundum ordinationem Humberti de Romanis.* Rome: A. Manuzio, 1927.

Rouvillois, Samuel. *Corps et sagesse: Philosophie de la liturgie.* Paris: Fayard, 1995.

Sainte-Marie, Joseph de. "L'eucharistie, sacrement et sacrifice du Christ et de l'Eglise: Développements des perspectives thomistes." *Divinitas* 18 (1974): 234–86.

Santogrossi, Ansgar. "Symbolisme liturgique et spiritualité biblique." *Catholica* 81 (2003): 126–29.

Schaefer, Mary. "Twelfth Century Latin Commentaries on the Mass: The Relationship of the Priest to Christ and to the People." *Studia liturgica* 15 (1983): 76–86.

———. "Latin Mass Commentaries from the Ninth through the Twelfth Centuries: Chronology and Theology." In *Fountain of Life*, edited by Gerard Austin, 35–49. Washington, DC: Pastoral Press, 1991.

Schmitt, Jean-Claude. *Le corps, les rites, les rêves, le temps: Essais d'anthropologie médiévale*. Paris: Éditions Gallimard, 2001.

Sölch, Gisbert. *Die Eigenliturgie der Dominikäner*. Düsseldorf: Albertus Magnus Verlag, 1957.

Taft, Robert F. "The Liturgy of the Great Church, An Initial Synthesis of Structure and Interpretation on the Eve of Iconoclasm." *Dumbarton Oaks Papers* 34/35 (1980–1981): 45–75.

———. *The Byzantine Rite: A Short History*. Collegeville, MN: Liturgical Press, 1992.

Taille, Maurice de la. *Mysterium fidei: De augustissimo corporis et sanguinis Christi sacrificio atque sacramento*. Paris: Gabriel Beauchesne, 1924.

Thibodeau, Timothy M. "Les sources du *Rationale* de Guillaume Durand." In *Guillaume Durand, évêque de Mende (v. 1230–1296): Canoniste, liturgiste et homme politique*, edited by Pierre-Marie Gy, 143–53. Paris: Editions du C.N.R.S., 1992.

Tirot, Paul. *Histoire des prières d'offertoire dans la liturgie romaine du VIIᵉ au XVIᵉ siècle*. Rome: Edizioni liturgiche, 1985.

Torrell, Jean-Pierre. *Saint Thomas Aquinas*. Vol. 1, *The Person and His Work*. Translated by Robert Royal. Washington, DC: The Catholic University of America Press, 2005.

———. *Le Christ en ses mystères: La vie et l'œuvre de Jésus selon saint Thomas d'Aquin*. Paris: Desclée, 1999.

———. *Le Verbe incarné*. 3 vols. Paris: Cerf, 2002.

Trainar, Geneviève. *Transfigurer le temps: Nihilisme-symbolisme-liturgie*. Geneva: Ad Solem, 2003.

Tremblay, R. "Le Mystère de la messe." *Angelicum* 36, no. 2 (1959): 184–202.

Turrini, Mauro. "Raynald de Piperno et le texte original de la *Tertia pars* de la *Somme de théologie* de saint Thomas d'Aquin." *Revue des sciences philosophiques et théologiques* 73 (1989): 233–47.

———. *L'anthropologie sacramentelle de saint Thomas d'Aquin*. Paris: Institut Catholique de Paris et Université de Paris-Sorbonne, 1996.

Vagaggini, Cipriano. *Il senso teologico della liturgia*. Rome: Edizioni Paoline, 1965.

van der Leeuw, Gerardus. *L'homme primitif et la religion*. Paris: PUF, 1940.

———. *Religion in Essence and Manifestation: A Study in Phenomenology*. Translated by J. E. Turner. Princeton, NJ: Princeton University Press, 2014.

van Dijk, Stephen J. P. "De fontibus 'Opusculi super missam' Fr. Gulielmi de Melitona." *Ephemerides liturgicae* 53 (1939): 291–349.

———. ed. *Sources of the Modern Roman Liturgy: The Ordinals by Haymo of Faversham and Related Documents (1243–1307)*. Vol. 2, *Texts*. Studia et documenta franciscana 2. Leiden: Brill, 1963.

————. *The Ordinal of the Papal Court from Innocent III to Boniface VIII and Related Documents*. Spicilegium Friburgense 22. Fribourg: Éditions universitaires, 1975.

van Dijk, Stephen J. P., and J. Hazelden Walker. *The Origins of the Modern Roman Liturgy: The Liturgy of the Papal Court and the Franciscan Order in the Thirteenth Century*. Westminster, MD: Newman Press, 1960.

van Steenberghen, Fernand. *Le mouvement doctrinal du XIᵉ au XIVᵉ siècle: Le XIIIᵉ siècle*. Paris: Bloud et Gay, 1951.

Vert, Claude de. *Explication simple, littérale et historique des cérémonies de l'Église*. 2 vols. Paris: Florentin Delaulne, 1697–1698.

von Gunten, Andreas F. "L'Eucaristia come sacrificio secondo San Tommaso e il Concilio di Trento." Course presented at the Pontifical University of St. Thomas Aquinas (Angelicum), Rome, 1995.

Vonier, Anscar. *A Key to the Doctrine of the Eucharist*. Assumption Press, 2013.

Vogel, Cyrille. *Medieval Liturgy: An Introduction to the Sources*. Translated by William George Storey and Niels K. Rasmussen. Washington, DC: Pastoral Press, 1986.

Walsh, Liam G. "Liturgy in the Theology of St. Thomas." *The Thomist* 38 (1974): 557–83.

————. "The Divine and the Human in St. Thomas' Theology of Sacraments." In Pinto de Oliveira, *Ordo sapientiae et amoris*, 321–52.

Weber, Edouard-Henri. *L'homme en discussion à l'université de Paris en 1270*. Paris: Bibliothèque thomiste, 1970.

Wilmart, André. "*Expositio missae*." In *Dictionnaire d'archéologie chrétienne et de liturgie*, edited by Henri Leclercq, vol. 5, part 1, 1014–1027. Paris: Letouzey et Ané, 1922.

Winzen, D. *Das Geheimnis der Eucharistie*. In *Die deutsche Thomas-Ausgabe*, vol. 30. Salzburg: Pustet, 1938.

David Wright, "A Medieval Commentary on the Mass: *Particulae* 2–3 and 5–6 of the *De missarum mysteriis* (ca. 1195) of Cardinal Lothar of Segni (Pope Innocent III)." PhD diss., University of Notre Dame, 1977.

Index

Series Editors: Matthew Levering
Thomas Joseph White, OP

Principles of Catholic Theology
Book One: On the Nature of Theology
Thomas Joseph White, OP

Reading the Song of Songs with St. Thomas Aquinas
Serge-Thomas Bonino, OP
Translated by Andrew Levering with Matthew Levering

Divine Speech in Human Words
Thomistic Engagements with Scripture
Emmanuel Durand
Edited by Matthew K. Minerd

Revelations of Humanity
Anthropological Dimensions of Theological Controversies
Richard Schenk

The Trinity
On the Nature and Mystery of the One God
Thomas Joseph White, OP

Catholic Dogmatic Theology, A Synthesis
Book I, On the Trinitarian Mystery of God
Jean-Hervé Nicolas, OP
Translated by Matthew K. Minerd